BEST RADIO
PLAYS OF 1

It is often said that radio plays are one of the subtlest, most imaginative yet most accessible forms of writing today. This anthology bears out this claim to the full and reveals the diverse and accomplished talent that is drawn to this immensely popular yet curiously neglected medium.

The six radio plays in this volume have been selected as the best of the year's output in 1978, and each has won a Giles Cooper award as the most outstanding play in its category. The categories are based on the BBC's familiar drama slots, and the winning plays are:

The Monday Play: *Daughters of Men* by Jennifer Phillips
Saturday Night Theatre: *Remember Me* by Jill Hyem
Afternoon Theatre: *Polaris* by Fay Weldon
Thirty-Minute Theatre: *Is It Something I Said?* by Richard Harris
Drama Now: *Episode on a Thursday Evening* by Don Haworth
and *Halt! Who Goes There?* by Tom Mallin.

BEST RADIO PLAYS OF 1978

The Giles Cooper Award Winners

EYRE METHUEN
In association with the BBC

First published in Great Britain in 1979 by Eyre Methuen Ltd
11 New Fetter Lane, London EC4P 4EE

Set IBM Journal by 🅰 Tek-Art, Croydon, Surrey
Printed in Great Britain by Cox & Wyman Ltd., Fakenham, Norfolk.

ISBN 0 413 45960 8 (Hardback)
ISBN 0 413 45970 5 (Paperback)

CONTENTS

THE GILES COOPER AWARDS: a note on the selection

Giles Cooper

As one of the most original and inventive radio playwrights of the post-war years, Giles Cooper was the author that came most clearly to mind when the BBC and Eyre Methuen were in search of a name for their new, jointly sponsored radio drama awards. Particularly so, as the aim of the awards is precisely to encourage original radio writing by both new and established authors — encouragement in the form both of public acclaim and of publication of their work in book form.

Eligibility

Eligible for the awards was every original radio play first broadcast by the BBC domestic services during 1978 (about 450 plays in total). Excluded from consideration were translations, adaptations and dramatised 'features'.

Categories

In order to widen the scope of the awards and to ensure that the resulting anthology volume would represent the broad variety of radio playwriting, the judges aimed to select at least one outstanding play from each of the four Radio 4 drama slots: the Monday Play (usually 90 minutes long), Saturday Night Theatre (90 minutes), Afternoon Theatre (60 minutes) and Thirty-Minute Theatre; and one or more plays from Radio Three's drama output (varying in length from 20 to 120 minutes).

Selection

The producer-in-charge of each drama slot was asked to put forward about seven or eight plays for the judges' consideration. This resulted in a 'short-list' of some 40 plays from which the final selection was made. The judges were entitled to nominate further plays for consideration provided they were eligible. Selection was made on the strength of the script rather than of the production, since it was felt that the awards were primarily for *writing* and that production could unduly enhance or detract from the merits of the original script.

Special Awards

Unanimously selected as one of the best radio plays of 1978, John Arden's *Pearl*, broadcast on both Radio 4 and Radio 3, was voted a Giles Cooper award winner irrespective of category but is not included in this volume as Eyre Methuen had already contracted to publish it separately.

In the Radio 3 category, the judges found it impossible to decide between the plays by Don Haworth and by Tom Mallin, and so two awards were given in this category. Both plays are printed in this volume.

Judges

The judges for the 1978 awards were:
    William Ash, BBC Radio Drama Script Unit
    Robert Cushman, drama critic, *The Observer*
    Nicholas Hern, drama editor, Eyre Methuen
    Gillian Reynolds, radio critic, *The Daily Telegraph*

EPISODE ON A THURSDAY EVENING

by Don Haworth

Don Haworth was brought up at Burnley, Lancashire. He served in the RAF and then worked in several parts of the world as a journalist, first for print and later for broadcasting. For the past twelve years he has divided his time between writing plays for radio and making documentary films for BBC television. Almost all his drama has been written for radio, though stage and television adaptations have been made of some of the plays. In all he has written twenty, which have been broadcast in thirty-five countries. Of his recent work, *On a Day in Summer in a Garden* won the Imperial Tobacco Award for Radio in 1976, and *Events at the Salamander Hotel* won the Play of the Month award of the Deutsche Akademie der darstellenden Künste in April, 1977. A collection *We All Come to it in the End* was published in 1972.

Episode on a Thursday Evening was first broadcast on BBC Radio 3 on 21st September 1978. The cast was as follows:

JERRY	Terry Scully
TOM	John Hollis
ROSE	Diana Bishop
PROCTOR	Lewis Stringer

Director: Richard Wortley

The bar of a pub. It is Thursday evening around 8 o'clock. ROSE, the barmaid, is drying glasses. PROCTOR, a customer, is playing 'We'll gather lilacs' on the piano. JERRY comes in. He is very anxious and preoccupied in his exchanges with ROSE and PROCTOR.

JERRY (*approaching, rather breathless*). Hello, Rose.

ROSE (*slightly surprised to see him*). Hello, Jerry.

JERRY. Tom been in?

ROSE. Not yet. Is he not at the cinema?

JERRY. I've just come from there.

PROCTOR. Five past he comes in for his pint. Five past on that clock.

ROSE. You know Mr Proctor at the piano, Jerry?

PROCTOR. We have met.

JERRY. Have we?

    PROCTOR *finishes with a trill of notes.*

PROCTOR (*moving*). You showed me the projectors when Tom gave me a bit of a tour back stage at your cinema.

JERRY. I remember.

PROCTOR. He'll be in any minute. What'll you have?

JERRY. I'm not staying.

PROCTOR. Go on, while you're here.

ROSE. Have a half lager.

PROCTOR. And a bitter for me, Rose.

    Glasses tinkle and fill as ROSE serves.

There's never anybody in on Thursdays.

ROSE. Not till the dogs finish.

PROCTOR. Not on Thursdays.

JERRY. No.

PROCTOR. We have a jar together most nights, me and Tom. Don't we, Rose?

ROSE. True.

PROCTOR. A pint and a pickle.

JERRY (*abruptly*) Look, I'd better go back to the cinema.

ROSE. You've just come from there.

JERRY. He might have got back to the office.

PROCTOR. He's always here at five past. Stay put.

ROSE. Use the phone if you like.

JERRY. Can I?

ROSE. Sure, don't traipse back.

JERRY *dials his number while* ROSE *serves the drinks.*

ROSE. Forty-two. Do you have the two, Mr Proctor?

PROCTOR. Here you are.

ROSE. Lovely. (*She rings up the till.*)

JERRY (*into telephone*). Elsie, is Tom there? No, he's not in the pub. I'm speaking from the pub. . . Do you know whether he's left? Well, look round for him. It's very urgent. I'll hang on here for two minutes. If you find him ask him to ring me, you know, immediately. (*He replaces the telephone.*)

ROSE. No luck?

PROCTOR. He'll be in any moment. Prost then.

JERRY. What?

PROCTOR. Prost. Skol. Your astonishing good health.

JERRY (*short apologetic laugh*). And yours.

They drink.

PROCTOR. When I come in here I leave my cares at the door. Don't I, Rose?

ROSE (*at a little distance*). What, Mr Proctor?

PROCTOR. Leave my cares at the door.

ROSE. Every time.

PROCTOR. So if there's anything bugging you.

JERRY. No.

PROCTOR. Agitating you.

JERRY. No.

PROCTOR. Eating you.

JERRY. No. No.

PROCTOR. Shattering your tranquility.

JERRY. No.

PROCTOR. Forget it. Drain that glass and then you can buy me one. You can reciprocate. (*He laughs in a friendly way.*)

> JERRY, *perceiving his kindness, also laughs but still under great restraint.*

PROCTOR (*kindly*). He'll walk in any time now. (*Tentatively, probing, making conversation.*) Are you thinking of selling the cinema?

JERRY. Did Tom say that?

PROCTOR. No, no. I forgot to ask him about it. There were a couple of blokes came in here last Tuesday — Wednesday would it be, Rose?

ROSE. Would what be?

PROCTOR. Those two blokes in camel-hair coats, talking about buying the flea pit.

ROSE. Goldilocks with the ginger toupé?

PROCTOR. That's right, the little 'un. He'd got thatched somewhere.

ROSE. Like a ginger rug on his head.

PROCTOR. Did you know about them?

JERRY. No. No.

PROCTOR. They gave the impression they were interested in your flea pit, asking questions.

ROSE. Quizzing. Did we get many in after the show? Do the police often come round for a eyeful? That kind of thing.

JERRY. I don't know. Look, Rose, do you mind if I use the phone again?

ROSE (*surprised*). No, help yourself.

He dials. Phone is heard ringing.

JERRY. Hello, Elsie did you — (*relieved*). Oh, that's good. . . He actually told her he was coming here, did he? No, I see. Thanks.

Receiver replaced.

He's on his way.

PROCTOR. I told you. Now drain that glass.

JERRY *gives a short laugh of acknowledgment and some relief.*

PROCTOR. Thing I've always meant to ask about blue movies. Stop worrying now — he's on his way. You come to a particularly good bit — and wump it's on and off before you've seen it.

JERRY. It's on for the proper time.

PROCTOR. But stills, a still photograph you can gaze upon it, you can study it from all angles, you can return to it any number of times.

ROSE. But that's a still.

PROCTOR. That's what I say, a still.

ROSE. Well that's not their business. They don't show blue stills. They show blue movies.

PROCTOR. Right, but why can't we have the best of both worlds? Why can't they stop the projector at selected spots and give people time to drink it in?

ROSE. It'd go on all night. Everything'd be as long as 'Gone with the Wind'.

PROCTOR. I'm only talking about highlights, moments of surpassing lewdness. Why can't the projector be stopped? They do on the telly.

ROSE. They stop the telly at moments of surpassing lewdness?

PROCTOR. No, football matches. But the same principle could apply. Isn't that right, Jerry?

JERRY (*not wanting to be bothered*) No, it's different.

PROCTOR. How?

JERRY. One's videotape and the other's film.

PROCTOR. I've seen films stopped. I've seen cinema films stopped.

JERRY. It's not done by stopping the projector.

PROCTOR. How is it done then?

JERRY (*trying to dismiss the subject*). It's a frozen frame. It's done when the film's made.

PROCTOR. All right then, why can't it be done just for those few delectable moments, as I say, of breathtaking prurience?

JERRY. They're not the same for everybody.

PROCTOR. There's a consensus.

JERRY (*dismissively*). There isn't a consensus.

PROCTOR. There must be — except for pederasts.

JERRY. Different things turn different people on. Let's leave it at that.

PROCTOR. All right, but if you want to make a bob or two, if you stopped the projector —

JERRY. People do not pay to see the projector stopped.

ROSE. It's movies, not stills.

PROCTOR. But if people could come back next morning and they were to run their projector down to a few well chosen spots.

JERRY. We don't do it.

PROCTOR (*suddenly remembering*). But you used to do morning shows.

JERRY (*crossly*). We did special shows for nut cases.

ROSE. They came in here.

JERRY (*in a rising voice*). The cleaners didn't like it. It didn't work out. We've stopped. Nobody is admitted in the mornings now except the employees. Is that clear?

PROCTOR (*taken aback*). All right. There's no need to be cross.

    Silence. TOM *comes in.*

TOM (*approaching*). Hello. . . What's up?

ROSE. Hello, Tom.

TOM. What's going on?

JERRY. Look, I want a word.

TOM (*surprised*). OK, Jerry.

JERRY (*moving*). In the snug.

TOM. OK, mate.

JERRY (*more distant*). Urgent.

TOM (*to* JERRY). Coming. (*Quieter, to* ROSE *and* PROCTOR.) What have you been saying?

PROCTOR. Nothing, have I, Rose?

ROSE. He just blew up.

TOM. Misunderstanding. (*Moving.*) Draw us a pint, love.

PROCTOR. I'm in the chair.

TOM (*moving and calling*). And some bread and cheese. (*Sitting and speaking quietly.*) Right, mate. Don't let Peter rattle you.

JERRY. No.

TOM. He means well.

JERRY. Yes.

TOM (*with a laugh*). Just comes a bit strong at times. Bit loquacious. . . What is it?

JERRY. We've had a bomb warning.

TOM. Here?

JERRY. No us, the cinema.

TOM (*frightened*). Who from?

JERRY. Don't know. Bloke on the phone.

TOM. When?

JERRY. Just now. Ten minutes ago.

TOM (*alarmed*) Threatening to plant a bomb?

JERRY. It's already planted.

TOM. There's a bomb ticking away in our cinema?

JERRY. Yes.

TOM (*frightened*). Good God! What'll we have to do?

JERRY. Get the audience out, eh?

TOM. Why didn't you do that straightaway?

JERRY. I wanted to ask you.

TOM. What did you come down here for?

JERRY. Couldn't find you. I looked all over.

TOM. I was mending a fuse. I was among the meters.

JERRY. I didn't look among the meters. I thought you'd come down here.

TOM (*after a pause*). Is it a leg-pull?

JERRY. Don't know.

TOM. Is somebody having us on?

JERRY. Possible.

TOM. And just when we've got these blokes interested.

JERRY. They were in here last week.

TOM. Who said?

JERRY. Proctor, Rose. Two blokes in camel-hair coats.

TOM. Telling Rose all about it?

JERRY. Sort of quizzing folk about —

TOM. Anyway we can't bother about them . . . I don't know.

PROCTOR (*calling from a distance*). Did you hear that, Tom?

TOM. What?

PROCTOR. The crusty bread's finished. Will you have sliced?

ROSE. You could have it toasted.

TOM. No, just plain.

ROSE. And pickles?

TOM. Sure, Rose, sure. (*Pause, then to* JERRY.) I don't know. (*Long pause, then with decision.*) It's a leg-pull, that's what it is. It's a hoax.

JERRY. Might be.

TOM. The Troc had a bomb warning.

JERRY. Yes.

TOM. False alarm.

JERRY. Yes.

TOM. And the Essoldo.

JERRY. Yes.

TOM. And Take Two in town, all false alarms. There's been a spate. It's some bloody hoaxer.

JERRY. But wasn't there something funny at the Essoldo?

TOM. There's always something funny at the Essoldo, the manager.

JERRY. Pately.

TOM. Defrocked priest.

JERRY. Is he?

TOM. Or a busted Group Captain, something. God, there's some odd blokes in this business. Morgan and his pal under his ginger mop they come negotiating with us like a couple of thieves in the night, not a word, don't breathe it, in the utmost confidence, then they're down here, telling Rose and bruiting it about. (*As though to dispose of the matter.*) I don't know.

JERRY (*after a pause, then diffidently*). Tom. . . What are we going to do?

TOM. It's a hoax, isn't it?

JERRY (*uncertainly*). In view of all the others, I suppose —

TOM (*after a pause*). Look, let's not panic. That's the first thing. Run over it. I've only got half a story.

JERRY. It's what I've said. This bloke came on the phone.

TOM. When? What time?

JERRY. Ten, fifteen minutes ago. Ten to eight.

TOM. Did he sound like a Paddy?

JERRY. I don't know. He was on and off.

TOM. Did he sound foreign?

JERRY. No, not foreign.

TOM. What exactly did he say?

JERRY. I can't remember exactly. It was unexpected.

TOM (*not unkindly*). Course it's unexpected, Jerry. We don't get an offer to blow us up every day.

JERRY (*with an apologetic laugh*). No, but —

TOM. Try to remember. Think.

PROCTOR. When to the sessions of sweet silent thought I summon up remembrance of things past.

PROCTOR *puts a glass on their table.*

Your pint, Tom.

TOM. Thanks, Peter.

PROCTOR. Evocative lines those, aren't they? Sweet silent thought. I don't know what's happened to your cheese and pickles. (*Moving away.*) Rose must have fallen into the jar.

TOM (*with a forced laugh, calls*). Mixed bathing. (*Speaks to JERRY.*) What did he say then? Keep your voice down. Old Big Ears there.

JERRY. It wasn't me that raised my voice.

TOM. No, it wasn't. Sorry mate. Did he give a time?

JERRY. What for?

TOM. When it's set to go off?

JERRY. I don't think he said a time.

TOM (*after a pause*). It's somebody trying to ruin our business.

JERRY. You think so?

TOM. The Troc, the Essoldo, they had these false alarms.

JERRY. Yes.

TOM. And there's nobody in. They're playing to no business.

JERRY. Yes.

TOM (*wryly*). He's a fickle bloke, your cinema client. He doesn't like being blown up.

JERRY. No.

TOM. Or even the remote spurious threat of it.

JERRY. So you think —

TOM. You say he didn't give a time?

JERRY. I don't remember him giving a time.

TOM (*after a pause*). He's a phoney.

JERRY. You're sure?

TOM. The Paddys, the Baader Meinhof buggers, the Japanese Red Army, all your pukka terorists, they give a time. It's an essential part of their operation.

JERRY. Is it?

TOM. Create the maximum disturbance. Publicity, bomb squad out, telly cameras. This isn't a pukka bloke.

JERRY. No.

TOM. It's the bloke who emptied the Troc and the Essoldo.

JERRY. Might be.

TOM. Some kid. I'd kick his backside.

JERRY. Might be.

TOM. Look, your instinct.

JERRY. My what?

TOM. Your instinct. I rely on your instinct. I've got a better head and you've got a better instinct.

JERRY. Sometimes.

TOM. When that bloke rang off the phone what was your instinct?

JERRY. To consult your head.

TOM (*laughs*). OK. Look, mate, you don't make mistakes. Morgan and his pal, I said they were funny blokes. They've been in here, we now learn, acting strange. To me, they're more than dubious. But you've thought all along they were seriously in for a deal. All right, despite what I think, I trust your instinct. You're seldom wrong.

JERRY. But in this case —

TOM. Look, if that bloke on the phone was authentic, you'd have sensed it instantly and without an iota of doubt. You'd have been straight on to the PA switch and you'd have emptied the place.

JERRY. I don't know.

TOM. You wouldn't have come calmly down here.

JERRY. Wasn't all that calmly.

TOM. You wouldn't be sitting here now with your lager.

JERRY. No. (*Pause.*) I panicked.

TOM. Anybody would, mate.

JERRY. Yes.

TOM. Anybody'd panic.

JERRY. Yes.

TOM (*after a pause*). It was never our game, the cinema game.

JERRY. No.

TOM. We should never have gone into it.

JERRY. No.

TOM. Vulnerable every way up, aren't you?

JERRY. Seem to be.

TOM. If we do sell the place it'll take ten years off me.

JERRY. Yes.

TOM. And it'll take twenty years off you. You're the worrier.

JERRY. It's my mother's money.

TOM. She's been very good to us, your mother, she's been very patient. We mustn't let it leak out, this bomb warning business.

JERRY. No.

ROSE (*calls from a distance*). Do you want it over there, Tom?

TOM. Eh?

PROCTOR (*calls from a distance*). Your cheese and pickels.

TOM (*calls*). We're coming over. (*Speaks to* JERRY.) So not a word to anybody.

JERRY. No.

TOM. Not even to your mother.

JERRY. No.

TOM. For the time being. If you don't mind.

JERRY. Sure.

TOM (*moving*). OK let's drift over. (*They start to move.*) Hang
on. (*Long pause and then with anxiety and deep feeling.*) Be a
dreadful thing if despite —

JERRY. Yes.

TOM. All those people.

JERRY. Yes.

TOM. The staff. Dick, Elsie.

JERRY. Mrs Alderson.

TOM. I don't know. God, it screws you up. It really screws you.

JERRY. Perhaps —

TOM. We are insured, aren't we? We are insured?

JERRY. We're insured.

TOM. But that pile of bills we put to one side, deferred.

JERRY. Yes.

TOM. Well, was the insurance premium not amongst them?

JERRY. No.

TOM. I don't remember signing the cheque.

JERRY. We don't sign a cheque. It's on a banker's order.

TOM. So it is. (*Laughs.*) Be one way of getting shot of the place
and collecting. But it's not a consideration, insurance.

JERRY. No.

TOM. It's just that instinctively you think of it when you're put
on the spot.

JERRY. Yes.

TOM. What we might do, what we could do: without disturbing
the audience, we could have a discreet snoop round, you
know, the offices, the foyer, the toilets, backstage.

JERRY. He said it was in among the audience.

TOM. In the darkness?

JERRY. Yes.

TOM. You didn't say that.

JERRY. It's what I meant. It's what he conveyed.

TOM (*after a pause*). So it's either nothing, or everyone out?

JERRY. Yes.

TOM. This is the ultimate refinement.

JERRY. Yes.

TOM (*after a pause*). It's not authentic. It is not authentic. Genuine bombers don't play games like this. They don't narrow down the area you've got to search. They don't give clues. They're not playing hunt the sodding thimble.

JERRY. No.

TOM. It's some kid, and he's done it before. He's got it figured out in every detail.

JERRY. Yes.

TOM (*after a pause*). I will not be pushed around. I will not break into a sweat to amuse some damned kid. Cinemas are in a bad enough way without this kind of buffoonery. Well, sod 'em, they've picked on the wrong blokes this time. Let's join the company. (*He gets up.*)

JERRY (*after a pause*). Perhaps I'll get back, Tom.

TOM (*composed*). Stay and have a jar. (*Moving and quietly.*) Act at your ease. Old big ears there. (*Loudly.*) OK, Peter lad, same again?

PROCTOR. Thank you, Tom.

TOM. Same again all round, Rose, and have one with us.

ROSE. Thank you, Tom.

ROSE *draws the drinks.*

PROCTOR. Hey, Tom, it hadn't occurred to me before.

TOM. What?

PROCTOR. Your names.

TOM. What about them?

PROCTOR. Tom and Jerry. That's what they call that cartoon cat and mouse, isn't it? You as flea pit moguls — it's like Happy Families — you know, Mr Feedus the Grocer, Dr Quack and so forth.

TOM (*with a slight laugh*). Yes.

PROCTOR. Something troubling you, Tom?

TOM. No.

PROCTOR. Something blown up?

TOM. No.

PROCTOR. Bit of a crisis blown up?

TOM. No, no, no. Routine matters. (*Laughs*.) Old age and poverty.

PROCTOR. The fate of us all if we're spared.

ROSE. You used to call it that, didn't you, Tom?

TOM. Call what what?

ROSE. Your cinema. You used to call it the Tom and Jerry.

TOM. One time.

JERRY. When we first took over.

PROCTOR. Why did you change it?

TOM. Created a wrong expectation. We're not exactly in the Tom and Jerry business.

ROSE. Those biddies in the school holidays.

PROCTOR. What was that?

TOM. Turned up with all their bambinos in the school holidays expecting to see cartoons, and what were we running, Jerry?

JERRY. Can't exactly remember.

PROCTOR. Something highly salacious, I don't doubt.

ROSE. They expostulated.

TOM. That's right. One expostulated with a brick through the windscreen of the van.

They all laugh.

PROCTOR. Bit strong.

TOM. And they sent Jerry's old Sunday School superintendent to tell his mother.

They all laugh. Telephone rings.

ROSE (*still laughing*). Excuse me. (*Into phone.*) Royal Victoria.

PROCTOR (*laughing*). No quarter given.

TOM (*laughing*). Mums, you know, at the end of their tether in the school holidays.

PROCTOR. A menace to the Queen's peace. (*He bursts out laughing.*) It's a sort of Tom and Jerry situation in itself, isn't it?

TOM. What?

PROCTOR. Kids wailing, wrathful biddies belting round your flea pit after you.

TOM (*laughing*). Not exactly.

PROCTOR. Scuttling past Rabelaisian scenes on the screen, wump with a brick through your windscreen, then the whole phalanx of 'em bearing down on Jerry's mum shaking like angry jellies. (*He laughs.*)

TOM *and* JERRY *also laugh. During the above exchanges* ROSE *is replying on the telephone to a person whom we do not hear. She has difficulty in hearing above the conversation and it is not easy for her to grasp what is being asked.*

ROSE (*into telephone*). Yes, that's right, the Royal Victoria. . . Who? Yes. . . I don't know. . . A what? When? I don't know. . . Look, hang on, I'll ask him. (*She puts the receiver down.*) Tom. (*Laughter stops.*) Tom, it's the *Express*. They say have you had a bomb warning at the cinema? (*Silence.*)

TOM. Is he on now?

ROSE. It's a woman.

TOM. I'll speak to her. (*Into telephone.*) Hello, Tom Baker here. . . When? When's this supposed to have happened? No, no, somebody's pulling your leg, love. . . No, I'd know, I've been there all night. . . No, I'll ring you back if I hear anything. (*He replaces receiver. Silence.* TOM is subdued and concerned.*) How much, Rose?

ROSE. What?

TOM. The drinks, my supper.

ROSE. One seventy, please, Tom.

TOM. Thanks.

ROSE *rings up the money in the cash register.*

Well, cheers.

PROCTOR. Cheers.

They drink.

TOM. Bloody kids.

PROCTOR. Bomb warning?

TOM. Hoax.

PROCTOR. Some prankster?

TOM. Been a whole spate of 'em, hasn't there, Jerry?

JERRY. At cinemas.

TOM. The Troc, the Essoldo, Take Two in town.

ROSE. Skating rink the other Saturday.

TOM (*encouraged*). I'd forgotten that. It's not funny. I'd kick their backsides.

> *Silence.*

PROCTOR. It's on now, is it?

TOM. That's the tale.

PROCTOR. You're sure it's a leg-pull?

TOM. It has all the hallmarks.

PROCTOR. Not worth disturbing the audience for?

TOM. That's what they want, isn't it? Sitting in the café opposite watching everybody panicking out.

ROSE. Don't play into their hands, that's what the boss said.

PROCTOR. How did he come to say that?

ROSE. Passing an opinion.

PROCTOR. Have you had one of these warnings?

ROSE (*with a laugh*). No.

PROCTOR. Come on. How many have you had? ·

ROSE. We don't want it spread around.

PROCTOR. Come on. When?

ROSE. We're speaking in confidence, aren't we?

PROCTOR. Course we are.

ROSE. Because it'd be bad for business if it got out.

PROCTOR. We're all friends. When did it happen?

ROSE. Once or twice, a few times.

PROCTOR. What did you do?

ROSE. We had a quick scout round without alarming anybody.

TOM. Which we can't do in a darkened flea pit.

ROSE. And we spotted nothing, so the boss said: 'Right, we'll brazen it out.'

PROCTOR. You never told me.

ROSE. We never told anybody. The banks don't.

PROCTOR (*accepting the joke*). I could have been blown to Kingdom Come with my pint in my hand.

TOM. Good way to go if you have to.

ROSE (*laughing*). We used you as a sort of gauge.

PROCTOR. A sort of gauge?

ROSE. I was very nervous.

PROCTOR. Naturally.

ROSE. The boss said: 'Just calmly go on with your work and from time to time keep an eye on Mr Proctor there. If his head's still on his shoulders at closing time you'll know it was a hoax.'

They all laugh.

PROCTOR. It's back to the Red Lion for me after this.

TOM. But seriously, Mr Dewer's right. If this sort of thing gets out it can be very harmful to business.

ROSE. That's why I said, in confidence.

TOM. And in our case likewise. We're all in the same boat with this sort of lark and we all know what sort of damage this kind of publicity can do.

ROSE. They were a long time picking up business at the Farmer's Arms.

TOM. I'd forgotten that.

PROCTOR. Sunday lunchtime job. Cleared a few score of tipplers out.

ROSE. And many of them still haven't gone back.

PROCTOR. So let your counsel be Yea, Yea, and Nay, Nay, as the Good Book says.

TOM. Or just Nay, Nay, thanks.

They laugh.

JERRY (*still worried*) Well, I think I'll get back, Tom.

TOM. You're all right. You haven't paid your round yet.

ROSE. We seldom have the pleasure of your company, Jerry.

PROCTOR (*invitingly*). Stay and pay your round.

TOM. Have a pickle.

JERRY (*laughs*). No thanks.

TOM. Well, come on, you're in the chair.

JERRY (*relenting*). Same again then?

PROCTOR. Please.

JERRY (*slight laugh*). Please, Rose.

ROSE *draws drinks*.

PROCTOR. Would be a hell of a thing though.

TOM. What?

PROCTOR. Bomb in a cinema.

TOM. Bomb anywhere.

PROCTOR. But especially in a cinema. Under a seat, among the empty ice cream cartons, ticking away but obviously inaudible while the sound track's running, your customers sitting back or whatever they do in the darkness — then wump, heads and arms and toffee wrappings flung up into the projector beam. What a way to go.

ROSE. Imagination, eh?

TOM (*slightly annoyed*). It wouldn't be like that.

PROCTOR. Like what?

TOM. People's heads flying through the projector beam.

PROCTOR. Why not?

TOM. If it was as bad as that the projector would be knocked out.

PROCTOR. Not necessarily. Blast is a funny thing. Or it might be that the projector would cop it, not stopped but badly knocked out of line. That would be a scene. Moaning and carnage down in the darkness and the projector churning away on its side throwing lewd images on the shattered walls above the dead and dying. Everybody —

JERRY. All right, that'll do.

PROCTOR (*surprised*). Sorry Jerry, no offence meant.

TOM (*aside and overlapping*). OK Jerry. (*Aloud.*) None taken, Peter. (*Mock seriously to restore harmony.*) But talking of heads I'm a bit bothered about yours.

PROCTOR. It lacks nothing but hair.

TOM. That psychiatrist, eh Rose?

ROSE. Him who brought the nutters?

TOM. The same.

ROSE. Vogelheimer.

TOM. He'd have been interested in Peter's head.

ROSE. His imagination?

TOM. No, this kink he has, this obsession.

PROCTOR (*with good humour*). What obsession?

TOM. You're always on about projectors.

PROCTOR. I've never mentioned them till just now.

ROSE. You did. You were on about it with Jerry earlier, wasn't he, Jerry?

JERRY (*agreeably*). It was touched upon.

TOM (*enlightened*). Hey, wait a minute. There was a contretemps in progress when I came in, wasn't there?

PROCTOR (*laughing it off*). No, not exactly.

TOM. Never mind not exactly, there was a contretemps. And I know what it was about.

PROCTOR. No, no.

TOM. You, Mr P., were putting to my friend and partner the proposition you put to me every other week.

PROCTOR (*laughing*). No. No. No. No. No.

TOM. You were putting the proposition could you come in some morning and we'd run the film for you and stop the projector at the juicy bits.

PROCTOR (*laughing*). No. No. No. No. No.

ROSE. Yes. Yes. Yes. Wasn't he, Jerry?

JERRY. Sort of.

TOM. You meet all the kinks in this business but this is the first we've ever had, isn't it, Jerry, who had a thing about the projector?

PROCTOR (*agreeably*). All right, you could have made a bob or two, but if you don't want the morning business —

JERRY. No thanks.

TOM. Not after the last lot.

ROSE. The nutters.

PROCTOR. What nutters? Who are you libelling now?

TOM. We're not libelling anybody. These really were fully paid up card-carrying nut cases.

PROCTOR. You let them in in the mornings?

TOM. Ran special shows for them.

ROSE.   ⎱ Then they came in here.
PROCTOR. ⎰ What for?

TOM. Therapy. This psychiatrist bloke —

ROSE. Vogelheimer.

TOM. Or Robinson, approached us. He thought some of our artistic offerings might be therapeutic for them.

JERRY. They were therapeutic for him.

TOM (*laughing*). By God, yes. Sitting there with the static crackling round his beard.

They all laugh.

PROCTOR. And they were a bit of a handful, were they?

TOM. They were all right. One or two of them forgot they were in public.

ROSS. The boss wouldn't serve 'em here.

TOM. And our cleaning ladies wouldn't stand them — they were prejudiced. And so, put briefly, there are no more morning shows either for certified nutters or for uncertified ones who want to see the projector stopped.

They all laugh.

ROSE. They should never have let them out.

PROCTOR. It's a democratic country.

ROSE. What's that got to do with it?

PROCTOR. Everything. It's a defining principle. In totalitarian countries they put sane people in lunatic asylums; in democracies they let the lunatics out.

ROSE. Oh, very clever.

TOM. Don't get on your political hobby horse. Here you are, pick up your pint. Cheers, Jerry.

PROCTOR. Cheers, Jerry.

ROSE. Seventy-four, Jerry.

She rings the till. They drink.

PROCTOR (*laughs*). It would be an embarrassing end, though, wouldn't it?

TOM. What?

PROCTOR. To be blown up watching a blue movie.

TOM. If you were blown up you wouldn't feel anything, would you, embarrassment or anything else.

PROCTOR. But the relations, the bereaved. Some poor woman having to tell the kiddies their dad had been translated while having a bit of a wallow.

ROSE. Here he goes again.

PROCTOR. Inserting a notice in the paper. 'Dear husband, father, brother, uncle, son, Suddenly while watching Prurient Passions.'

TOM. Yes, yes.

PROCTOR. One moment enjoying your bit of smut, the next on a fizzer at the Judgment Seat.

ROSE. You've got to go sometime. You might as well go happy.

PROCTOR. Not if you care about being in a state of grace.

TOM. Do you care about being in a state of grace?

PROCTOR. I don't but other blokes do. They wouldn't care to be scythed down in a state of mortal sin.

TOM. Mortal sin, watching pictures?

PROCTOR. It could be.

TOM. Rubbish.

PROCTOR. Well, it's not the good death for which we all pray.

TOM. The good death for which we all pray. You're not a Catholic. You're some sort of a communist.

PROCTOR. I can still pray for a good death if I want to.

TOM. No.

PROCTOR. I can apply, I'm not debarred.

TOM. All right, carry on. Do you think it'd have been a good death if you'd been blown off that stool with a pint in your fist?

PROCTOR. At least when I'm in here I'm where my wife thinks I am.

TOM. So am I when I'm in the cinema.

PROCTOR. But your customers aren't, many of them, that's all I'm saying, and it'd be a profound shock to their near and dear ones to find their remains in the rubble of a blue movie house.

TOM. All right. Jerry's mother doesn't know he goes into pubs.

ROSE. He very seldom does.

TOM. And it'd be a profound shock to her to find his remains in the rubble of a pub, which from the number of warnings they've apparently had is a deal more likely than at our flea pit.

PROCTOR (*arguing*). Perhaps so —

TOM. But whatever rubble he reposed in the fact of his having passed on would be infinitely more upsetting to his mother than the location where he chose to do it.

PROCTOR. OK.

TOM. She'd have nobody to play golf with.

They all laugh. They drink and TOM *eats.*

JERRY. Well, I think I'd better get back now.

TOM. Hang on two minutes till I finish my nosebag. I'll come with you.

PROCTOR (*with insight but in a friendly way*). Has it come at a rather awkward time for you?

TOM. What?

PROCTOR. Tonight's little episode.

TOM. Any time would be an awkward time.

PROCTOR. I shan't bruit it around.

ROSE. Tell anybody and you've told everybody.

PROCTOR. You can depend on me.

TOM. I know we can, Peter.

> *Silence.* TOM *eats.*

PROCTOR. The reason I ask would it be an awkward time —
there has been a certain amount of rumour that you're looking
to sell the place.

TOM. No.

ROSE. There's always rumours.

PROCTOR. Not booming, bit of a millstone.

TOM. No. No. No. No.

PROCTOR. I was telling Jerry there were a couple of blokes in
here wearing camel-hair coats.

ROSE. He told you he didn't know them.

PROCTOR. One with a ginger toupé, obviously weighing up
business at your cinema.

TOM. No. . . They wouldn't come in here if they were interested
in buying the place. They'd come and see the books.

PROCTOR. They talked as though they had done.

TOM (*laughs. He speaks with some affection*). All right, you sod,
all right. Look, this really is in strictest confidence.

PROCTOR. Don't tell me if —

TOM. No, but entirely entre nous. Rose?

ROSE. Oh, entre nous.

TOM. Put it this way, the place is not for sale, not in the sense
that —

JERRY. We're not peddling it.

TOM. Quite. Your car, for instance, that's not for sale?

PROCTOR. No.

TOM. But if somebody offered you two thousand quid.

PROCTOR. They could have my wife as well.

TOM. Same with our cinema. It's ticking over, it's doing nicely, it's not advertised for sale, but these blokes are inquiring, they're interested.

PROCTOR. The gents in the camel coats?

TOM. Yes, and at the kind of money they're talking about we've got to listen, haven't we, Jerry?

JERRY. We've got to listen.

TOM. So to that extent this bomb scare has come at a very awkward time.

ROSE. They hurt business at any time.

TOM. And if it got out it would certainly hurt the prospects of any deal that might just conceivably be arrived at. So I would take it kindly, Peter, as one old friend to another if in view of the delicate balance of things —

PROCTOR. Tom, you can depend on me.

TOM. I know I can, Peter. Rose, let's have another round.

JERRY. I'll get back, Tom.

TOM. Just one round now I've ordered it and I'll come with you.

JERRY. I think I'd better —

TOM. Sit tight, you worry too much Jerry. . . Hey, isn't that you mother's car standing outside?

JERRY. My own's in for service.

TOM. But you drove here from the cinema?

JERRY. Yes.

TOM. You got in the car and you drove 100 yards?

JERRY (*laughs, self-consciously*). I was in a hurry.

TOM. I see. . . You shifted your mother's car in case there was a bomb ticking away there and you left me down among the meters to perish in the rubble.

TOM, PROCTOR *and* ROSE *laugh.*

JERRY (*amused and slightly embarrassed*). No, I thought you'd already gone. I looked for you everywhere.

TOM (*joking*). Straight out and into his mother's car.

JERRY. Turned back for it actually.

TOM. Turned back to the holocaust to rescue his mother's car.

Everybody laughs through TOM's *dialogue.*

TOM. He's more afraid of his mother than he is of the bomb. . .
O death where is thy sting. . . She's a kind old lady. She'd
have written a nice letter to my widow.

Everybody laughs. When they stop there is a brief silence, then
JERRY *says —*

JERRY. Tom, perhaps we should tell them.

TOM. Tell who?

JERRY. The people in the cinema, we should perhaps tell them.

Silence.

TOM. This is right about face. What's brought this on?

JERRY. We should tell them.

TOM. We've been over it, haven't we? We've been minutely over
it.

JERRY. Yes.

TOM. Well, then.

JERRY. Well talking in here is one thing, but it seemed altogether
different when I was trying to start my mother's car.

TOM. What way different?

JERRY. Well, ominous.

TOM. But you panicked. You said that. You were rattled.

JERRY. So rattled I tried to unlock the door with the ignition
key.

TOM. All right, I was rattled when you first told me.

ROSE. The boss was rattled when it happened here.

PROCTOR. Anybody'd be rattled. They do it to rattle folk.

TOM. I'd kick their backsides. Come on, Jerry, drink up.

They drink.

PROCTOR. Strictly speaking, though, I suppose in a perfect world people would be entitled to know they were in danger of being blown to Kingdom Come.

TOM. How?

PROCTOR. It seems a basic human right.

TOM. In a perfect world it'd be a basic right not to be blown to Kingdom Come.

PROCTOR. Granted.

TOM. But we don't live in a perfect world. We've got to use judgment.

ROSE. Don't play into their hands. That's what the boss said.

TOM.   ⎱ Exactly.
PROCTOR. ⎰ Whose hands?

ROSE. Terrorists.

TOM. Exactly. If they could get buildings evacuated on the strength of a phone call they could paralyse the civilised world from a telephone box.

ROSE. You've got to keep a sense of proportion. There's scores of spoof calls every day. It's a fashionable yobbos' hobby. The big hotels and banks and whatnot don't react any more and we wouldn't hear if it happened again.

JERRY. But it's still worrying.

ROSE. Course it is. You know there must be a thousand of these spoofs to every genuine alarm call and the chance of anybody, however crackpot, picking on a pokey little flea pit —

TOM. Luxury cinema, do you mind?

ROSE. Or a rundown suburban boozer like this, it's so utterly remote, but it still nags, doesn't it, Jerry? You can't completely put it out of your mind once that phone has rung. I know how you feel, Jerry.

PROCTOR. Anguish.

ROSE. What?

PROCTOR. Anguish. That's the name of the game.

ROSE. What game?

PROCTOR. It's a product every time of the system, isn't it?

TOM. What's the system got to do with it?

PROCTOR. Well, if nothing else, it's created these mobs of unemployed yobbos with nothing to fill their time but spoofs of this sort.

ROSE. They should call 'em up for the Army. That'd sort 'em out.

PROCTOR. And if we get down to basics it's the system that's bred terrorism.

TOM. } No, no, no.
ROSE. { Come off it.

PROCTOR. Terrorism has grown out of injustice.

TOM. What injustice?

PROCTOR. Well, the Paddys have had their landlords tugging their roofs off.

TOM. That's bloody ages ago.

PROCTOR. It can rankle, it can fester. And the Palestinians they were given the heave-o off their native sod.

TOM. Me and Jerry didn't give 'em the heave-o, we didn't tug their roofs off.

PROCTOR. I'm not saying you did.

TOM. All right then, what right have they to come and bomb our flea pit?

PROCTOR. You say they're not bombing your flea pit.

TOM (*genially, breaking off the argument*). Well, drink up then and buy us a pint.

They both laugh.

JERRY. Tom.

TOM. Jerry.

JERRY. Tom, I think at least we should get the staff out.

TOM (*after a pause*). OK. . . That's reasonable.

JERRY. I'll go back and —

TOM. Hang on. (*In a joking voice.*) It's quicker by phone. Rose, could I —

ROSE. Help yourself.

TOM dials number.

TOM. Elsie? It's Tom. Look, love, there's something come up, sort of practical joke, I'll explain later. Anyway, what I want you to do, I want you to leave the cinema, just for a few minutes. Collect Mrs Alderson and the two girls and see Dick in the projection room and all of you go and wait in the café opposite or better still go down to the Coffee Pot. It's a spoof, somebody trying to get at us. Go to the Coffee Pot. Order whatever you like all of you and I'll see to the bill when I come. . . Good. (*He puts the telephone down. Silence.*)

What's up, Peter?

PROCTOR. Nothing.

TOM. Come on.

PROCTOR. Well it's not my business, Tom, but since you press me. I think that was an error of judgment.

TOM. To get the staff out?

PROCTOR. And leave the audience in. It could look bad in retrospect.

TOM. How?

PROCTOR. If the worst comes to the worst, if the whole flea pit goes up.

TOM. It's not going to go up.

PROCTOR. Why disturb the staff if you're 100 per cent sure?

TOM. I'm not 100 per cent sure. What's anybody 100 per cent sure of? Are you 100 per cent sure there isn't a bomb wired up to your car ignition at this moment, are you 100 per cent sure your wife isn't in bed with the window cleaner, are you 100 per cent sure the sun will come up tomorrow?

PROCTOR (*with good humour*). Well, I don't know what you might know about the window cleaner —

TOM (*with a laugh*). Just an example.

PROCTOR. But of the other two propositions I'm sure beyond a reasonable doubt.

TOM. Fair enough, then. I'm as sure as that.

ROSE. And in any case it's different for staff.

PROCTOR. How?

ROSE. We're more often exposed.

TOM. Exactly. If there is a slight element of risk, slight as it is, it's multiplied for the staff by the number of occasions they're exposed to it.

ROSE. We've had four warnings here, false alarms. You were only in for two of them.

PROCTOR. And the boss rightly judged they were false alarms and rightly or wrongly said nothing.

ROSE. Rightly.

PROCTOR. But this is the point, what's sauce for the goose is sauce for the gander. You didn't evacuate yourselves and leave us here.

ROSE. That's exactly what we did. We went down to the air raid shelter.

PROCTOR. What air raid shelter?

ROSE. In the cellar, what they had built during the war.

PROCTOR (*affecting indignation*). You went creeping down there and left me at the bar?

ROSE. You weren't at the bar. You were playing the piano.

PROCTOR. You should have mentioned it. I'd have played Abide with Me.

ROSE. You did better. You were playing wartime tunes. The boss said it was just like the blitz, sitting down in the shelter.

PROCTOR. I'm glad I kept you entertained. How long did this go on?

ROSE. We went down five minutes before.

PROCTOR. Before what?

ROSE. The time the warning was given for, quarter to ten. We were very glad to enjoy your melodies without interruption.

PROCTOR. And I'm very glad, now I'm aware of the circumstances, that I was spared to continue them without interruption.

ROSE. And you were still alive and hammering it out at ten to and the boss said: 'Old Proctor's still hard at it up there. I suppose we can assume the All Clear's gone?'

They all laugh.

PROCTOR. Happy days.

ROSE. But subsequent times we just haven't bothered. We put it out of our minds — or we try to — and just go on serving.

TOM. You've got to.

ROSE. Course you have.

PROCTOR. All the same, Tom, I'd be worried about the construction that might —

TOM. Peter, we've sorted it out and we don't want to go on debating it.

PROCTOR. All right.

TOM. Look, we're a couple of little businessmen with a piddling little suburban flea pit. We know nothing about politics or terrorists or the psychological problems of unemployed youth —

ROSE (*sympathetically indignant*). You shouldn't be bothered.

TOM. It's not our scene and it's not our size. We run a little cinema and before this we ran a little snack bar and before that an unprofitable launderette. The biggest crisis we've ever dealt with in all our lives was when some kids put a cat in one of the driers.

ROSE (*shrieks*). Don't tell me!

JERRY. Went in ginger and came out white.

ROSE (*shrieks*). Stop it! I'm not listening.

TOM (*laughs*). Bit dizzy but otherwise —

ROSE. Stop it! Cruelty, that's one thing I can't stand.

JERRY. Boys, you know.

ROSE. Should give 'em a good hiding.

PROCTOR. But what's that got to do with —

TOM. I'm telling you, that's on our scale. We can cope. It's in the dimensions of our scene, cats in driers. But this thing it's a preposterous thing to saddle us with. We can't be held responsible.

PROCTOR. But if you don't tell 'em you have taken responsibility, haven't you? You've used your judgment on their behalf.

TOM. All right then, what are you advocating?

PROCTOR (*after a pause*). It's difficult.

TOM. All right, it's difficult. The seconds are ticking away. You tell me what to do.

PROCTOR. Give 'em the option, then the responsibility's theirs, not yours.

TOM. The option?

PROCTOR. Yes, there need be no panic. A calm announcement. Say frankly that you've had this warning and frankly you give it little credence. But if anyone of a nervous disposition chooses to depart the doors are now open etcetera and after a brief intermission, during which sweets and ice cream will be on sale, the film will resume for patrons who choose to remain.

TOM (*laughing*). Peter, if there was a bomb it would have gone off before you'd said that lot.

ROSE. It's his ploy to get the projector stopped.

They all laugh.

TOM. No, that's the worst of both worlds.

ROSE. Course it is. You've left the customers in and you've damaged the business.

PROCTOR. Would it actually damage the business so much?

TOM. You ask 'em at the Troc and the Essoldo.

ROSE. You ask 'em at the Farmers' Arms.

PROCTOR. But even so, weighed in the balance against people's lives.

ROSE. False alarms don't kill people.

Silence.

PROCTOR (*prepared to drop the subject*). No.

Silence.

TOM (*suddenly anxious and angry*). God, it screws you up. If the aim of this clown was to create the maximum anguish and anxiety I'd just like him to know he's succeeded 100 per cent.

ROSE. They should flog 'em.

PROCTOR (*sympathetically*). It's the system. It screws everybody.

ROSE. Aw, politics.

PROCTOR. All right, politics, but we're all victims of the system. The blokes who plant bombs —

ROSE. They're psychopaths, not victims.

PROCTOR. That's only a different word for it, Rose. And the people who are killed and maimed they're —

ROSE. Who's killed and maimed?

PROCTOR. And Tom and Jerry they're victims of the system.

ROSE. They're not victims of any system. They're victims of a hoax.

PROCTOR. Which the system turns into anguish.

ROSE. How do you mean?

PROCTOR. If there were no considerations of a capitalist nature, if there were no commercial motives, there'd be no problem..

ROSE. If there were no commercial motives there'd be no cinemas.

PROCTOR. There are cinemas in socialist countries.

TOM. Where they don't get blokes in asking to stop the projector.

ROSE. Not for those sort of films.

TOM. You wouldn't want a private peek-a-boo, Peter lad, at a saga about pig iron production in Bulgaria.

PROCTOR (*laughs*). I don't get a private peek-a-boo at anything. But granted, in the specific area of serving our common lechery, capitalism works best. But in practically every other sphere it lands people in a nasty pickle.

ROSE. Who's in a pickle?

PROCTOR. Tom's in a pickle. Jerry's in a pickle. We're all in a pickle. We're making stabs at judging what can't be judged, we're watching the minutes tick away, we're fiddling perhaps while Rome burns, we're swigging pints sitting on a keg of dynamite. That's what —

JERRY. All right, all right. That'll do.

ROSE. You get carried away, Mr. Proctor.

PROCTOR (*after a pause*). I'm sorry.

Silence.

TOM (*after a pause, then quietly*). Perhaps you're right, Peter. (*Very worried.*) I don't know.

ROSE. He'd come to a reasonable decision and you've upset him now.

TOM. Is it reasonable, Jerry?

JERRY. I don't know.

PROCTOR. If I might suggest —

TOM. All right, Peter, you're obviously clearer than we are.

PROCTOR. I'm not saying that.

TOM. We've discussed it, we've carefully weighed the possibilities and we've come to a decision. Right or wrong now I'm going to sweat it out. I'm going to sit tight. But as I said this sort of situation is beyond our scale, isn't it, Jerry?

JERRY. It is.

TOM. And if it's clear to you we're wrong, then you do what's right.

PROCTOR. It's not my responsibility.

TOM. Peter, if a hundred people get blown up in the next half hour are you going to argue it wasn't your responsibility?

ROSE. If you know about it, you're responsible.

PROCTOR. Look, this isn't my decision. You can't fob this off on to me.

TOM. I'm not fobbing it off. I've told you what we're going to do — or rather what we're not going to do. You don't have to agree. You don't have to comment. But you know as much or as little as I do, you've as good ground for forming an opinion, and if you strongly feel I'm wrong, I'm willing to be over-ruled. I won't stand in your way.

ROSE. That's fair.

Silence.

TOM. So which way is it going to be?

PROCTOR. I don't know. . . I don't know. . . I'd look a right donkey if I took it upon myself and then nothing. . . I don't know. . . On balance, on balance I support you, Tom. Looked at realistically, in the sober light of day, I go along with you. You're right.

Silence.

ROSE (*gently*). People don't want to be troubled, you know, Mr Proctor.

PROCTOR. No.

ROSE. If we were told of everything that might threaten us, we'd never stop worrying.

PROCTOR. No.

ROSE. I'd sooner not know. We never told my mother and she was happy until the last weeks when the pain —

PROCTOR. I remember your mother, Rose.

ROSE. You can't spend your life running away from death.

PROCTOR. No.

ROSE. It's got to come some day, and whether it's a bit earlier or a bit later doesn't matter much.

PROCTOR. Doesn't it, Rose?

ROSE. Because when it does come we shall see God in his glory, as my mother did.

Silence. The telephone rings. There is an apprehensive pause before ROSE *picks it up.*

Royal Victoria. . . No, he's out for the evening and Mrs Dewer's with him. . . He might be at his brother's. . . Yes. . . Righto. . . Goodbye.

TOM. I shouldn't have put you on the spot like that, Peter.

PROCTOR. Fair enough, Tom. I perhaps made rather bold with my comments.

ROSE (*pleasantly*). As ever.

TOM. You're quite right though. I take your point. We do have commercial motives.

ROSE. Who doesn't?

TOM. If only on the crudest level. I don't want to have to pawn the children's bicycles and he doesn't want to put his mother in the workhouse. But it goes a bit deeper, doesn't it, Jerry?

JERRY. At the present moment.

PROCTOR. You don't have to justify yourself, Tom. You've explained.

TOM. At any other time we'd pass on this scare, wouldn't we, Jerry?

JERRY. Yes.

TOM. Knowing it to be spurious, we'd give the alarm.

JERRY. Yes.

TOM. We'd stand the loss. But it has come at an absolutely critical time.

PROCTOR. I understand.

TOM. We seriously think those blokes are ready to buy. All that separates us is a very narrow gap, a few quid. They're going to come back to us next week.

He stops and the others wait to see whether he will continue. Then PROCTOR, *as though to close the matter, says* —

PROCTOR. Ill-timed. An ill-timed incident.

TOM. Yes. . . Look, we've known each other a long time, you're good friends. I said they were making us a good offer. Well, that's not strictly true. All we want is a rock-bottom price and they're trying to get it for less. We're nearly bust and they know it.

PROCTOR (*sympathetically*). I'd no idea —

TOM. It's all right on the surface. We're eating, we're paying the wages, we're meeting the bills, some of them.

JERRY. When they come printed in red.

TOM. To outward appearances we're turning over but in fact, in the accountant's book, we've been running down from the beginning. We've now had twelve thousand pounds in tax allowances for depreciation so there should be twelve thousand pounds in the depreciation account and in fact there's nothing.

ROSE. What's that mean?

TOM. It means, Rose, we're living on what we've been allowed for depreciation and when the time comes for capital replacement, we haven't got the money, we fizzle out, bankrupt. That's our own money gone, plus six thousand pounds Jerry's mother lent us.

PROCTOR. So you need to get out?

TOM. We need to get out.

PROCTOR. And these blokes —

TOM. They're in a buyer's market. They've been round looking. There isn't a cinema within 50 miles they couldn't buy tomorrow.

PROCTOR. It's come at a desperately bad time.

TOM. They'd just turn their interest elsewhere. But even if it wasn't for that — and I'm being absolutely frank with you every way up —

PROCTOR. You are, Tom.

TOM. Whatever way we might then feel free to act, I'd still come to the same conclusion. I've vaccilated and I've had a hot flush or two and I know I don't carry Jerry with me 100 per cent, but when I face it calmly, I simply do not believe there's a bomb in that cinema. It's a leg-pull.

PROCTOR. You're right, Tom. I talk too much. I'm sure you're right.

ROSE. 'Course he's right. If we'd ever seriously thought anything different we wouldn't have spent the night talking about it.

TOM. Jerry?

JERRY (*after a pause, calmly and sincerely*). I agree with you, Tom.

Telephone rings. They stand silent, then ROSE *lifts it.*

ROSE. Royal Victoria. . . He said he was going to his brother's. . . I see. He'll be back about 11. Could you ring him then, or in the morning. . . OK I'll tell him. (*She replaces receiver.*)

PROCTOR (*thoughtfully*). Figuring it out, Tom.

ROSE. Oh come on, Mr Proctor, order some drinks. We've had enough figuring.

PROCTOR. I just want to say this in the light of what you've disclosed. I'm sure now this is a hoax and I suspect it's not a simple hoax.

TOM. How?

PROCTOR. Somebody's deliberately trying to do dirt on you.

ROSE. But not personally.

PROCTOR. Yes, personally.

ROSE. It's got blown up out of all proportion. This sort of thing happens scores of times a day.

PROCTOR. I'm not saying it doesn't.

ROSE. It's not personal spite. It's a yobbos' hobby. It wasn't somebody personally trying to do dirt on Mr Dewer.

PROCTOR. We don't know who it was.

ROSE. It's not somebody personally trying to dirt on the skating rink or the banks.

PROCTOR. But a little suburban cinema at the very time when they're in desperate negotiations. It's somebody who knows, somebody with a score to pay off.

TOM (*laughs*). Anybody who watches our films has a score to pay off.

ROSE (*laughs*). Or maybe one of the nutters because you stopped their morning show.

TOM. That was ages ago.

Telephone rings over TOM's words. ROSE lifts receiver.

ROSE. Royal Victoria.

PROCTOR. They have long memories, nutters, like elephants.

ROSE (*overlapping*). Yes, hold on. (*To* TOM). For you.

TOM (*reluctant*). Who is it?

ROSE. Elsie.

TOM. Hello, Elsie. . . But you have found Mrs Alderson? Good. . . And Dick and the girls have gone? Well, you and Mrs Alderson get off straightaway now. . . Who told her that? Yes, well as I said, it's a hoax and we don't want a word said to anybody because it's upsetting. . . But just as a super precaution you and Mrs Alderson get off and wait in the Coffee Pot till I come up. . . Don't fiddle around. Leave things and go.

He replaces receiver. Silence. From now on the conversation is quiet, considered and serious and on TOM's side a little weary.

JERRY. What did she say?

TOM. She had to look round for Mrs Alderson.

JERRY. But she has found her?

TOM. Yes. . . Mrs Alderson had heard something.

JERRY. Who from?

TOM. Perhaps the reporter, the *Express* woman. Presumably she rang there before she rang me here.

JERRY. I see.

TOM. Apparently Mrs Alderson asked Elsie: 'Have you heard this rumour there's a bomb in here due to go off at nine o'clock?'

JERRY. So there was a time stated then?

TOM. Yes.

JERRY. Five minutes from now.

TOM. Yes.

JERRY. So what do you think?

TOM (*after a pause*). We've made our choice, Jerry. It's too late to be wrong. I stick by my judgment. (*Pause, then arguingly.*) Look, suppose there is a bomb, suppose we evacuate everybody out to the car park, that's what they'd expect, isn't it? Well, the bomb might be on the car park.

ROSE (*quietly*). That's what happens when you run away.

Silence.

JERRY. Tom, I want to ring and give the warning.

TOM. There's nobody to answer, Jerry. The staff have gone.

JERRY. I'll go back, Tom.

PROCTOR. If there is a bomb set for nine, Jerry, it'll go off in your teeth now.

JERRY (*moving — he has decided to go*). All the same.

TOM (*accepting that* JERRY *will go*). OK Jerry. OK.

JERRY (*by way of justification*). Tom, I know you're right and you convince me, but whenever that phone rings I remember the tone of the bloke's voice.

TOM. All right, Jerry, I still think it's the wrong move, but I won't stand in your way.

JERRY (*moving*). I'll give you a ring, Tom.

He goes through the door.

PROCTOR (*after a pause, quietly*). He's a worrier, your partner.

TOM. Yes.

PROCTOR. You can't change your nature if that's how God made you.

TOM. No.

Silence.

ROSE. Well, come on, cheer up. We'll have people coming in soon. Give us a tune.

PROCTOR (*diffidently*). I don't know if Tom —

TOM (*making an effort to brighten*). Sure, let's have a tune.

ROSE. Not too boisterous, Mr Proctor.

PROCTOR *plays first line of 'We'll gather lilacs' and continuing to play asks —*

PROCTOR. How's that?

ROSE. Nice.

PROCTOR (*quietly sings two lines*).
'Until our hearts have learned to sing again
When you come home once more.' (*He stops singing, continues to play and says soberly by way of final review —*) You know, Tom, I do think somebody is trying to do dirt on you.

TOM (*having had enough of the subject but not crossly*). Ah well.

PROCTOR (*leisurely*). And I think I know who it is, too,

ROSE. You know who it is?

PROCTOR. I think so.

ROSE. Who?

PROCTOR. The blokes in the camel-hair coats.

He stops playing.

ROSE. They really were weird blokes.

PROCTOR. Two pence for a phone call to knock a few hundred quid off the price — not a bad transaction.

ROSE. What do you think, Tom?

TOM. It's far-fetched but the whole business is far-fetched. As I said, it's beyond me.

PROCTOR. I'd put a quid on it.

ROSE. They really were weird blokes.

Silence.

TOM (*suddenly decided*). Look, give me the phone, I'll have a word with Jerry.

TOM *dials, and the number is heard ringing.*

ROSE. Not there yet?

TOM. I'll hang on.

Telephone is heard ringing. ROSE *by way of making conversation says quietly to* PROCTOR.

ROSE. They really were odd balls. The big one ordered a whisky Mac, and the little one, the one with the ginger rug on his head, he said did we do vodka Macs, then they both went off laughing. Weird blokes.

Phone is heard ringing.

TOM (*to himself*). Come on, Jerry.

ROSE. Perhaps he's said his piece already.

PROCTOR. Hardly be there yet.

Phone is heard ringing. Ringing stops.

TOM. Jerry. . . Have you done anything yet? Yes, I know it's nine o'clock, mate, but listen, before you rush into it, won't take a second. Peter here has had a thought what's behind this business. He thinks it's the blokes in the camel-hair coats, you know, Morgan and Walters, trying it on to screw the price down. He could be right, Jerry. What do you think, mate? (*He stops talking and listens.*) All right, Jerry. All right, if that's your decision. I'll come up. (*He puts the telephone down. Pause.*)

ROSE (*diffidently*). What did — what did he say?

TOM (*resigned*). He's going on with it.

PROCTOR. He's getting everybody out?

TOM. It's what he wants to do.

ROSE. Pity.

PROCTOR. It's unfortunate. It is. It's a classic dilemma. Whatever you'd have done would have been wrong, Tom.

TOM (*resigned*). Ah, well.

ROSE. You can't win 'em all, Tom.

TOM. No.

PROCTOR. Would you like a short?

TOM (*after a pause*). No thanks, I'd better go back. . . He's probably right. His instinct's better than mine. He's probably right.

ROSE (*sympathetically*). Worrying evening for you.

TOM (*tired laugh*). They come and go.

PROCTOR. It'll blow over, Tom.

TOM. Sure.

PROCTOR. Tomorrow the birds'll sing.

TOM. Sure.

> *The cinema blows up.*
>
> (*Quietly.*) Good God.

PROCTOR. It's gone up, Tom. (*Moving.*) Good God, Tom, the roof's burning.

TOM (*quietly and slowly*). No. No. No. No. No.

ROSE. Oh, Tom. It's not your fault, Tom.

TOM (*dazed*). No. No.

ROSE. Don't blame yourself.

> TOM, *dazed, continues to repeat the word 'No'.*

ROSE. You did your best.

PROCTOR (*dazed*). We all did our best.

ROSE. You can't win 'em all, Tom.

PROCTOR (*dazed*). According to our lights.

ROSE. We're all fallible, Tom. ·

PROCTOR (*dazed*). In the light of the information available.

ROSE (*protesting*). We're only human. We're not omniscient. We can't always be right.

TOM. No. No. No.

ROSE (*with great kindness*). Have a short, Tom. Have a short both of you. Have a short on the house.

Sirens of police cars and ambulances approach.

Mix to: 'We'll gather lilacs' played on the piano, over which the closing announcement is made. Music ends in the clear.

HALT!
WHO GOES THERE?

by Tom Mallin

Tom Mallin was born in 1927 in the Midlands. After boarding-school he was a student at the Birmingham College of Art. His education having been interrupted by military service, he moved to London where he married the painter Muriel George. In 1955, together with their two sons, Simon and Rupert, they moved to Suffolk where Tom earned his living as a picture restorer. At the age of thirty-five, he began to write. With the production of his first stage play, *Curtains*, in 1970, he became a full-time author. Although he continued to write stage plays, — *The Novelist, As Is Proper, Mrs Argent*, and novels — *Dodecahedron, Erowina, Knut, Lobe, Bedrok*, his work most regularly appeared as radio drama. The BBC has so far broadcast *Curtains, Downpour, Rooms, Vicar Martin, The Lodger, Two Gentlemen of Hadleigh Heath, Spanish Fly, Halt! Who Goes There?* and *Rowland*. In the fifteen years before his sudden death in 1977, Tom Mallin wrote over forty plays and novels.

Halt! Who Goes There? was first broadcast on BBC Radio 3 on 26th March 1978. The cast was as follows.

ARNOLD BUTTERWORTH	Clive Swift
MR ASHDOWN	Maurice Denham
MRS RUBIN	Stella Tanner
MATRON	Rosemary Leach
JOCK MACGILBIE	Robert Trotter
DICK TWIST	Jonathan Scott
LOUIS PALMERSTON	Leonard Fenton
MRS WESLEY	Brenda Kaye
MRS SNELL	Kathleen Helme
ABIGAIL WHITE	Hilda Kriseman
CELIA	Anne Rosenfeld
ELLEN	Katharine Page
NURSE FULTON	Heather Bell
MR GRIMWADE/PORTER	Rod Beacham
DRIVER	Kenneth Shanley

Director: Richard Wortley

The play is set in 'Cliff Tops', a convalescent home.
    The male ward. Music (120 secs) is the music with which, at the time of writing — the 10th June 1977, BBC Radio 4 begin their morning transmission at 6.15 a.m.

ANNOUNCER (*over*). 'Halt, who goes there?' A play for radio by Tom Mallin.

MATRON (*over, approaching*). 'Morning, gentlemen. (*Greeting.*) Mr Palmerston.

Sound of curtain being dragged on runners.

Sleep well?

LOUIS *moans.* JOCK *blows his nose.*

ANNOUNCER (*over*). The part of the starchly aproned, unbending, steely-eyed, good looking Matron, is played by . . . The half-blind, hard of hearing, trembling octogenarian, Louis Palmerston, by . . . .

LOUIS (*who speaks throughout without his teeth*). Dreamt I w's tap dancin'. Ha! Tap dancin'. . .

MATRON. With Ginger Rogers? Here's your tea.

Sound of cup and saucer rattling.

The female ward. Sound of water pouring into wash basin.

ANNOUNCER (*over*). . . . . plays the prematurely grey, blue-eyed, buxom Nurse Fulton.

NURSE (*approaching*). Come on, ladies. Tea up. Stir yourselves.

Sound of tea cups and saucers and spoons stirring sugar. Over, all moan.
MRS SNELL *coughs.*

NURSE FULTON. Hairdresser comes this morning remember.

Sound of curtain being dragged on runners.

MRS SNELL (*over — and speaking throughout with chewing gum in her mouth*). Ha, bleedin', ha.

ANNOUNCER. The parts of the three, partially-sighted spinsters, Ellen, Celia and Abigail, are played by. . . . , ... and . . . . .

ELLEN. What's the weather like out?

CELIA. Bound to be raining.

ABIGAIL. Wish we could see.

MRS SNELL *coughs.*

The male ward. Sound of curtain being dragged on runners.

ANNOUNCER. . . . . . plays the part of the over-weight, pugilist-faced Jock MacGilbie.

Sound of tea cups and saucers.

MATRON (*over*). How d'you feel this morning?

JOCK. Noo bad, Matron. Wee bit. . . (*sound of aerosol spray.*) . . . hot.

MATRON. Mr Ashdown?

ANNOUNCER. Played by . . . . .

ASHDOWN. Didn't sleep.

MATRON. You slept soundly.

Sound of electric razor.

ASHDOWN (*over*). Got this pain in my chest.

MATRON (*withdrawing*). I'll be round with the pills shortly.

Sound of curtain being dragged on runners.

DICK TWIST. I feel like I've got six heads, this morning.

MATRON. I've only brought one cup of tea, Mr Twist.

ANNOUNCER. The part of the tenacious but redundant Dick Twist is played by . . . . .

MATRON (*close*). Mr Laughton? How's the bed this morning? Dry?

ASHDOWN (*distant*). I don't think I want to get up this morning, Matron.

MATRON (*withdrawing*). No one stays in bed, Mr Ashdown.

The female ward.

ANNOUNCER. The grey and wan Mrs Lynn Wesley is played by . . . . .

Sound of cups and saucers.

MRS WESLEY (*over*). Some of us, Nurse, like lemon tea in the mornings.

MRS SNELL *coughs.*

MRS RUBIN (*over*). And some of us like pork sausages for breakfast, but when you're overweight already and religion forbids you, what you get? Crisp bread. (*Fading.*) Every day, crisp bread.

ANNOUNCER (*over fade*). . . . . plays the part of the fat, waddling, short-legged perspiring Mrs Ida Rubin.

MRS SNELL. Could I 'ave an n'asprin?

Sound of curtain being dragged on runners.

NURSE FULTON (*passing*). Start the day as you intend to go on, Elsie.

MRS SNELL. Tha' mean no?

Sound of curtains, one after the other being dragged on runners.

NURSE FULTON (*over, distant*). It means, get up, wash, dress and get yourself and your moans downstairs, Mrs Snell.

ELLEN *gargles.*

ANNOUNCER (*over*). The part of the bony, cheerless, forever-coughing Elsie Snell, is played by . . . . .

MRS SNELL. 'Onest, they treat yer like bleedin' prisoners. Or delinquents.

Sound of bucket and mop.

ANNOUNCER (*over*). The Porter is played by . . . . . ; the Driver of the hospital car . . . . . and the role of imperious Mr Arnold Butterworth by . . . . .

Rapid fade out of all sounds except music.

MATRON. There'll be one new admission today, Nurse.

NURSE FULTON. Male or female?

MATRON. His name is Butterworth.

Music ends. Pause.

The main entrance hall — with echo sound of doorbell followed by impatient knocking.

PORTER (*approaching*). Knock, knock, knock. (*Raising voice.*) Wait on!

Sound of door chains and bolts being slid.

PORTER. It's a peculiar characteristic the sick have — when on the road to recovery — im-bloody-patience.

Sound of heavy door opening. Exterior — windy acoustics.

PORTER (*snapping*). Yes?

DRIVER. Butterworth.

BUTTERWORTH. Still locked and bolted midday?

PORTER. Who are you?

BUTTERWORTH. Butterworth.

PORTER. Aren't you Butterworth?

BUTTERWORTH. He drove me here. You haven't answered my question.

PORTER. So few people go out, Mr Butterworth, it hardly seems worthwhile sliding the bolts. Where do I sign?

DRIVER. Against his name.

BUTTERWORTH. There. . .

PORTER. Here?

BUTTERWORTH. . . . . hospital number, double-two-seven, nine, two 0.

DRIVER. Ta. I'll leave his suitcase.

PORTER. Got his documentation?

BUTTERWORTH. This what you want?

PORTER. You shouldn't have that.

DRIVER (*withdrawing*). See you then, Squire.

PORTER. Give it here.

BUTTERWORTH (*calling after*). Many thanks.

PORTER. This envelope is clearly marked, Arnold Butterworth. It also says — look — in big letters. . . Are you looking? Con-fid-ential.

BUTTERWORTH. Nurse, the envelope is sealed. The flap stuck down. Gummed.

PORTER. Come in. Leave the suitcase.

BUTTERWORTH. Outside?

Sound of car being driven away down gravel drive.

PORTER. You mustn't lift.

BUTTERWORTH. Aren't you the nurse?

PORTER. Porter.

MATRON (*advancing*). Mr Butterworth?

Sound of outer door slamming shut. Ending of exterior acoustics. The beginning of the interior echo.

PORTER (*over*). It's a Mr Butterworth.

MATRON. Welcome to Cliff Tops Convalescent Home, Mr Butterworth. Pleasant journey?

BUTTERWORTH. I came via the coast road. Very wild.

MATRON. Here at Cliff Tops we prefer to call it bracing.

BUTTERWORTH. Yes. I've read the brochure.

MATRON. Oh, I am glad. Not many bother.

BUTTERWORTH. I got as far as the do's and dont's.

MATRON (*laughingly*). There are very few, Mr Butterworth, and all intended to make your stay here both enjoyable and beneficial.

BUTTERWORTH. I'm a firm believer in home being where a person responds best to warmth and love, Matron; amongst his intimates and family.

MATRON. It may surprise you, Mr Butterworth, but many patients are reluctant to return home when their time comes to leave. Follow me, would you?

PORTER. Follow Matron.

Sound of footfall on wooden floor.

MATRON (*over*). Got your papers?

BUTTERWORTH. The Porter has them.

PORTER. Give these to Matron.

MATRON. Thank you.

BUTTERWORTH. I inadvertently stuck the flap of the envelope down.

MATRON. Did your documentation make interesting reading?

BUTTERWORTH. Not very.

PORTER. Watch where you're going.

MATRON. In here, Mr Butterworth.

PORTER. In there.

Sound of footfall and echo fades.

The male ward. Sound of general conversation.

MATRON (*over*). May I have your attention, gentlemen?

Conversation hushes.

MATRON. This is Mr Butterworth. (*Withdrawing.*) Say how d'you do.

Silence.

ASHDOWN (*close, quietly*). Name's Ashdown. Shake hands.

Sound of distant curtain being drawn on runners.

MATRON (*over, distant*). This is your cot, Mr Butterworth.

BUTTERWORTH (*aside*). Cot?

LOUIS. Her thinks we'm all babbys. Ha! Babbys. . .

ASHDOWN (*close, whispering*). I conclude from your handshake, you're not er, ha-hum.

BUTTERWORTH. Not what?

ASHDOWN (*close, whispering*). I'm the only man here who is.

PORTER (*passing*). I've put your name on your cot, Professor.

ASHDOWN (*close*). I had a heart attack, you know.

MATRON (*distant*). Mr Ashdown, you can discuss your symptoms with Mr Butterworth later.

ASHDOWN. You a Professor?

BUTTERWORTH. No, Squire. (*Whispering.*) Nor a freemason.

NURSE FULTON (*distant*). Matron, could you spare a moment? Mr Laughton has fallen.

MATRON (*advancing and passing*). Wait there, Mr Butterworth.

Slight pause.

MR TWIST (*approaching*). Any guards on the main gate today, Mr Butterworth?

BUTTERWORTH. Is it that bad?

JOCK. Were you in the Army? (*Sound of aerosol spray.*) This is ten times worse. Seen the barbed wire everywhere?

BUTTERWORTH. Surely, that's to stop people climbing in.

ASHDOWN. You try getting out.

A general laughter.

JOCK. Y'need a pass signed by the camp commandant herself.

A sound of aerosol spray.

MATRON (*approaching*). Is Mr MacGilbie telling the tired joke about there being observation towers along the perimeter; mines laid either side of the drive and how guard dogs roam the grounds at night? (*Pause.*) You're perfectly free to leave, Mr MacGilbie. Anytime.

JOCK (*meekly*). Yes, Matron. (*Sound of aerosol spray.*) I hav'na had m'pills yet.

MATRON. Nurse is on her rounds.

ASHDOWN. She's eight minutes late.

JOCK. Ten, by my watch.

Sound of aerosol spray.

MATRON. Neither of you are going to drop dead because Nurse is a few minutes late. (*Withdrawing.*) And do put away that deodorant spray, Mr MacGilbie.

MR TWIST (*distant*). He could always try taking a bath.

ASHDOWN. I can't climb stairs. My heart.

JOCK (*boastful, moving away*). Back home, I take a bath every week.

MATRON (*distant*). Over here, Mr Butterworth.

JOCK (*distant*). On a Sunday.

ASHDOWN (*over, close*). Takes three nurses to wash me all over.

MR TWIST (*distant*). You're lucky to have a tin bath, mate.

JOCK (*distant*). Tha's no tin. Tha's a proper bath.

MR TWIST (*distant*). Aw lis'n tay Jock Mac Bath. His bath is naw tin. . .

MATRON (*close, over*). This is your bedside cupboard, Mr Butterworth. Slippers — when not worn, in the bottom drawer, please. Two towels. Any valuables? Hand them in for safe keeping. I'll give you a receipt. And this is your tray. Keep it covered with this cloth. For privacy. Underneath, as you see, are all the various things you will need. A kidney bowl. . .

A sound of metal instruments in metal bowl.

BUTTERWORTH (*taken aback*). Tweezers?

MATRON. Everything. Are you still discharging?

BUTTERWORTH (*dismissively*). Hardly worth bothering about.

MATRON. Let me be the best judge of that, Mr Butterworth. Now. We rise at six-thirty, breakfast at eight. At twelve, we dine. Have you eaten?

BUTTERWORTH. Yes.

MATRON. Good. Six o'clock is supper time. Bed, usually nine.

BUTTERWORTH (*surprised*). Nine?

MATRON. As it's your first day, I'd like you to be in bed by eight-thirty. After you've unpacked, hop into bed.

BUTTERWORTH (*astonished*). Now?

MATRON. No need to undress. Slip off your shoes and lie under the quilt.

BUTTERWORTH (*protesting*). It's only half past twelve.

MATRON. Until two. (*Moving away.*) Come along, Mr MacGilbie. You too, Mr Ashdown. You both know the routine. In you pop.

Sound of aerosol spray.

MATRON (*returning, close*). The staff lunch, Mr Butterworth, is between one and two. Surely you don't begrudge us time off to eat?

BUTTERWORTH. Would it upset your digestion knowing I was sat, in what the brochure describes as a large, spacious lounge with comfortable armchairs, reading, or trying to catch up on my correspondence?

MATRON (*withdrawing*). Don't disappoint me, Mr Butterworth.

BUTTERWORTH (*calling after*). I won't sleep.

MATRON (*distant*). Have a pleasant rest, gentlemen.

ASHDOWN. You don't know when you're well off, Mr B. I look forward to my after-lunch nap.

JOCK. Me too.

Sound of aerosol spray.

BUTTERWORTH. It's quite foreign to my nature.

MR TWIST (*approaching*). A new life style always takes some getting used to. I'm Dick Twist.

BUTTERWORTH. How d'you do.

MR TWIST. The first day here is a bit like prison. But take heart, after the first day, it gets steadily worse.

Laughter. Fade.

The bathroom. Sound of water filling bath tub — held.

MATRON (*over*). Clothes all off? Good. Let me look.

Pause.

BUTTERWORTH (*apprehensive*). Something wrong?

MATRON. Trying to equate what I see with your hospital report. Any bleeding?

BUTTERWORTH (*with slight panic*). Where?

MATRON. You may from time to time.

BUTTERWORTH. Much?

MATRON. The thing to remember is to keep yourself scrupulously clean. Managing in all other respects?

BUTTERWORTH (*with nervous laugh*). Child's play.

MATRON. Any anxieties, Mr Butterworth, you've only got to say.

BUTTERWORTH (*unconvincingly*). Everything's fine. The only thing. . .

Pause.

MATRON. Yes?

BUTTERWORTH. Nothing. It was my wife's idea I convalesce here. Myself, I felt I might be denying a more senior citizen the chance of a well-deserved rest — in pleasant surrounds.

MATRON. Everyone is entitled, Mr Butterworth. Turn round please.

BUTTERWORTH. You want me to bend?

Pause.

MATRON. Very neat.

BUTTERWORTH. I'm in good company, so I'm told. Showbiz personalities. Royalty.

MATRON. The majority of diseases cut across class barriers, Mr Butterworth. Those which reveal a preference for a particular social group are generally caused by poverty or overcrowding. (*Withdrawing.*) You may take your bath now.

BUTTERWORTH (*calling after*). I've never voted Tory in my life!

The taps are turned off.

NURSE FULTON. You're very brown. Been sunbathing?

BUTTERWORTH. What do you want?

NURSE FULTON. To supervise your bath.

BUTTERWORTH (*tartly*). I can wash myself, thank you.

NURSE FULTON. Convince me. (*Pause.*) Mr Butterworth, why not take advantage of the fact that here, you are outnumbered by women?

BUTTERWORTH. Oh, very well. You may handle my elbow.

NURSE FULTON. I'll go one better — and wash your back.

Sound of water disturbance.

NURSE FULTON (*over*). And that's something only a woman can do really well.

Fade.

The long hall — with echo. Sound of three walking sticks tapping on wooden floor — approaching slowly.

ELLEN (*over*). Where are we?

CELIA. Don't you know?

ABIGAIL. I'm following you two.

ELLEN. Must be near.

ABIGAIL. Have a look.

ELLEN. Shall I?

CELIA. You mustn't.

ABIGAIL. Be a devil.

Sound of stick tapping stops. Pause.

ELLEN (*surprised*). We're in the long hall.

MATRON (*approaching*). Ladies! You must *NOT* remove your dark glasses. (*Pause.*) What mustn't you do?

ELLEN.
CELIA. } (*meekly*). Remove our dark glasses.
ABIGAIL.

MATRON. And?

Pause.

ELLEN. Sit facing the light.

CELIA. Watch television.

Pause.

ABIGAIL. Look out of the window at the beautiful garden.

ELLEN. I said that.

Pause.

MATRON. One more thing you're forbidden to do.

ELLEN. Read and write.

MATRON. Correct.

ABIGAIL (*close, whispering*). That's two things.

MATRON. Please remember.

ABIGAIL (*aloud*). I had a letter this morning. . .

MATRON (*ignoring*). Now, run along.

ABIGAIL (*raising voice*). . . . Could be bad news.

MATRON (*moving away*). And stay out of mischief.

ABIGAIL (*calling after*). He's not strong! (*Quietly.*) How'm I going to look after him?

ELLEN. Who, dear?

ABIGAIL. My father.

CELIA (*surprised*). He's still alive?

ABIGAIL. Selfish old . . . !

ELLEN. You're better off here, dear.

ABIGAIL. Don't I know it.

CELIA. We all are.

ELLEN. Hold tight, ladies. Let's press on. Grab my cardigan, Celia.

CELIA. Got it. Come on, Abigail.

Sound of three walking sticks tapping on wooden floor — receding.

ABIGAIL (*over*). Where we going?

ELLEN (*moving away*). The sun lounge.

CELIA (*moving away*). Last time, you mistakenly led me into the gentleman's lavatory.

ABIGAIL (*moving away*). How did you know it was the gentleman's lavatory?

ELLEN *and* CELIA, *moving away, laugh. Pause.*

NURSE FULTON (*close*). Cataracts. You'll see them sat outside Matron's office four times a day waiting for their drops.

BUTTERWORTH (*close*). On lump sugar?

NURSE FULTON. What? (*Pause.*) In their eye, silly. (*Pause.*) Drum the gong.

BUTTERWORTH (*distant*). This?

NURSE FULTON. For supper.

Sound of gong being struck timidly.

NURSE FULTON (*over, approaching*). We are timid.

Gonging stops.

NURSE FULTON. Give it here. (*Pause.*) Before you leave, I'll have you begging me to let you strike it — like *this!*

Sound of furious and loud gonging quickly fading.

The dining hall. Sounds — hum of conversation, dishing of plates, cutlery — continuous.

MATRON (*over*). Sit at this table, Mr Butterworth.

BUTTERWORTH. With the men? Surely, Matron, segregation in the dining hall could be construed as sex discrimination.

MATRON (*raising voice*). Quiet! Quiet, please! (*Silence.*) Mr Butterworth here, wants to sit with the ladies.

MRS RUBIN (*distant*). And Mrs Rubin here, wants to marry Sacha Distel. So that makes two of us what's disappointed.

Distant, light laughter.

MATRON (*over*). Is there a lady willing to give up her seat to make room? (*Silent pause.*) No one? Carry on.

Dining hall sounds return — surging.

MATRON (*over, moving away*). Sit down, Mr Butterworth.

Pause.

JOCK. Same in the sun and TV lounge.

ASHDOWN. Every chair occupied.

MR TWIST. By a woman — or her handbag.

BUTTERWORTH. Is there no intermingling?

MR TWIST. Even when we have visitors, there's an unspoken agreement the men confine themselves to the 'smoke room'. . .

JOCK (*cutting in*). Well, I dunna mind. There's nay one o' them you cude call a great beauty. An' near on all is as old as me granny.

MR TWIST. Pass the bread.

Light laughter.

BUTTERWORTH (*over*). Have you a wife, Mr MacGilbie?

JOCK. I'm no married.

BUTTERWORTH. By choice?

JOCK. Wha's tha' got t'do wi' you?

MR TWIST. Jock, cock, pass the marge.

JOCK. Wha'?

MR TWIST. Marge.

JOCK. Here.

MR TWIST. Ta, me old tartan. Tell Mr Butterworth about your house.

ASHDOWN. You should see my bungalow. Both garages have central heating.

MR TWIST. Jock does his own cooking.

JOCK. An' baking. Sponge cake. Drop scones.

LOUIS. Ha! Drop scones. . .

JOCK (*with pride*). Even biscuits.

ASHDOWN. All forbidden eating.

JOCK. Aye, I've been told I got t'lose weight. This m'second heart attack.

ASHDOWN. My third.

JOCK. I was at the bottom of the garden.

MR TWIST. Looking for fairies?

JOCK. Pulling rhubarb.

LOUIS. Ha! Pullin' 'is rhubarb. . .

JOCK. I was holding a knife. Good job I didna fall on it.

BUTTERWORTH. Where were you fated to have your heart attack, Mr Ashdown?

PORTER (*cutting in*). Right. Who's low-residue? Mr Butterworth? Boiled fish.

BUTTERWORTH. Thank you.

PORTER. You boiled fish, Mr MacGilbie?

JOCK. And him.

NURSE FULTON. The rest are all fried.

BUTTERWORTH. How long have you been living on the wrong side of the border, Mr MacGilbie?

MR TWIST. Thorrity ye-arrr the noo.

JOCK. And I'm noo goo'n back up there.

BUTTERWORTH. No relatives?

MR TWIST. None what is 'tee-tottal'.

JOCK. I know wha' drink c'n do tay a man.

MR TWIST. And woman.

JOCK. You hist or I'll. . .

MATRON. Everyone happy?

Pause.

MATRON (*withdrawing*). Remember, only one slice of bread, Mr MacGilbie.

Pause.

BUTTERWORTH. Tell me, Mr MacGilbie — Jock, an engineer, were you?

JOCK. Aye.

MR TWIST. Ditto. But Louis here, worked on the land. Dug dirt.

LOUIS. Dug dirt. . . Ha!

BUTTERWORTH. And you, Mr Ashdown? What's your occupation?

MR TWIST. Bailiff.

ASHDOWN. Was.

BUTTERWORTH. Landholder's steward?

ASHDOWN. No. I came under the Sheriff.

MR TWIST. Issued writs, didn't you?

ASHDOWN. Processes. A few arrests.

BUTTERWORTH. Oh.

MR TWIST. Keen on law and order is our Mr Ashdown.

ASHDOWN. My ambition was to be in the police force.

MR TWIST. Too short, weren't you, eh? Mind you — they all know him.

BUTTERWORTH. The police?

ASHDOWN. Came to me for advice. Information.

Pause.

MR TWIST. Go on, Ashy — tell him.

ASHDOWN (*confidentially*). I helped convict a murderer when they still had the death penalty. Hung, he was. On my evidence.

BUTTERWORTH. Myself, I am of the opinion. . .

ASHDOWN (*cutting in*). I know what you're going to say. Could I do the hangman's job?

Pause.

BUTTERWORTH. Could you?

Pause.

JOCK. You all right, Ashy?

MR TWIST. Ashy?

ASHDOWN. Heartburn.

LOUIS (*laughs*). Heartburn. . .

MR TWIST (*close, quietly*). It never fails to get a laugh.

Pause.

BUTTERWORTH. Better?

ASHDOWN. Where was I? Oh, yes. If I had my way. . .

BUTTERWORTH. Take your time.

ASHDOWN. The bloody blacks have started to do it now.

BUTTERWORTH. Do what?

ASHDOWN. Squat.

Pause.

BUTTERWORTH. Look, drink some water. (*Pause.*) All right now?

Pause.

ASHDOWN. There's one won't try it on anymore.

BUTTERWORTH. Thump him, did you?

ASHDOWN. Her.

BUTTERWORTH. A woman?

ASHDOWN. You think you've heard filthy language. (*Pause.*) She 'said' she was pregnant. It was a (!) cushion!

BUTTERWORTH. And you lost your temper. (*Pause.*) Was that when you had your heart attack?

ASHDOWN. I still get a pain just thinking about it.

BUTTERWORTH. In the stomach?

ASHDOWN. Heart.

BUTTERWORTH. Traditionally, conscience pains the intellect.

ASHDOWN. I'm a common sense man, Mr Butterworth. Like you. And we aren't in the minority. There are thousands who think the same.

BUTTERWORTH (*aside*). God forbid.

ASHDOWN. If you'll excuse me. . .

Pause.

BUTTERWORTH. What happens after supper?

JOCK. You c'n watch tele.

MR TWIST. Get a quick snooze in before bedtime.

LOUIS. Ha! Snooze. . .

MR TWIST. For the more adventurous, there's conversation. (*Pause.*) I tell you, it's all go.

Fade.

The male ward. Sound of curtain being dragged on runners.

MATRON. Sleeping pill, Mr Butterworth?

BUTTERWORTH. No, thank you.

MATRON. I don't want you ringing your bell in the middle of the night complaining you can't sleep.

BUTTERWORTH. Matron, I could sleep curled up on top of the wardrobe. . .

LOUIS (*distant*). On top of the wardrobe. . . Ha!

BUTTERWORTH. . . . . I don't have any difficulty sleeping.

MATRON. Turn off your light then.

BUTTERWORTH. I'm reading.

MATRON. Your light keeps the others awake. (*Pause.*) Mr Butterworth, do you wish me to remove the light bulb?

Sound of light switch.

MATRON. Thank you. Good night.

Sound of curtain being dragged on runners.

MATRON (*withdrawing*). Good night, gentlemen. Sleep well.

Mumbled 'Good nights', and a few farts. Fade.

The long hall. Sound of telephone being lifted off cradle, dialling, pause, money being inserted.

BUTTERWORTH. Hello? Grace? It's me . . . Arnold. Your husband. Come and take me away. . . From Cliff Tops. . . This morning. By ambulance car. . . Much as expected. A large, private house. By the look of it, lifted straight out of an old Hollywood film set. Remember *Double Indemnity*? Barbara Stanwyck and Fred MacMurray? Only this seems to be built of sea shells and tiles arranged in patterns. Inside, queer bits of William Morris joinery. . . *Very* close to the cliffs. . . Yes. Freezing. Wind comes straight off the sea. When the driver stepped out of the car this morning, it blew out one of his contact lenses. True. The wind. . . Fellow patients?. . . What?. . . Grace, it is I who am at odds with the world. . . What d'you mean? 'Startling confession'. I can't hear other people's pain. Besides, if you must know, in comparison they make my ailment seem, well, insignificant. And it's during this period *I need* sympathy. . . Come and fetch me. It was a mistake coming. . . What?. . . I've had four weeks of people deciding what's good for me. . . Hello?. . . Yes. . . Saturday? Not sooner?. . . All right. In the morning. Fine. Yes. . . What d'you mean, how are you?. . . Hello? Grace? . . . Oh!

Sound of telephone being replaced on cradle.

BUTTERWORTH. Did I disappoint her by not dying? Or has my illness upset her well-ordered routine? We'll never know.

MATRON (*approaching*). Mr Butterworth, what are you doing out of bed at this time of night?

BUTTERWORTH 'This time of night' is when most people are settling down to watch an evening's television.

MATRON. Kindly return to your ward.

BUTTERWORTH. Impossible. Listen.

Sound of men snoring.

BUTTERWORTH (*over*). How'm I expected to sleep through that cacophony?

MATRON (*lowering voice*). I asked if you required a sleeping pill.

BUTTERWORTH. Matron, at the risk of repeating myself. . .

MATRON. Shhh. . .

BUTTERWORTH (*whsipering*). I don't need pills to make me sleep.

MATRON (*whispering*). Mr Butterworth, it would appear that you do. You are the only one awake.

BUTTERWORTH. Matron, I was asleep. Their snoring woke me.

Pause.

MATRON. I could, I suppose, allow you to sleep on your own. There is an empty room in the attic.

BUTTERWORTH. And risk alienation?

MATRON. Mr Butterworth, I'm offering you a choice.

BUTTERWORTH. It would be seen as a privilege.

MATRON. Then it's a pill or nothing.

BUTTERWORTH. How about a cup of tea?

MATRON (*with emphasis*). Good night, Mr Butterworth.

Sound of snoring surges.

JOCK (*whispering*). Hey, mate. Want some advice? You'll nay get roon' the ol' hag be bletherin'.

BUTTERWORTH. Weren't you given a sleeping pill?

JOCK. I'll swallow it doon when I'm gude 'n' ready.

Sound of aerosol spray.

BUTTERWORTH. Ever thought of leaving? Just walking out?

JOCK. Since I first come here.

BUTTERWORTH. I've arranged to be fetched Saturday. But I've a good mind to leave now. (*Pause.*) You game? There's nothing to prevent us.

JOCK. Oh, aye? You got money f'a taxi then? Mebbe a bus an' a train?

BUTTERWORTH. No. But all we have to do is get to the main road then hitch.

JOCK. How far c'n you walk?

BUTTERWORTH. I could make it.

JOCK. Carryin' a suitcase? Talk sense, mon. This y'first day oot a hospital.

BUTTERWORTH. So — I'll go empty-handed.

JOCK. An' leave y'bits and pieces?

BUTTERWORTH. I'll stuff what medical odds and ends I need into my pocket.

JOCK. Oh, aye? Well, I canna come.

Sound of aerosol spray.

BUTTERWORTH. Why?

JOCK. Where'm I going t'get heart tablets this time a night?

BUTTERWORTH. Steal them.

JOCK. I'm no breakin' inta Matron's office.

BUTTERWORTH. I'll do it.

JOCK. It's nay just heart tablets I need.

BUTTERWORTH. Write me out a list.

Pause.

JOCK. Look, if I leave, wha' chance'll I have a convalescin' again?

BUTTERWORTH. What makes you think there'll be a need to?

JOCK. Wi' this heart, I'm fated.

Pause.

BUTTERWORTH. You wouldn't necessarily be sent here.

JOCK. But they'd have me name, wouldn't they? It'd be on m'record card. In big letters. 'Buggered awa' one cood neet.'

Pause.

BUTTERWORTH. I'll go on my own.

JOCK. You do tha'. An' gude luck. It's just begun tay snow.

Sound of aerosol spray.

NURSE FULTON (*quietly and/or whisperingly throughout scene*). Is that you talking, Mr Butterworth?

BUTTERWORTH (*quietly and/or whisperingly throughout scene*). To myself.

NURSE FULTON. I've brought you a cup of tea.

BUTTERWORTH. Nurse Fulton, you're an angel.

Sound of cup and saucer rattling. BUTTERWORTH *sips tea.*

NURSE FULTON. Nice?

BUTTERWORTH (*sips*). Delicious. (*Sips.*) You must be a mind reader. (*Sips.*)

NURSE FULTON. Wasn't my idea.

BUTTERWORTH (*sups*). Whose was it? (*Sips.*)

NURSE FULTON. Matron's.

BUTTERWORTH (*sips*). Matron's? (*Sips.*)

Sound of tea cup and saucer rattle.

BUTTERWORTH. Oh, no. No. . .

NURSE FULTON. Yes.

BUTTERWORTH. In my tea?

NURSE FULTON. You'll sleep like a log now. (*Very whisperingly.*) Goodnight, Mr. Butterworth.

Sounds of snoring surges. Stops. Sound of electric razor.

PORTER (*over*). Keep still, Mr Palmerston, if you want a nice, close shave.

MRS RUBIN. As a porter, he makes a better barber. Aren't you? Such fingers. Like a bank cashier I knew. Could watch him count money all day. Same dexterity. Like he was a card sharper.

PORTER. My admiration was for our grocer. Watching him slice bacon. (*Sound of electric razor stops.*) Zzzzzzip. Zzzzzz-i-p. Piece after piece of bacon falling away in thin slices.

Sound of electric razor.

PORTER (*over*). Wonder was he never lost a finger.

MRS RUBIN. But you hoped. Me too. But who ever saw a bank cashier drop money?

Sound of electric razor stops.

PORTER. There we are, Mr Palmerston. Feel better?

LOUIS. Like a wet shave best. Wi' a cut-throat. (*Makes sound of having throat cut.*). Ha! Cut throat. . .

PORTER. You watch out for the women now you've had a shave. They'll be wanting to kiss you.

MRS RUBIN (*withdrawing*). So why don't I? Poor old boy. Mmmmm. . . (*Sound of a kiss.*) There.

LOUIS. This me mouth. 'Ere.

MRS RUBIN (*aside*). You suck your own gums.

LOUIS. Wha'?

PORTER (*over*). Leave the men alone, gorgeous, and come and sit down.

MRS RUBIN (*approaching*). Gorgeous, he calls me. Ida Rubin, you are entrusting the last of your good looks to a blind man.

PORTER. Only love is blind, Mrs Rubin.

MRS RUBIN. But in my case?

PORTER. I shall make an exception.

MRS RUBIN. And I love you too. Here?

PORTER. Just sit down.

MRS RUBIN. Like this?

PORTER. And put your chin up.

MRS RUBIN. Chin, he says. Which one?

Sound of electric razor.

PORTER (*over*). Soon have you done.

Fade.

The long hall.

BUTTERWORTH (*approaching*). You are looking very dapper this morning, Louis. (*Withdrawing.*) Very smart. Had a shave?

LOUIS. Me an the bearded lady. Ha! Bearded lady. . .

ASHDOWN. She's a Jewess — Mrs Rubin.

MR TWIST. Her husband was an artist. Painted nudes.

JOCK. Tha' a fact?

MR TWIST. Him and Dick Van Dyke.

BUTTERWORTH (*approaching*). Back home, I'd just be coming up to Poslingbroke corner.

ASHDOWN. Know why Jewish women have moustaches?

MR TWIST. Don't you know any clean jokes, Ashdown?

BUTTERWORTH (*withdrawing*). Never walk less than five miles a day. Helps me stay in trim. (*Returning.*) Besides, every effort must be made to stop ourselves becoming institutionalised. Am I right?

ASHDOWN. I mustn't walk far, puts too much strain on my heart.

MR TWIST. Then how 'bout a leisurely jog trot round the ludo board? (*Withdrawing quickly.*) Say a ten p. stake. You game, Louis? Jock?

BUTTERWORTH (*over*). Well, don't you agree?

MATRON (*approaching*). Mr Butterworth, may I ask why you have been pacing up and down all morning?

BUTTERWORTH. Exercise.

MATRON. You will wear our one strip of carpet thin if you go on much longer.

BUTTERWORTH. I had hoped to go out for my walk.

MATRON. The weather forecast speaks of dry, sunny periods towards the end of next week.

BUTTERWORTH. Matron, I intend to keep to a *daily* schedule.

MATRON. One recommended by the physiotherapist?

BUTTERWORTH. One I worked out for myself.

MATRON. I would warn against excess, Mr Butterworth.

BUTTERWORTH. Me and my body, Matron, have a meaningful dialogue going.

MATRON. The body, Mr Butterworth, has a habit of giving late warnings. As you have reason to know. Otherwise your cancer would have been detected sooner.

Slight pause.

BUTTERWORTH. Will you stand aside, please. I have to pace out another thirty-two lengths by when I shall have walked exactly one mile.

MATRON. You are going to have to alter your schedule, Mr Butterworth.

BUTTERWORTH. Are you asking or requesting me to?

MATRON. Ordering. You will confine your marathon to the other side of this mark. (*Withdrawing.*) Carry on.

Pause.

The games room. Sound of snooker balls clicking, one being potted.

BUTTERWORTH. She cut off eight feet. Sixteen, there and back.

Sound of snooker balls clicking, one being potted.

MR TWIST (*distant*). That's the blue down. Now for the pink.

BUTTERWORTH. That's nearly nine hundred feet in every mile she's trying to deny me.

Sound of snooker balls clicking, one being potted.

BUTTERWORTH. You know why — she doesn't want me to see her sitting in her comfortable little chintz-draped parlour, feet up, a fag in her mouth, drinking tea and reading the newspaper. Or darning her tights.

MR TWIST. Needle pointing.

BUTTERWORTH. Pardon?

MR TWIST. She embroiders. Very good. Odd. Off duty she drives a motor bike at speed. Handles a boat pretty well too — so I'm told. And mad keen on archery.

BUTTERWORTH. You know a lot about her, Mr Twist.

MR TWIST. We're all secretly in love with Matron. You'll grow to depend on her too. And this place. It's a safe haven from life's storms outside.

Sound of snooker balls clicking, one being potted.

MR TWIST. And the black. That's a quid you owe me.

BUTTERWORTH. I still say she's got it cushy. Found a little domain over which she can lord it.

MR TWIST (*distant*). Double or quits?

Sound of snooker balls being got ready in wooden triangle former.

BUTTERWORTH (*over*). And she knows, I know, she knows she's in an unassailable position if she chose to exercise authority.

MR TWIST. We could play ping pong — if you'd prefer.

BUTTERWORTH (*preoccupied*). Mmmm? What?

MR TWIST. Ping pong.

BUTTERWORTH. Is there a net?

MR TWIST. Plenty of cobwebs.

BUTTERWORTH. Well-appointed games room, the brochure said.

MR TWIST. We can use this plank.

BUTTERWORTH. The 'library' consists of a book shelf and two Readers Digests.

Fade.
Sound of a rhythmical game of table tennis.

BUTTERWORTH (*over*). The staff eat the same food as us. The only difference is, *they* pay for it.

The rhythm is broken.

MR TWIST (*distant*). Nineteen, seven. Serve.

Sound of a rhythmical game of table tennis.

BUTTERWORTH (*over*). The first meal I sat down to I spotted what they were up to.

MR TWIST (*distant*). Tell me something I don't know.

The rhythm is broken.

MR TWIST. Twenty, seven. Serve.

Sound of a rhythmical game of table tennis.

BUTTERWORTH (*over*). There you are then. If the patients got together. . . took concerted action. . .

The rhythm is broken.

MR TWIST (*distant*). Twenty-one, seven. Game.

BUTTERWORTH. Why not?

MR TWIST. I stood up for my rights, once.

Sound of ball being bounced on bat.

MR TWIST. Tried to clear my name. Did. Judge found me innocent. But it cost me my life's savings. Not only *my* savings — my wife's my wife's mother's, and all the money half a dozen relations could lay their hands on beside. I ended up worse off than when I started.

BUTTERWORTH. But you righted a miscarriage of justice; got back your self-respect.

MR TWIST. Mr Butterworth. . .

Sound of ball being trapped under bat.

MR TWIST. I lost my home, my wife, children, my small business,
the lot. All I got in compensation was ulcers. And know what
I learnt? Don't rock the boat. If you do, if you draw attention
to yourself, show the system up for what it is, some nameless,
faceless B. is going to shout, 'time's up, numner five. Come on
in'. And brother, you'd better row for the shore. Or else.
And I'll tell you something else. Compared to the mangy hostel
I'm forced to live in, Cliff Tops is paradise. So who am I to
complain? Good luck to the staff if they're fiddling the system
and getting away with it. The system killed me.

Pause.

BUTTERWORTH. How much do I owe you?

MR TWIST. You look pale.

BUTTERWORTH. I must have overdone it.

MR TWIST. Go and lie down.

BUTTERWORTH. Perhaps I will.

MR TWIST (*fade*). You do. I'll give you a good thrashing
tomorrow. . .

Pause.

The male ward. Sound of curtain being dragged on runners.

MATRON. Off that bed.

BUTTERWORTH *groans.*

MATRON. Up.

BUTTERWORTH. I'm all in.

MATRON. *Both* feet on the floor, please. (*Pause.*) Mr Butterworth,
stop play-acting — or do you want me to call the porter?

BUTTERWORTH. I'm ill.

MATRON. This is a convalescent home, not a hospital. Kindly
get up.

BUTTERWORTH. What d'you dislike about me?

MATRON. I do not have time to form likes and dislikes.

BUTTERWORTH. You married? (*Pause, moving away*.) No, wait. Answer me a question.

MATRON (*close*). Kindly let go my arm. (*Pause.*) Thank you. (*Pause.*) You're proving to be a great disappointment Mr Butterworth. And you, of all people.

BUTTERWORTH. What's so special about me?

MATRON (*bitterly, with regret, whisperingly*). Nothing.

Sound of footfall on wooden floor — receding.

BUTTERWORTH (*calling after*). What's your Christian name?

Sound of distant door slamming shut. Pause.
Sound of knock on door. Door opening.

MRS RUBIN (*distant*). Mr Butterworth? Mr Arnold Butterworth? (*Approaching.*) Your wife telephoned. Such a nice voice. Give him a message. Tell Mr Butterworth I can't fetch him Saturday.

BUTTERWORTH. Did she say why?

MRS RUBIN. Busy. Too busy.

BUTTERWORTH (*withdrawing*). I'll telephone her.

MRS RUBIN. She ain't in, Mr Butterworth.

BUTTERWORTH (*returning*). Did she say when she would be?

MRS RUBIN. Why is it we ladies don't see you in the sun or TV lounge, Mr Butterworth? You and the other men got something against women?

BUTTERWORTH (*persisting*). When, Mrs Rubin. Did she say?

MRS RUBIN. The train she was catching was going to Edinburgh. (*Pause.*) D'you know Edinburgh? Me — I don't. Got no interest in Edinburgh. Can't even *spell* Edinburgh. . .

BUTTERWORTH (*cutting in*). Thank you, Mrs Rubin. You have delivered the message.

MRS RUBIN. . . . What's so special about Edinburgh anyway? Why thank me? How was I to know it was wrapped round a brick?

Sound of distant door closing.

BUTTERWORTH. How indeed. . .

Fade.

The sun lounge. Sound of subdued, female conversation — held.

NURSE FULTON. Mr Butterworth has decided to abandon his marathon walks.

BUTTERWORTH. For the time being.

NURSE FULTON. He's put in a request for occupational therapy.

MATRON. Are you bored, Mr Butterworth?

BUTTERWORTH. The brochure lists various handicrafts.

MATRON. Unfortunately. . .

BUTTERWORTH. } *(in unison)*. . . . owing to unforeseen economic
MATRON.   } difficulties. . .

MATRON. . . . some activities have had to be suspended — temporarily — yes.

Pause.

NURSE FULTON. Mr Butterworth still has a choice of decorative lampshades or raffia work.

MATRON. The female patients find ball-winding relaxing.

NURSE FULTON *(explaining)*. Pom-poms from scrap wool.

BUTTERWORTH. I had hoped to make a basket to hold bread rolls.

NURSE FULTON. As a general rule, only those with failing eyesight weave.

MATRON. I suggest he stuff toys. Teddy bears, Mr Butterworth.

BUTTERWORTH. And what, precisely, is the therapeutic value in that?

MATRON. Our target is one thousand by Christmas.

BUTTERWORTH. May I wish you both, every success.

MATRON. Thank you. *(Withdrawing.)*. The money from their sale will go to the Golden Home for Incurables.

BUTTERWORTH *(aside)*. Oh, Charity, thy name should be blackmail. *(Aloud, resigned.)* Give me an empty teddy. Or should I have asked for a fur fleece?

NURSE FULTON. Here's a boxful, and a large bag of foam filling. Good stuffing.

General female cackle.

BUTTERWORTH. May I sit here?

MRS SNELL. Be my guest.

MRS RUBIN. Welcome to the sun lounge, Mr Butterworth.

BUTTERWORTH. Have you all been roped in?

MRS WESLEY. Work for idle hands, Mr Butterworth.

Pause.

BUTTERWORTH. How does one go about 'stuffing' a teddy bear?

MRS SNELL. First, find the h'aperture. (*General female cackle.*) The other end, dummy.

BUTTERWORTH. Bit small, isn't it?

MRS SNELL. You braggin', deary, or this y'first time?

General female cackle.

BUTTERWORTH. Despite your innuendo, Mrs. . . ?

MRS SNELL. Snell. Elsie Snell.

BUTTERWORTH. I was under the impression teddy bears were masculine.

MRS SNELL. Yeah, well, tha's why when y'go down inta the woods wiv 'em you're sure'f a big surprise, en it? (*Laughs — ends coughing.*)

General female cackle.

BUTTERWORTH. And when I've done?

MRS SNELL. Yeah, well, I sew up 'is 'ole. Mrs Rubin 'ere affixes 'is legs 'n' arms. Then 'e gets a ribb'n an' a brush up fr'm Mrs Linsey-Woolsey.

MRS WESLEY. Lynn Wesley. (*Quietly, exasperated.*) Not, Linsey-Woolsey.

BUTTERWORTH. Quite an industry.

MRS SNELL. Bleddin' unpaid labour.

MRS RUBIN. Listen, don't no one talk to me about sweated labour. I once worked for Greenbaum making dresses. For my life, it was a sixty-hour week in that stinking basement. Know what I got paid? Not enough. Then, one day, this man, Harry

Rubin, the only friend Izzy Greenbaum never deserved, he come to me and said, Ruby — my name's Ida — Ruby, he said, why's a nice girl like you working for Izzy Greenbaum? One week Izzy pay you this. Next week he pay you that. How can you live with such uncertainty? Marry me and every week I guarantee to pay you nothing. Sounded too bad to be true. So I did. Besides, I liked the way he said, guarantee. That was forty years ago. After ten year, I give up trying to convince him my name was Ida. Who was I to disillusion a man who'd set his heart on marrying a Ruby?

Pause.

MRS SNELL. Nice weddin', was it?

MRS RUBIN. Nice? Please believe me when I tell you no Bozkowiski ever give such a wedding. And the food! That was something to remember.

MRS SNELL. Yeah, well, they say the way to a man's heart. . .

MRS RUBIN. ⎫
MRS SNELL. ⎬   is through his stomach.
MRS WESLEY. ⎭

MRS RUBIN. Never in your life. Through his pride. Every man got his pride.

MRS SNELL. Yeah, well, got a stomach too, en'e?

MRS RUBIN. For a man to lose his pride, Mrs Snell, is like losing his — (*Slight pause.*) — you know.

MRS SNELL. Balls?

MRS WESLEY. Did she say that? Mr Butterworth, did Mrs Rubin say that? There was absolutely no call, Mrs Snell, to use such (!) language.

MRS SNELL. It's wha' she meant.

MRS WESLEY. We do not, Mrs Snell, always say what we mean. Least of all Mrs Rubin.

MRS RUBIN. I don't?

MRS WESLEY. No disrespect, Mrs Rubin, but your grasp of our language is not exactly — well, it wasn't learnt at Rodean.

MRS RUBIN. Rodene? Ain't Rodene some sort of rat poison?

MRS SNELL. Tha's Warfarin, what 'ospitals give t'stop y'blood clottin'.

MRS WESLEY. Rodean is a girls' school, Mrs Rubin, where they teach the King's English. Or is it the Queen's? Not that I went there, but I do pride myself in knowing there are some words which should never be used. Words which are not in any dictionary I've looked them up in.

MRS RUBIN. Who uses language anymore anyway? Now, my Harry — there was a man who could speak English like what Shakespeare never wrote. But with such diction! Like he was born with a whole canteen of silver cutlery in his mouth not just a spoon. And he give words such expression. Words like. Like — mish-mash — become real meaningful. Same with, gentile. (*Pause.*) But, like everything, words has undergone revolution. If you have the English, no one listens. And who has anything to say? It's all been said. And which of us is being the wiser for having heard? I'm telling you, it is better to be like those three donkeys. Don't hear nothing. Don't see nothing. Don't even say nothing.

MRS WESLEY. Not donkeys, Mrs Rubin — monkeys. Three wise monkeys.

MRS RUBIN. Mrs Wesley — please. I know what it is I am saying. It is donkeys what is stupid. A wise man don't stay so silent. (*Long pause.*) You see? So peaceful — it makes you want to *scream!*

Laughter.

MRS SNELL (*after coughing*) Yeah, well, why was you in 'ospital?

BUTTERWORTH. Me?

MRS SNELL. Most people 'ere don't need askin' — they're into their reminiscences an' back up on the op'ratin' table 'fore you c'n say, anaesthetic.

BUTTERWORTH. I'd rather not discuss it.

MRS SNELL. Wouldn't embarrass me, mate.

BUTTERWORTH. It would me.

MRS SNELL. Yeah, well, suit yer'self. (*Pause.*) I 'ad breast cancer.

BUTTERWORTH. Oh. (*Pause.*) I never would have guessed. Not by looking.

MRS SNELL. It's foam.

BUTTERWORTH. The same . . . ?

MRS SNELL. As wha' you're stuffin' teddy wiv — yeah.

BUTTERWORTH (*aside*). Poor Christopher Robin.

MRS SNELL (*not hearing*). Wha'? Don't ya believe me? (*Pause.*) You feel. (*Pause.*) Go on. (*Pause.*) Well?

BUTTERWORTH. Could have fooled me.

MRS SNELL. I jus' did. Tha's me real one! (*Laughs — ends coughing.*)

MRS RUBIN (*over*). All us three ladies is lop-sided, Mr Butterworth.

MRS WESLEY (*disapprovingly*). Oh, really, Mrs Rubin!

MRS RUBIN (*laughingly*). And me more than most; on account I'm O.S.! (*Laughs.*)

BUTTERWORTH. At least you're cheerful.

MRS RUBIN. Cheerful? No. Nerves, Mr Butterworth. Nervous.

MRS SNELL (*quietly*). Nervous she'll lose the other. Right, Ida?

MRS RUBIN. Who'd have thought I'd become so possessive of the one remaining? When I had two, I never give neither a thought. But when y'lose something. . . (*Pause.*) You lose anything, Mr Butterworth?

BUTTERWORTH. My anus.

Slight pause.

MRS RUBIN. Did I hear right?

BUTTERWORTH. Yes.

MRS RUBIN. A person can lose a leg, an arm, but that he can lose an anus, I wouldn't have believed. That's some loss, Mr Butterworth. Now I am really nervous.

BUTTERWORTH. No need to be. They found me another.

MRS RUBIN (*delighted*). Listen to him! Ain't that the happiest ending? Like a fairy tale what come true. They find him another.

BUTTERWORTH. I had a colostomy.

MRS RUBIN. He had a colostomy. (*Pause.*) What is with this 'colostomy'?

MRS WESLEY. If you'll excuse me, I'm going to sit in the television lounge.

MRS RUBIN (*protesting*). Why? Don't you want to hear of surgery what might benefit hundreds?

BUTTERWORTH. More like, thousands.

MRS RUBIN. You hear? Millions.

MRS WESLEY (*close to tears*). Why can't you show some respect for all the pain and suffering we're having to endure, instead of this endless joking?

MRS RUBIN. Take my word, the human condition ain't never been comical, Mrs Woolsey, but who's to say a sense of humour ain't beneficial? Because, and believe me, Mrs Linsey-Woolsey, when you're suffering, the Divine meaning to life come to seem like a badly told joke.

MRS WESLEY (*over the top*). My name is *not* Linsey-Woolsey! Its *Lynn Wesley*. (*Pause. Cry of despair. Exit.*)

Sound of door slamming shut.

MRS RUBIN. Poor soul. It takes people differently. Some, like her, they don't say hardly a word. Like they was dumb. But when they scream? Aye-yi-yi, do they scream? And d'you know the worst kind of scream, Mr Butterworth? One when you open your mouth and nothing come out. And d'you know where you go to do that kind of screaming, Mr Butterworth? (*Whispering.*) In the mad house. (*Pause.*) That's one place I don't want never to end up in. Put me in an old people's home — okay, in hospital — I don't mind which, but a mad house? Know why, Mr Butterworth? That's failure. And I don't never mean to fail — even when it come to dying.

Pause.

MRS SNELL. I'm goin' 'ome, Monday.

BUTTERWORTH. That'll be nice.

MRS SNELL. Wish I could stay.

MRS RUBIN. Who don't?

BUTTERWORTH. It seems to be a desire most people here have and one I'm beginning to share. What's your reason?

MRS SNELL. My old man hates the sight of me.

BUTTERWORTH. Oh, come. Give him time to adjust to your operation.

MRS RUBIN. That's it. Tell her love ain't just a pretty face. Think she don't know already?

MRS SNELL. He knocks me about. And the kids. Beat me eldest unconscious 'cause her stayed out late. (*Pause.*) 'Alf-past nine. And 'e thumped 'er.

BUTTERWORTH. How old's your daughter?

MRS SNELL. Eighteen.

MRS RUBIN. Eighteen. There's an age. When I was that age I thought I was old. Now I'm old, it don't seem like I was ever eighteen.

BUTTERWORTH. At eighteen, I would have thought a daughter legally entitled to leave home.

MRS SNELL. Yeah, well, she can't, can she? Anyway, he'd thump 'er. And who'd look after the baby?

BUTTERWORTH. Whose baby?

MRS RUBIN. Listen to him. Her daughter's. Who else's?

BUTTERWORTH. Oh. . .

MRS SNELL. Illigit, en it?

BUTTERWORTH. Perhaps that's why your husband. . . In a way he's trying to protect your daughter.

MRS SNELL. Protect her? It's 'is bleedin' child.

BUTTERWORTH. You do have problems.

MRS RUBIN. Mr Butterworth, believe me, the woman who don't have none, ain't been born yet.

PORTER (*distant*). Tea and biscuit. (*Fading.*) Who wants tea and biscuit?

Pause.

MATRON's *office.*

MATRON. And that's what she said?

BUTTERWORTH. You don't appear shocked.

MATRON. Are you?

BUTTERWORTH. I haven't become callous.

MATRON. You think I am? (*Pause.*) Mr Butterworth, the nurse who is continually running into the sluice room to dry her eyes and blow into a handkerchief is a dead loss to the profession.

BUTTERWORTH. The King is dead. Long live the King.

MATRON. If it will set your mind at rest, Elsie Snell and her problems are well documented.

BUTTERWORTH (*ironically*). How reassuring to know she's a number.

MATRON (*correcting*). A problem. A social problem. When she leaves here, she will be met by a qualified social worker who will escort her home for the inevitable confrontation with her husband.

BUTTERWORTH (*lightly*). Who, in a drunken rage, will black her eye.

MATRON. Wrong. Elsie's husband is teetotal; sexual jealousy motivates his rage. And he won't black her eye. More likely than not, he will try and strike her on the head with a hammer. He has before. Didn't you notice? Elsie wears a wig.

BUTTERWORTH. You are saying — the Snells are inadequate.

MATRON. If you think sentiment will win the day, Mr Butterworth, be warned. Elsie doesn't wield a hammer, she attacks with anything sharp. (*Pause.*) As you can see, the wound is nearly healed. (*Pause.*) Before you go, Mr Butterworth. . .

BUTTERWORTH (*distant*). Yes?

MATRON. I understand you haven't had any visitors.

BUTTERWORTH (*approaching*). My wife, Matron, like you, is a professional woman. She cannot take time off just when she chooses.

MATRON. You have only to ask, Mr Butterworth, and I can arrange for a welfare officer to visit your home.

BUTTERWORTH. As a shot in the dark, it's gone wide off the mark, Matron.

MATRON. I do hope so, Mr Butterworth. It pains me to turn on the light and find there is blood to mop up. Enjoy your weekend.

Fade.

The long hall — with echo. Sound of hurried footfall approaching on wooden floor.

NURSE FULTON (*approaching*). Morning, Mr Butterworth. You look down in the mouth today.

Footfall ceases.

BUTTERWORTH. The place is strangely quiet. Where's Matron?

NURSE FULTON. On holiday.

BUTTERWORTH (*peeved*). For how long?

NURSE FULTON (*crossly*). I don't know.

BUTTERWORTH. She didn't say anything to me yesterday about taking a holiday.

Sound of receding footfall on wooden floor.

NURSE FULTON (*over, withdrawing*). Since when did Matron take to consulting with you.

Pause.

The sun lounge.

MRS WESLEY. Good morning, Mr Butterworth. Come to join us in the sun lounge?

BUTTERWORTH. Good morning.

MRS SNELL. Mornin'. (*Coughs.*)

MRS RUBIN. Morning, Mr B.

BUTTERWORTH. Good morning, Elsie, Mrs Rubin.

MRS RUBIN. Call me Ida. Sit down.

ELLEN.   Good morning. (*Separately.*)
CELIA.   Good morning. (*Separately.*)
ABIGAIL.   Good morning. (*Separately.*)

BUTTERWORTH. Morning, ladies.

MRS RUBIN. Make yourself comfortable. Have a toffee.

Sound of paper bag rustle.

CELIA. Is that Mr Palmerston?

BUTTERWORTH. Butterworth.

ABIGAIL (*whispering to* ELLEN). Who did he say?

ELLEN (*whispering*). Butterworth.

ABIGAIL. Good morning, Mr Butterworth.

BUTTERWORTH. Morning. (*Pause.*) Well. . .

MRS RUBIN. Well?

BUTTERWORTH. Heard the bad news? Matron's gone.

MRS RUBIN. You say it like she was dead.

BUTTERWORTH. Without her, this place is — present company excepted.

MRS RUBIN. Excepted, nothing. You think I don't miss her? Mrs Snell here? Mrs Wesley too? The others? Who else should we go to for reassurance, uh? Whose word can we trust? believe in? Who else got time to listen?

BUTTERWORTH. Staff nurse. . .

MRS RUBIN. Mr Butterworth, outside — back home, when you got trouble, who do you turn to? Saint George? Never. You talk to the head of the firm direct. To God.

BUTTERWORTH. For me, Mrs Rubin, he is seldom, if ever, in.

MRS RUBIN. Mr Butterworth, this your lucky day. For you, it is Sunday.

MRS WESLEY. Already?

ELLEN. How time flies.

MRS SNELL. When you're 'avin' fun. But oo is? I ent. Nor likely to. T'morro', I go 'ome.

MRS RUBIN. So, put your feet up. Relax. Have a toffee.

Sound of paper bag rustle.

MRS RUBIN (*over*). Tell yourself Monday's next week.

Pause.

CELIA. Are you, by any chance, going to church, Mr Butterworth?

BUTTERWORTH. You want taking?

ABIGAIL. I don't like my vicar. His socks are too short.

CELIA. Is it far?

BUTTERWORTH. The church?

MRS WESLEY (*withdrawing*). Back home, I never miss. Go to both the morning *and* evening services.

MRS SNELL (*aside*). Holier than bleedin' thou, she is.

BUTTERWORTH (*to* CELIA). I wouldn't know.

MRS WESLEY (*distant*). The vicar's a friend of the family.

BUTTERWORTH (*to* CELIA). Ask Mrs Wesley.

MRS SNELL. She's over-watering the plants again.

MRS WESLEY (*approaching*). I'm watering the plants.

CELIA. Did you say his socks were too short?

MRS RUBIN. Could be his trousers aren't long enough.

Sound of paper bag rustle.

MRS RUBIN (*over*). Toffee anyone?

ELLEN. Whose socks?

MRS SNELL. Cardinal Wolsey's.

MRS WESLEY. Wesley.

ELLEN. I think I shall listen to morning service on the wireless.

ABIGAIL. I don't think he's a Wesleyan.

MRS SNELL. Anyone want a fag?

ELLEN. What about you, Celia?

CELIA. I don't smoke, dear.

ABIGAIL. She's Church of England.

ELLEN. No. The wireless. Will you listen?

ABIGAIL. I prefer television.

CELIA. We're not allowed to watch.

ABIGAIL. Songs of Praise. I always join in at home. Abide with Me's my favourite hymn.

MRS SNELL. Tha's wha' they sing at the Cup Final, en it? 'Ow's it go?

MRS WESLEY (*over*). This is beginning to flag.

ABIGAIL. . . . The darkness deepends, Lord with me abide;
          When other helpers fail, and comfort flees,
          Help of the helpless, O abide with me.

MRS SNELL. She kills 'em off. Pot plants visitors 'ave brung as pressies for relatives, she drowns 'em. (*Raising voice.*) You don't water gloxinias fr'm the top, Mrs Wesley.

ELLEN. Hush, Abigail.

ABIGAIL *stops singing.*

MRS WESLEY. My late husband had a greenhouse.

MRS RUBIN. He should have taken time off and told you that flowers, like fish, can drown.

MRS WESLEY. My husband, Mr Wesley, was a hard-working man.

MRS RUBIN. So what made your husband different from mine?

MRS WESLEY. He had green fingers. . .

MRS RUBIN. He was different.

MRS WESLEY. . . . but he never lived to enjoy his retirement. Or his greenhouse. Two weeks before he was due to retire, he passed away.

BUTTERWORTH. Unexpectedly?

MRS WESLEY. Shovelling snow. (*Beginning to sob.*) And, d'you know. . . (*Sobs.*) His insurance policy. . .

Pause.

MRS RUBIN. They wouldn't pay?

MRS WESLEY (*controlled*). There should be a law. . .

MRS RUBIN. If I was in your shoes, I'd be sorry for me too.

MRS WESLEY. His whole life, he'd looked forward to retiring. And he was denied.

MRS RUBIN. My Harry despised retirement. Who can live on a pension? he said. Only someone who's not interested in living. Ha! It would break his heart to see me now. Loved life did Harry.

BUTTERWORTH. He's dead too?

MRS RUBIN. And how is he dead. He was killed by hooligans, Mr Butterworth. Tied up with football scarves, he was put on display in his own shop window. Died of suffocation.

Pause. Sound of water dribbling onto floor, held.

ELLEN (*over*). Is that you, Abigail?

MRS SNELL (*warning*). Mrs Wesley. . .

MRS WESLEY (*distant*). Someone call?

ABIGAIL. Is that me what?

MRS RUBIN. It's dribbling onto the floor, dear.

ELLEN. Why didn't you say, Abigail?

ABIGAIL. Say what?

Sound of another dribble of water, held.

MRS WESLEY (*approaching*). Where's all that water coming from?

MRS SNELL. Where d'ya think?

CELIA. Up you get, Abigail.

MRS WESLEY. There's quite a puddle.

MRS SNELL. Yeah, sev'ral.

ELLEN. Hold onto me, Abigail. I'll take you.

Sound of yet another dribble of water, held.

ABIGAIL. Take me where? (*Tetchily.*) I was nicely settled.

MRS SNELL. Careful where y'put y'feet.

ELLEN. How embarrassing. Do excuse us. (*Withdrawing.*) Come along, Abigail. This way, I think.

CELIA (*withdrawing*). We could have got you there in time, if you'd said.

ABIGAIL. In time for what?

MRS WESLEY. Where are you three going?

Sound of three walking sticks tapping floor — receding.

ELLEN (*distant*). The toilet.

BUTTERWORTH. Hadn't someone better get a cloth?

Sound of dripping water begins to slow.

MRS WESLEY. Did I make that mess?

MRS SNELL. Ev'ry saucer filled t'over-bleedin'-flowin'.

MRS WESLEY. I thought they looked dry.

MRS SNELL. From yesterday?

MRS WESLEY. I don't like to see plants neglected.

MRS SNELL. You 'aven't stopped fussin' 'em since y'bleedin' come.

MRS WESLEY (*at crisis*). It gives me something to do! Something to take my mind off it!

MRS RUBIN (*kindly*). Calm down, calm down. There's no need to get all hot and bothered. You overdid it, that's all. Like with life. What we love, we are killing with kindness. Be thankful they was only flowers. Relax. Have a toffee.

Sound of paper bag rustle.

MRS RUBIN (*over*). Anyone else?

BUTTERWORTH. Mrs Rubin, tell me. . . Oh, thank you. Tell me, do you know why your husband was set upon by hooligans?

MRS RUBIN. The police said they guessed it was because Harry wouldn't sell them metal combs.

MRS SNELL. Steel combs?

BUTTERWORTH. But didn't anyone see him sitting in the shop window tied up with scarves?

MRS RUBIN. People must have. But who is understanding what they see? Mmm? We don't know real from real no more. On your television, people in a make-believe play die with as much conviction and blood as a man what they show dying on the news.

BUTTERWORTH. But your husband was on view to the public, alive, behind glass; perhaps struggling, turning red in the face, his breath forming a condensation on the glass. . .

MRS RUBIN. Mr Butterworth, now'days advertising is all gimmicks.

BUTTERWORTH. I can't believe people are so insensitive; gullible.

MRS RUBIN. Me neither. But who wants to get involved? Huh? It's the age of avoidance, Mr Butterworth. The age of avoiding.

Pause.

BUTTERWORTH. What kind of business was your husband engaged in before his untimely death?

MRS RUBIN. What kind? Honest. (*Laughingly*.) So now you know why we never got rich. (*Laughs*.)

MRS WESLEY. You said it was a shop.

MRS RUBIN. So what's unusual about an honest shop?

MRS WESLEY. A shop at which could be bought — what?

MRS RUBIN. Silver. All kinds. Clocks and watches. Jewellery.

MRS WESLEY. And he sold combs?

MRS RUBIN. This some sort of inquest? 'Cause he sold combs?

MRS WESLEY. *Steel* combs? In a jewellers?

MRS RUBIN. Did I say it was a jewellers?

MRS WESLEY. You've carefully avoided mentioning what kind of shop.

MRS RUBIN. Okay. So it was a pawn shop. You want I should be ashamed my Harry was a pawnbroker? Go ahead, make jokes about his three, brass balls. I know them all. Some, you ain't ever heard. But I aint ashamed. Me? I can remember when our small town couldn't do without their Harry Rubin and his wife. Every week they come to us. Times are bad, they said — like we lived on a different planet and didn't know times wasn't so good. How much you give us on our best teapot? Or maybe it was a set of fish knives. A watch. Clock. . . Come Friday, back they'd come. Please, Mrs Rubin, may we have our teapot? That damned teapot — or whatever, went backward and forward across the counter so many times it made you dizzy. Good business, they said. Ha! If they knew so much about business, how come they was always borrowing?

MRS WESLEY. You didn't do too badly.

MRS RUBIN. We didn't do so well, either. All that silver gilt getting scratched every time it come in and out. And what happen on the day they don't come to claim no more? Eh? What have you got? Junk.

MRS WESLEY. You didn't starve like some people I know.

MRS RUBIN. Listen, Mrs Linsey-English-Woolsey, I could name you people what become prominent town councillors — not your socialists either, so-called respectable men who *still* owe money from them days. Money, Harry, out of the goodness of his heart, lent to men what didn't have no security. Then — it was, 'Good morning, Mr Rubin. How is the beautiful wife

this morning?' But they was all promissory men. You know.
Promise you this. Promise you that. 'Put in a good word for
you at the golf club, Harry. Promise.' And always crossing
their hearts and hoping to die. Know something? They should
have, then Harry need not have bankrupted himself in the
hope that one day he get to play a round of golf. Not that he
would leave the shop, what with the Fascists prising up paving
stones. Remember the Fascists. Mrs? Remember how windows
got broken? Not only windows. Heads too. All because we
was Jews. Or was it because we was Jews what did business?
People wasn't too keen on the Rubins for a while. Then when
Harry come back from the war, you got your welfare, so who
needed a Rubin anyhow? Thank God Harry never forgot how
to mend clocks. So, we managed. A little mending here, a
little selling there. A bit of costume jewellery on the side. You
know, what's called a flourishing one-man business. Only it
didn't flourish and was one-man because we don't have no
children on account God give me the outside shape of a
woman but missed out on the internals. That's life. We manage.
Then you want he should sell metal combs. You seen how
they can cut? I've seen how they can cut. And I tell you,
Harry's face I am not ever forgetting. You want to frighten
someone? Be combing your hair when I open the door. Me?
I will show you how quick an old woman drops dead.
But dead I ain't. Maybe I wish I was. Maybe I wish I was.
Who needs a fat, old Jewish widow who's got a moustache
and only one tit, eh? Or maybe you think I see myself as part
of some master plan. Okay. I got a sense of humour. I see
the funny side. Maybe God too. But tell me, why is no one
laughing? Huh? (*Pause.*) Mr Butterworth?

BUTTERWORTH. It was never ever funny.

MRS RUBIN (*withdrawing*). So excuse me while I cry, huh?

Sound of high-heeled shoes receding on wooden floor.

MRS RUBIN (*over*). Just this one luxury before this old woman
gets furious with her God, herself, and you damned women.

Pause.

MRS SNELL. Yeah, well, when y'reckon on dinner?

MRS WESLEY. It was her own fault. And so emotional — the
Jews. (*Fading.*) It's one of their weaknesses. Now, take the
English. Much more phlegmatic. . .

Pause.

NURSE FULTON (*close, confidential*). Off somewhere, Mr Butterworth?

BUTTERWORTH (*close*). Off out of it, Nurse Fulton. Off out of it. Better I confine myself to the company of men.

NURSE FULTON. Well don't go far. It's time for lunch.

BUTTERWORTH. Let me gong for it.

NURSE FULTON. No.

BUTTERWORTH. Oh, please, Nurse. Just this once. (*Pause.*) I can?

NURSE FULTON. Now.

BUTTERWORTH. With pleasure.

An ear-shattering gonging, only gradually fading to silence. Pause.

The TV lounge. Sound — TV programme 'Crossroads', held.

BUTTERWORTH (*over*). How long have you smoked?

LOUIS. Fust World War.

BUTTERWORTH. Were you in the second?

LOUIS. Desert rat. Ha! Desert rat. . .

BUTTERWORTH. You were?

LOUIS. Wounded. (*Pause.*) Wan' t'know where I w's wounded? (*Laughs.*) Weren't in the 'ead! (*Laughs.*)

BUTTERWORTH. What unit?

LOUIS. Artillery. (*Slight pause.*) That's why I'm —

Pause.

BUTTERWORTH. Deaf?

LOUIS. Wha'?

BUTTERWORTH. The gun fire.

LOUIS. Made me deaf. (*Pause.*) Bbum! Ha! (*Laughs. Pause.*) In Germany too.

BUTTERWORTH. As a gunner?

LOUIS. Know Krupps? (*Pause.*) Krupp.

BUTTERWORTH. Oh — Krupp — steel engineer. Big armament factory. Yes?

LOUIS. Captured his hum.

BUTTERWORTH. Krupp's what?

LOUIS. Hum. (*Pause.*) Pheeeewwww. . .

BUTTERWORTH. Big?

LOUIS. Coooooor. . . Furnitures. Paintin'.

BUTTERWORTH. Whereabouts?

LOUIS (*laughing*). Everyone grab, grab, grab. . .

BUTTERWORTH. Loot?

LOUIS. There w's two horses. S'big. Black. Looked well on my mantlepiece they would.

BUTTERWORTH. You nicked them?

LOUIS. Off'cer saw me. (*Laughs.*) 'Ad one under each arm.

BUTTERWORTH. What happened?

LOUIS. Put me under close arrest.

BUTTERWORTH. The officer?

LOUIS. Said he'd shoot me. (*Laughs.*)

BUTTERWORTH. But he didn't.

LOUIS. Ha! 'Course 'e didn'. (*Laughs.*) Know wha'? He got me to make he boxes. Hundreds a boxes. (*Laughs.*) Bloody wood'n crates ev'rywhere. All goo'n hum. His hum in England. Surrey, or somewhere. (*Laughs.*)

BUTTERWORTH. What happened to the two bronze horses?

LOUIS. I crated 'em up for 'im, didn' I? (*Laughs.*) Two, nice hosses, they w's. Workin' on a farm, I reckon I know'd 'bout horses, an' they w's two nice 'uns. I really fancied they. Only thin' I ever did fancy. They two black horses.

BUTTERWORTH. You gave in too easily, Louis. You should have stuck to your guns.

LOUIS. I did. Had to. I w's in Artill'ry, weren't I? Ha! (*Laughs.*) Stick t'me guns . . . Tha's a good'n.

MRS WESLEY (*distant*). Will you two men keep your voices down. We're trying to watch Crossroads.

Pause. Fade.

The male ward. Sound of curtain being dragged on runners.

ASHDOWN. I've been on television.

BUTTERWORTH. Gracious, I *am* impressed. I came to get my book.

ASHDOWN. Twice.

BUTTERWORTH. Twice!

ASHDOWN. King Wonder and his talking budgerigars.

BUTTERWORTH. *You,* Mr Ashdown? A full-time, strong-armed Bailiff with a sneaking for am-at-eur theatricals?

ASHDOWN. Police balls. Children's parties. You know the sort of thing. I've got a way with animals.

BUTTERWORTH. Born with it, were you?

ASHDOWN. One of God's gifts.

BUTTERWORTH. But hard work nevertheless.

ASHDOWN. Patience and kindness bring their own reward, Mr Butterworth.

BUTTERWORTH. My sentiments exactly. Applicable to humans too. Have you see my book?

ASHDOWN. Train anything, I can.

BUTTERWORTH. Donkeys?

ASHDOWN. Taught one to count.

BUTTERWORTH. Really? And here's me still adding up on my fingers. The book's got a lurid cover.

ASHDOWN. Nearly turned professional.

BUTTERWORTH. You should have.

ASHDOWN. I had the patter.

BUTTERWORTH. Jokes?

ASHDOWN. Specially written.

BUTTERWORTH. Get-a-way! Who by?

ASHDOWN. Ah, that would be telling. (*Pause.*) Paid as much as a pound each for some jokes.

BUTTERWORTH. Sounds expensive.

ASHDOWN. Pays to buy the best.

BUTTERWORTH. I'm sure Max Bygraves would agree.

ASHDOWN. Some were a bit. . .

BUTTERWORTH. Risqué?

ASHDOWN. Near the knuckle.

BUTTERWORTH. Say no more. Now, this book. . .

ASHDOWN (*lowering voice*). Some, I wouldn't even tell the wife.

BUTTERWORTH. That strong? My name's written on the fly leaf. In blue.

ASHDOWN (*over*) Stag night stuff.

BUTTERWORTH. Ah.

ASHDOWN. When it's all men together.

BUTTERWORTH. I know the feeling.

Pause.

ASHDOWN. Heard the one about the short-sighted Irishman who went to bed.

BUTTERWORTH. With a Chinese girl who'd got a cleft palate and wore a surgical leg iron?

ASHDOWN (*disappointed*). You've heard it.

BUTTERWORTH. Perhaps I saw your act. (*Pause.*) This book. . .

ASHDOWN. My best was a troupe of acrobatic dogs.

BUTTERWORTH. What was their particular forte? Two on a see-saw?

ASHDOWN. Back somersaults. Feigning dead.

BUTTERWORTH. Feigning dead?

ASHDOWN. Leap frog.

BUTTERWORTH. That, I imagine, was a trick fraught with temptation, if the doggies were in any way excited.

ASHDOWN. Pushing baby in the pram. Always ended with a fashion parade.

BUTTERWORTH. Your wife make the clothes?

ASHDOWN. Sewed every sequin by hand.

BUTTERWORTH. What patience.

ASHDOWN. Great artistry.

BUTTERWORTH. In the act herself?

ASHDOWN. That's a sore point, Mr Butterworth.

BUTTERWORTH. Didn't mean to pry, old sport. Sorry. If I could find my book, I'd let you get on with your undressing.

ASHDOWN (*confidentially*). It's her legs.

BUTTERWORTH. Her legs? Oh — legs. Too short? What? (*Pause.*) Fat?

ASHDOWN. Fish nets.

BUTTERWORTH. Pardon?

ASHDOWN. Wouldn't be seen dead in them.

BUTTERWORTH. Even under a split satin skirt?

ASHDOWN. Gracious — no. Worse. A very modest woman, the wife.

BUTTERWORTH. But a perfect little treasure.

ASHDOWN. Even though I say so myself. Yes. Know what earned a round of applause? And her idea entirely.

BUTTERWORTH. Do tell.

ASHDOWN. The animals in swim-wear.

BUTTERWORTH. Bikinis?

ASHDOWN. Each bitch wore a little padded bra.

BUTTERWORTH. It's those imaginative touches, which make for the professional, Mr Ashdown.

ASHDOWN. To give the act variety, I used to black up, sometimes.

BUTTERWORTH. Ah, a smudge of the old burnt cork, eh?

ASHDOWN. Billed myself as Old young King Cole.

BUTTERWORTH. Get a lot of laughs?

ASHDOWN. Went down a treat. Would like to have auditioned for the Black and White Minstrels.

BUTTERWORTH. Why didn't you?

ASHDOWN. The old ticker.

BUTTERWORTH. Ah. . .

ASHDOWN. I nearly died, you know.

BUTTERWORTH. How nearly?

ASHDOWN. Three times I was given up for dead.

BUTTERWORTH. Three times.

ASHDOWN. Three times.

BUTTERWORTH. Someone must have your name in that great box office in the sky, Mr Ashdown, to have allowed you to survive three times.

ASHDOWN. I think so too.

BUTTERWORTH. Ever trained fleas?

ASHDOWN. What?

BUTTERWORTH. Fleas.

ASHDOWN. No.

BUTTERWORTH. Bet you've caught a few though.

ASHDOWN. Pardon?

BUTTERWORTH. In your job.

ASHDOWN. No.

BUTTERWORTH. But surely, as Bailiff, you've had to force your way into unwholesome premises on occasion.

ASHDOWN. Frequently.

BUTTERWORTH. Supervised the removal of bits and pieces of furniture — mattresses, some of them lively with fleas.

ASHDOWN (*laughingly*). Often.

BUTTERWORTH. And a flea's never jumped you?

ASHDOWN (*laughingly*). Never.

BUTTERWORTH. So, you've never trained a flea.

ASHDOWN (*quietening*). No.

BUTTERWORTH. How about a debtor.

ASHDOWN. What?

BUTTERWORTH. A long-haired squatter.

ASHDOWN. What you on about?

BUTTERWORTH. Haven't you trained one?

ASHDOWN. To do what?

BUTTERWORTH. Somersault downstairs, jump out of a bay window, vault the corrugated iron barricade, say a few, choice words and go (*Blows a raspberry.*) to you, mate.

ASHDOWN (*withdrawing*). I thought you were a joker.

BUTTERWORTH (*calling after*). Where you going, Mr Ashdown? Come back.

ASHDOWN (*distant*) I've got better things to do.

BUTTERWORTH. Like what, for instance? Telling jokes about one-legged girls?

NURSE FULTON (*close*). That was very unkind.

BUTTERWORTH (*surprised*). Where d'you spring from?

NURSE FULTON. Ever thought Mr Ashdown might feel inadequate?

BUTTERWORTH. Nurse Fulton, the Ashdowns of this world are dangerous. Not because they have power, but the support they give those demagogues who do.

NURSE FULTON. I've brought back your book.

BUTTERWORTH. You don't believe me.

NURSE FULTON. Mr Ashdown is a very sick man.

BUTTERWORTH. *You* are telling *me?* I get it twice a day from him how near to death's door he came.

NURSE FULTON. Did he also tell you his only two children, his two daughters, are dead? Killed in the car he was driving at the time of his heart attack.

BUTTERWORTH. For that, you want I should be compassionate?

NURSE FULTON. True compassion is for those we despise; have come to loathe. Isn't it?

BUTTERWORTH. Possibly. Most people pull away from giving the kiss of life when the mouth to which they have to press their lips has collapsed with age, is rotten and the interior repellant with acidic fumes. We turn to you. . .

NURSE FULTON. The professionals.

BUTTERWORTH. Angels, so-called. But society also has its dustmen, sewerage workers, coal miners, rat catchers. . . always someone willing to undertake the tasks no one else will perform.

NURSE FULTON. Mr Ashdown is a Bailiff. Was.

BUTTERWORTH. Mr Ashdown, like all of us, is many other things besides. And it is the sum total which makes us the person we are. Having totted up Mr Ashdown's score, I find no redeeming feature which would make me feel compassionate towards him.

NURSE FULTON. Not, one aspect?

BUTTERWORTH. One. He is human. And therefore, is weak, pitiful, corruptible; thoroughly deserving of Christian compassion. There. I've said it. Not that I believe it to be true. Always at odds with society, the ideas and motivations which keep it alive, I have, unfortunately, weakened since my radical days — sneeringly, I could be called liberal, but one can compromise once too often. I feel I have. So, I propose to do what the ostrich does, and bury my head in the sand. (*Withdrawing.*) I am altogether too tired, Nurse Fulton. Too dreadfully tired.

Pause.

The TV lounge. Sound of TV programme 'Blue Peter'. Hold.

MR TWIST. This time last week, Mrs Snell went home.

BUTTERWORTH. Mrs Snell?

MR TWIST. Thin woman. Coughed a lot. (*Pause.*) Wore a wig.

BUTTERWORTH. Oh — her. Had breast cancer.

MR TWIST. Went home this time last week.

BUTTERWORTH. Get-away.

MR TWIST. This time last week.

LOUIS. I go t'morro'.

MR TWIST. Home? You?

BUTTERWORTH. You don't want to go home, do you?

MR TWIST. You're better off here, Louis.

BUTTERWORTH. Even Ashdown can't face the prospect of not being able to mow his immaculate lawn and having to sit watching his rose beds slowly disappear under a strangle of weeds.

LOUIS. Tha's proper place f'man. His hum.

BUTTERWORTH. I thought you were a widower.

MR TWIST. He lives in an isolated, tumble-down cottage in the middle of nowhere. So he said.

BUTTERWORTH. On his own?

LOUIS. Meals on wheels come twice a week.

BUTTERWORTH. And on other days?

LOUIS. Do me own cookin'.

BUTTERWORTH. But you're. . . (*To* MR TWIST, *quietly*.) Is he registered as blind? (*Aloud*.) How much can you see?

LOUIS. Some.

BUTTERWORTH. Enough?

Sound of coins.

LOUIS. Tha's a two bob bit, en it?

MR TWIST. Ten p.

LOUIS. Ten p.? Ha! An' I thought it were a two bob bit.

BUTTERWORTH. This is ridiculous. (*Appealing*.) Louis, your one good hand — it shakes.

LOUIS. I never were left-handed.

BUTTERWORTH. In the dining room, you sugar the table cloth never your tea.

MR TWIST. He can't even see to pour milk in his cup.

LOUIS. Had a stroke. Ha! Stroke. . .

BUTTERWORTH. How d'you manage to do your own cooking?

MR TWIST. On a primus, he told me.

BUTTERWORTH. Good grief! Imagine — a pan of boiling fat balanced precariously, and him with a fit of the violent trembles!

LOUIS. Know wha' I'm lookin' forw'd to when I git hum? Shave. Nice wet shave. Wi' a cut-throat. Ha! Cut throat. . .

MR TWIST. He'd qualify for a home help. (*Addressing* LOUIS.) Wouldn't you?

BUTTERWORTH. D'you have a home help, Louis?

LOUIS. S'ppose t'come three times a week.

BUTTERWORTH. Does she?

LOUIS. Little ol' dear come ev'ry day.

BUTTERWORTH. Good.

LOUIS (*confirming*). Har is tha'. Real nice gal. (*Slight pause*.) Make good egg custard.

BUTTERWORTH. Lucky you.

LOUIS. Eighty-two.

BUTTERWORTH. You are?

LOUIS. She is.

BUTTERWORTH (*aside*). Oh — no. . . (*Aloud*.) Can she cope?

LOUIS. Got a wood'n leg. Ha! Allus catchin' fire.

BUTTERWORTH. Her leg?

LOUIS. Sets there pokin' the fire.

BUTTERWORTH. With her leg?

MR TWIST. He's having us on.

BUTTERWORTH. You having us on, Louis?

LOUIS. Give a man a good shave, her can. Better'n a barber. Whispers cut-throat like she blowin' in yar ear. Ooooo. . . Ha! Feathers. . .

MR TWIST. He's mad. (*Aloud*.) You're cuckoo.

LOUIS. Tha's a good job I is, boy. Know why? I got a nest egg under me mattress I'm a keepin' warm f'when I git married 'gain. Ha! Nest egg. . .

Fade up music — theme preceding BBC TV News.

MR TWIST. That the news?

BUTTERWORTH. Who cares? Let the world go hang.

MR TWIST. Hear, hear.

Pause. Sound of Richard Baker reading the news.

LOUIS. Know wha' I'm lookin' forward to most when I git hum? Havin' me back rubbed. True. After me bath, Mrs Marsley allus rubs me back wi' a bit a old sackin'. Ooooo. . . tha's nice.

BUTTERWORTH. Having your back rubbed?

MR TWIST. With sacking?

LOUIS. Bring it up like an ol' piece linol'um, she can, wi' not an itch on't. Lovely.

BUTTERWORTH. Won't be long, then. You go home tomorrow.

LOUIS. An' real happy I'll be. Real happy.

Sound of distant gonging.

BUTTERWORTH. Give me your arm, Louis. (*Explaining.*) Dinner.

LOUIS. Supper?

MR TWIST. Food.

LOUIS (*withdrawing*). Eat a horse, I could.

MR TWIST (*withdrawing*). You've read the menu!

LOUIS (*laughs*). Read the menu. . . (*Laughs.*)

Fade.

The dining hall. Sound of cutlery, crockery, hushed conversation.

ASHDOWN. Thought I'd avoid the crush. Got here first. Like a zoo it is, sometimes. Feeding time.

BUTTERWORTH (*approaching*). Keep a firm grip, Louis. Hold on.

ASHDOWN. You have to watch out for yourself. No one else takes a blind bit of notice.

BUTTERWORTH. Now sit yourself down. S-l-o-w-l-y.

ASHDOWN. Another heart attack would kill me. Been sat here half an hour.

MR TWIST. Half an hour?

ASHDOWN. Me and Jock.

JOCK. Half a bloody hour waitin' fer the gong.

Sound of sudden crash of chair, table, cutlery, crockery smashing.
Silent pause.

BUTTERWORTH. Louis? (*Calling.*) Nurse! Come quickly!

NURSE FULTON (*approaching*). Don't try and lift him. (*Calling.*) Porter! Bring the chair!

PORTER (*approaching*). Stand away, all of you. Keep back.

Sound of squeaking wheels approaching, stopping.

PORTER. You too, Butterworth.

NURSE FULTON. I'll take his legs, Leslie.

PORTER. Got him.

NURSE FULTON. A-n-d — *Lift* -him-into-the-chair.

ASHDOWN. It's got wheels on the back legs.

Sound of squeaking wheels — receding.

PORTER (*over, withdrawing*). Matron's office?

NURSE FULTON (*withdrawing*). I'll start resuscitation. You phone the hospital. And hurry.

Pause. Sound of conversational hum returning as patients scrape back chairs and sit.

MR TWIST. That was quick.

ASHDOWN. Reassuring to know they're efficient in an emergency.

JOCK. Aye, but wha' aboot us?

MR TWIST. We'll get fed, sooner or later.

JOCK. I c'n get along fine wi'out fud, but I have t'take m'heart tablets regular.

BUTTERWORTH (*disapproving*). Oh, Jock. . .

JOCK. S'true. I need m'pills.

ASHDOWN. We both do.

JOCK. Otherwise they'll be sendin' a stretcher chair fer the two on us. Right Ashy?

ASHDOWN. Right, Jock.

BUTTERWORTH. But what about Louis? They can't see to both him *and* you.

JOCK. There's nay point on wastin' time on an ol' man what's dead — is they? They canna do anythin' for him, once he's dead.

MR TWIST. Jock has a point, Butterworth. The living come first.

JOCK. Are y'with me then, Ashy? Altogether, eh? (*Bangs knife and fork on table in time to:*) Why are we waiting. Oh, why are we waiting, (*etc.*)

ASHDOWN (*picking up time from* JOCK). Oh, why are we waiting, (*etc.*). . .

Sound of all the patients assembled in the dining hall slowly taking up the chant started by JOCK. *Banging, not only their cutlery, but stamping their feet.*

MATRON (*over, distant*). Quiet!

BUTTERWORTH (*enthusiastically*). It's Matron.

MATRON. Silence, I said! *Silence!*

Silence.

BUTTERWORTH (*quietly, with enthusiasm*). Matron's back!

MATRON (*approaching*). In all my years as Matron, even during my time as junior nurse, I have never, ever witnessed such disgraceful behaviour.

Sound of distant protest.

MATRON. Hold your tongue!

Silent pause.

MATRON. If there is a reoccurance — however slight, I shall not hesitate to take disciplinary action against the person or persons involved. They will be put out, bag and baggage. Do I make myself clear. It will be — out! (*Mumurs of acknowledgement.*) Good.

MRS WESLEY (*distant*). How's Mr Palmerston?

MATRON (*ignoring*). The Porter will be here directly to help dish up the food. . . (*Surge of sound.*) Quiet.

Sound of distant telephone ringing.

MATRON (*over*). Mrs Wesley, Mrs Cadugan, (*Pause.*) and Mr Butterworth. You three will help serve.

JOCK. Who's go'n t'gi' us our tablets?

Sound of distant telephone bell stops.

MATRON. I will, Mr MacGilbie.

JOCK. When? It's near on twenty minutes after six.

ASHDOWN. Twenty-two.

MATRON. I will come round with the medication trolley when I decide, Mr MacGilbie. And not before.

NURSE FULTON (*distant, calling*). Telephone for Mr Butterworth.

MATRON. Mr Butterworth, kindly inform your friends that they must not telephone during supper.

BUTTERWORTH. Probably my wife.

MATRON. Just tell her.

BUTTERWORTH. Yes, Matron. Welcome back.

MATRON (*withdrawing*). Stop dithering, and get on with it. You've got the meal to help serve.

Fade.

The long hall.

BUTTERWORTH. Butterworth speaking. . . Oh, hello, Grace. . . I sound what? . . . No, I'm all right. . . Saturday? *Last* Saturday? . . . You *didn't* go. . . So you wouldn't have been able to come and taken me away even if you *had* gone to Edinburgh. . . I see. And he's staying? . . . There now . . . No, I don't want to speak to him. . . Of course I'm not jealous. . . What d'you mean? Not like me. . . Yes. What? . . . I shouldn't bother. . . Yes. Might as well stay now I'm here. . . Yes. . . Love to you to. . . Hello? (*Pause.*) Gone.

Sound of telephone being replaced on cradle.

MRS RUBIN (*approaching*). Your lady wife?

BUTTERWORTH. Turn out the one, remaining spot, Mrs Rubin. Let the space go dark.

MRS RUBIN. Pardon me?

BUTTERWORTH. Ring down the curtain.

MRS RUBIN. I guessed you was maybe theatrical. But why the dramatics? Bad news perhaps?

BUTTERWORTH. I am going to accept Matron's offer and move up into the attic.

MRS RUBIN. And sleep on your own? Mr Butterworth, it's only chickens what goes broody.

BUTTERWORTH. Mrs Rubin, it's further to fall.

MRS RUBIN. From the third floor? Listen, I've known people what survived a drop of four floors — not altogether nicely, but they was grateful. So why not wait 'til you can jump from a really tall building, uh? Do the job properly?

BUTTERWORTH. The taller the building, Mrs Rubin, the more time for second thoughts as you fall.

MRS RUBIN. So — put a bullet in your head — but *after* you've helped serve supper, please?

BUTTERWORTH. I've lost my appetite.

Sounds from dining hall have, by now, begun to assert themselves.

BUTTERWORTH. In fact, I couldn't face food.

MRS RUBIN. You think that's what all them 'dummkopfs' are clammering for? No. Sure it's a hunger, but it's a hunger which ain't got no definition. No shape. But, if you don't feed it, then — aye-yi-yi — are you in trouble.

BUTTERWORTH. What you on about? Feed it with what?

MRS RUBIN. You think I got the answer? Listen, greater brains than mine have puzzled this question. You know what? I tell you. They don't have the answer neither. But — well, we got the main thing, eh? Okay, so you and I ain't so complete as we once was — bits of us is missing, but we got life, Mr Butterworth. We got life.

BUTTERWORTH. It's not enough, Mrs Rubin.

MRS RUBIN. Not enough, he says. Mr Butterworth, it's the *only* thing we got.

BUTTERWORTH. But it always comes gift-wrapped in death.

MRS RUBIN. That — you've just found out? Listen. . . You been in the Army? Yes! Okay. Imagine yourself on sentry duty. It's night. Dark. You're on guard. Okay? (*Withdrawing.*) You hear a footstep. Friend or foe, you wonder. How you going to find out?

ANNOUNCER. That was, 'Halt, who goes there?' by Tom Mallin.

MRS RUBIN (*fading*). You challenge him. Why? You think the enemy going to say, 'Death here'? Never in a hundred years. And who wants to live that long anyhow?

ANNOUNCER *over.*

Fade out sound.

THE MONDAY PLAY

DAUGHTERS OF MEN

by Jennifer Phillips

Daughters of Men was first broadcast on BBC Radio 4 on
Monday 1st May 1978. The cast was as follows:

KATE LISTER	Judi Dench
DAPHNE KERSHAW	Diana Bishop
SALLY LISTER	Jean Rogers
EDDIE MARCHANT	Peter Pacey
BAHAMA KELLY	Liza Ross
ANNE TROUBRIDGE	Jane Knowles
BOY KRUSCHEFSKI	Harold Kasket
DAVID LISTER	Malcolm Gerard

Director: Richard Wortley

Jennifer Phillips has had over forty of her plays produced. She
has had four of her own comedy series — two on radio and two on
television, and was the first woman in this country to be employed
as a comedy script writer. Her first full length stage play *The
Backhanded Kiss* was produced at the Pheonix Theatre, Leicester
in 1969. Three years later *Bodywork* was also directed by Robin
Midgley there, and given a different production at the Hampstead
Theatre Club. Her play *Instrument for Love* directed by Liane
Aukin opened the first women's theatre festival at the Almost
Free Theatre. Nikolas Simmons directed her next full length stage
play at the Haymarket Studio Theatre in Leicester. As is the case
with many British playwrights, Jennifer was given her first break
by BBC Radio with a play called *Fault on the Line* which starred
Beryl Reid and Pat Hayes; she continues to be given opportunities
there to write plays as diverse as, for example, *Stone Boy* and *The
Fixed Smile* for Radio 3 and *Henry Enjoying Himself* and *Blow
Your House In* for Radio 4. A stage version of *Daughters of Men*
opened at the Hampstead Theatre Club in January 1979.

Fade up slowly — the office of senior social worker, MRS DAPHNE KERSHAW. *At her desk she reads aloud from a file before her. The fact that it is late afternoon, that she never relishes this aspect of a report, and that* KATE LISTER *is already growing restless — have already increased the pace of her reading. . .*

MRS KERSHAW (*reads*). 'B. I have also had discussions with the respondent four times. Twice in the co-respondent's house whe re he is at present residing on September 29th and October 9th. Twice in his office on October 7th and October 20th.'

KATE. People ask too much of social workers.

MRS KERSHAW (*pressing on*). 'C. The child — once in the company of her mother on October 8th, once in the company of her father October 9th. Twice in my office — November 1st and 10th.'

KATE. Would you mind if I took my shoes off?

MRS KERSHAW. Oh, no. Nice colour red.

KATE. They're new.

MRS KERSHAW. Very nice.

KATE. They're new. Bit high though.

MRS KERSHAW (*continuing, fast*). 'D. The co-respondent once in my office on November 6th. E. The Headmistress of Catlin Primary School, once in her office on October 10th. F. Miss Anne Troubridge, a close friend of the petitioners, at my office on November 12th.' Obviously there should be an addition to F. now but that's left till the end — the Supplementary Welfare Report.

KATE. How many more pages are there?

MRS KERSHAW. Twelve. None of which you have to listen to.

KATE. I'm listening.

SALLY (*calls. Off. Distant*). Mummy?

MRS KERSHAW (*not reacting*). And which I'm in no way bound to read to you. It's just that in the interests of fairness. . .

KATE. Of course.

MRS KERSHAW. I like to give each party the chance to contradict or comment on the observations I have made.

KATE. Do continue.

MRS KERSHAW. And I will make a note of those comments. . .

KATE. I didn't mean to interrupt.

MRS KERSHAW. Or relevant interruptions and endeavour to include them in the final draft of my report. (*She turns her attention to the file again.*) Er. . . oh, yes. . . 'Number 3. Background relating to the Child. On 2nd April 1965, after having lived together out of wedlock for the nineteen months previously, the parties were married. Two years later on May 8th, 1967, the child, Sally, was born. Until then the couple's home had been the husband's bachelor apartment. Larger accommodation was now sought and a four bedroomed house bought in both their names for £17,950. The deposit being made up by the sale of the lease of the husband's flat and money saved by the wife. This left the couple with mortgage repayments of £60. 40p. per month. Initially paid out of their joint account — this joint account was cancelled when friction began to develop within the relationship. Each starting their own account on 11th April, 1970 and from thereon paying £30. 20p each per month towards the mortgage. Friction came to a head on March 15th, 1974, when the husband moved out of the matrimonial bedroom.'

SALLY (*calls, off, more insistent*). Mummy!

KATE. I heard it again.

MRS KERSHAW. What?

KATE. Didn't you hear. . . ?

MRS KERSHAW. I'm sorry. . . But I must press on, Mrs Lister, or we'll never get through before they lock the offices up. (*Reads on.*) 'From this point on other household bills were also divided. Rates of £201 being paid half yearly — first by the wife then by the husband. At first gas, electricity, water rate, food bills were all equally shared. But this provoked too many arguments so the wife took the gas bill and the husband the electric and water rates. Though Mr Lister pointed out that his wife paid the additional charge for the garden hose and sprinkler. (*Beginning to fade.*) The causes for friction differ in accounts given to me by the. . .

Fade.

Sound of front door slamming off. The living room of KATE's *house.*

SALLY. Mum? (*Calls.*) Mummy.

KATE (*off*). Darling? (*Approaching.*) My perfect latchkey child! (*Kiss.*) Oh, you found the doughnut then.

SALLY (*with a mouthful*). Very easy.

KATE (*moving off to kitchen area*). I don't know how you do it. I'd never have thought of looking behind the Oxford Dictionary.

Sound of kettle being filled.

SALLY. I sniff. (*She sniffs noisily.*) All round the room.

KATE (*slightly off*). You ought to blow your nose, Sally.

SALLY. Dad rang. (*Sniffs again.*)

KATE (*approaching*). Do blow your nose.

SALLY. Doesn't need blowing now, Mum.

KATE. He would. As soon as you got in, I suppose, and before I got back.

SALLY (*moving off slightly*). Can I use your felt tips?

KATE. Mmm, he would. (*She sits heavily.*) Oh, I must get some new shoes.

SALLY. Get high ones. Get red.

KATE. All right. It's not just my feet though. It's my thighs. From the waist up I'm fine. But in the mirror from the waist down I seem to be standing in a pool of water. You know how water magnifies? And that would account for my squashy shoes. Did he say he wanted to see me? I'd better ring him.

SALLY. No, don't stand up — I'm drawing you.

KATE. I don't want to ring him. I'm depressed enough because it's nearly my birthday.

SALLY. I got you your. . . (*She gasps.*)

KATE. My present! My . . . ! Oh, please don't tell me what it is, Sal, I forgot to forget when you told me last year. Give me one guess though?

SALLY. I'll show you if you like.

KATE. I wouldn't look.

SALLY. They're wrapped up. You couldn't tell what they were from the shape of the parcel.

KATE (*going to switch kettle off*). Ugh! Who's that you're drawing?

SALLY. You.

KATE. I see.

SALLY. Your idea — standing in a pool of water. How old are you, Mum?

Sound of water poured into mug.

KATE. I know how old you are — to the minute.

SALLY. The wrapping paper is blue with gold flowers on. The paper cost 12p.

KATE (*approaching*). It's a pair of. . .

SALLY. How did you know?

KATE. 'They' you said, a few moments ago, 'they'.

SALLY. I don't care. You'll never find them.

KATE. Where did you get the money?

SALLY. Dad. I'll give you a clue.

KATE. The best present I ever had was you. Every present since has been a bit of an anti-climax.

SALLY. Were you glad? When the doctor said. When I came out. Tell me.

KATE (*moving off slightly*). Oh, damn — I should've got the steak and kidney pie out of the freezer this morning. Oh, look, I did, how clever of me! I can relax another five minutes then.

SALLY. I got it out.

KATE. Darling, thanks. Shall we have a record on? The doctor said, 'If any person knows any cause or just impediment why these two should not be Mother and Daughter. . . ', 'I do', I murmured, 'Surely this must be the daughter of a king. . . '

SALLY. Was Daddy there?

Sound of record on, volume low, some Tchaikovsky.

KATE. 'And yet I have laid with no kings or princes.' You asked David once if he knew any princes and when he said, 'No,' you burst into tears. You were so angry. You wanted to marry one, you said, with a cloak and long hair. It was the first time he let you down.

SALLY. Are you going to ring him?

KATE. Well, as I don't know where he rang from. . . And as I feel like dancing. . . (*She hums to music, stops abruptly.*) This is something I cannot tolerate. I will not tolerate you slinging your things just anywhere. Look at your coat on the floor. I shan't tell you again, Sally, it's sluttish. Oh, not so important in itself perhaps. But it's one of these things like swearing, these outward signs that other people judge you by. You have to know how to behave and it's up to me to show you how — or other people won't like you as I know they should. They'll draw the wrong conclusions. (*Moving off slightly.*) More fool them. But that's how it is.

SALLY. Where are you going?

KATE. To hang your coat up.

SALLY. Take yours too then.

KATE. Where is mine?

SALLY. Over there, on the *floor*.

KATE (*approaching*). You take after me, that's what it must be. (*Moving off.*) I can't take after you.

SALLY (*calling after her*). You never say I take after David.

KATE (*calling, off*). Well, maybe you do.

SALLY. How could I? He's a man.

KATE (*approaching*). He was there when you were born. They gave him a piece of ice in some gauze. I think he was meant to be cooling my head with it. I think it was meant to be therapy for him. How did you know my size?

SALLY. I looked. . . oh, you pig!

KATE. Since you said 'they' then that means a pair of. . .

Volume up on music.

SALLY. I can't hear!

KATE (*shouts*). Turn it down! I don't want to know! Honestly, I swear! Then dance with me!

A certain amount of thumping and panting.

Mind the conservatory door! No, Sally, be careful! Mind the drinks trolley!

Sound of bottles and glasses rattling together.

End of rest and relaxation period!

Music stops.

SALLY. I might go round to Jane's.

KATE. Don't be late though, Sal.

SALLY. Or I might not. I like steak and kidney pie.

KATE. That will be too late. Anyway they're boring business people.

SALLY. I don't mind.

KATE. Americans.

SALLY. I won't take any notice of them.

KATE. Which is why I am doing traditional English cooking.

SALLY. Anne cooked it all.

KATE. She's got more time than me. And anyway it's the style with which one presents the meal, the finishing touches that makes it an aesthetic experience.

SALLY. I'll go to bed. If I can have the telly till nine and a beef-burger. No, two. In a soft roll. Tomato sauce. No onions.

KATE. Should I allow myself to be blackmailed?

SALLY. Yes.

KATE. Shall I be setting a precedent?

SALLY. Yes.

KATE. Will she, in later years, blame me for spoiling her, for her spotty skin, her teeth full of holes, her bitten nails and hopeless addiction to tomato sauce?

SALLY. Yes.

KATE. All right.

SALLY. But, Mum, first come upstairs. I'm not saying it is upstairs mind you. . .

KATE. Oh, no! Not 'hunt the parcel'!

SALLY. I shan't say anything except 'Hot' or 'Cold'.

KATE. But suppose I found it?

SALLY. Or I'll hide with it.

KATE. But just suppose?

SALLY. You won't find it as easily as I found my doughnut because you won't see me hiding it.

KATE. D'you mean you. . . ?

SALLY (*moving off*). I always watch you hiding it through the crack in the door.

KATE (*moving off*). The cheek! D'you often spy on me through the crack in the door? Right, be warned! I shall be hunting in earnest.

Fade.

Fade up slowly on MRS KERSHAW's *office — as before.*

MRS KERSHAW. We now come to heading number 4. (*Reads.*) 'The Petitioner.' Mrs Lister I wonder if you'd mind not wandering around the office all the time — I'm finding it increasingly difficult to concentrate.

KATE. Should I read it to myself?

MRS KERSHAW. Well, no, as I haven't had it typed up yet. (*Reads.*) 'Age — thirty-seven years.' Oh, there, I've left your name out.

KATE. I know my name.

MRS KERSHAW. In the interests of accuracy. (*Writes.*) Mrs Kate Lister. (*Reads.*) 'Age — thirty-seven years.'

KATE. How cruel of you.

MRS KERSHAW. What?

KATE. Repeating my age. A joke.

MRS KERSHAW. Oh. (*Reads.*) 'Self-employed advertising and commercial art agent. Offices in Maida Vale. Gross annual income of £6,500, being the average taken over a three year period. One child, Sally, aged ten and a half years. The petitioner states that she is making no claim for maintenance for either herself or the child, being in need of none. But states she does need the house from the point of view of security and continuity in the child's life. The husband's share of the house being her entitlement anyway in view of the fact that for several years she was the chief breadwinner.

I have observed a friendly and relaxed atmosphere between the petitioner and the child, Sally. Though some laxity of discipline complained of by the respondent and corroborated by Sally's headmistress is apparent — I would suggest that the petitioner has the best interests of the child at heart. On the other hand it should be noted that the petitioner has spent surprisingly little time with her child. Being a successful career woman has meant that she has employed a succession of 'au pair' girls or relied on the amenability of the respondent who has often been out of work or attending courses for the mature student which have given him holidays running concurrently with those of Sally's holidays at school. This also means that she is rarely free to take or collect the child from school. In fact the Headmistress states that although she has met Sally's father at school functions etc. she has no recollection of having met Sally's mother.

KATE. What rubbish.

MRS KERSHAW. I'll make a note of your contradiction, Mrs Lister. Would you care to elaborate?

KATE. She's got a wart on her nose.

MRS KERSHAW. Oh? (*Reads on.*) 'Initially the petitioner was most insistent that she was not living with anyone. . . '

SALLY (*calls, off, distant*). Mummy?

MRS KERSHAW (*not reacting*). 'Or indeed had any relationship with any member of the opposite sex, and certainly no relationship that might develop into a lasting one. (*Beginning to fade.*) The events that disproved this assertion are, for reasons that will become apparent later, dealt with under the heading. . . '

Fade

Fade up. KATE's *house as before.* KATE *is running downstairs.*

KATE (*calls*). It's no good. Can't find you, I'm giving up. Unless. . . (*Approaching*.) you're in the conservatory. I saw a plant move!

Door being opened.

(*Calling, sing-song*). Sally? Sally?

EDDIE. It's me!

KATE. Eddie! What the hell are you doing here?

EDDIE. I've brought you a new plant. Look, take it — go on — take it. I let myself in by the side door, you gave me a key for it, remember?

KATE (*hissing at him*). Sally's here. Go.

EDDIE. I should not necessarily introduce myself to her as your lover.

KATE. Hurry!

EDDIE. And you needn't sigh and stroke my hand or press your lips to my cheek — any of that sort of thing. Not in her presence anyway.

KATE. And give me the key back.

EDDIE. Show me the spare room.

KATE. What?

EDDIE. The one you were thinking about getting a lodger for.

KATE. You're mad.

EDDIE. I'll be the plumber then. Or if you prefer the truth — an artist on your agency books who wants to talk to you out of office hours.

KATE. The key.

EDDIE. And what else d'you want back. Anything? Everything?

KATE. I only let you take it on the understanding you came after Sally's bedtime at eight.

EDDIE. And after eight you seem to do a lot of entertaining that also excludes me.

KATE. My first concern is to protect her.

EDDIE. And deny me. Deceit is only a temporary form of protection.

KATE. Yes. Two months and we needn't bother any more.

Sound of front door slamming off.

(*Calls.*) Sally? I wonder . . . ? She sometimes spies on me through the crack in the door. She's gone round to her friend Jane's.

EDDIE. Two months! I just hope you realise the risks you're running. There's a blonde upstairs from me with tits so big I can hear them bouncing on the floor.

KATE. Oh, shut up.

EDDIE. I can hear something anyway.

KATE. You don't have to wait.

EDDIE. Just want you to know — the day to day strains I'm subjected to. Just want you to know I'm everything you accuse me of being — impatient, impulsive, greedy and above all — young.

KATE. Oh, Eddie, it's nearly my birthday.

EDDIE. I'm going to buy you something as well as the plant. The plant cost nearly three pounds.

KATE. I realise it's not fair on you and your student mentality. But I . . . I want to keep myself clean for it.

EDDIE. For what? The divorce?

KATE. For when I appear before the judge.

EDDIE. You could turn into the most godawful saint. Kate. It happens to women whose passions are fierce. They deny, deny, deny themselves till in the end it's the self-denial that gives them most kicks. You must allow me to be your devil's advocate. You must lust after me without shame. D'you understand?

KATE (*laughing*). Oh, yes.

EDDIE (*moving off*). Then I'll go.

KATE. Eddie? The wall can-opener is broken.

EDDIE. Just give you time for one wildly erotic fantasy about me before your guests arrive.

KATE. I must get the cans opened and out of sight.

EDDIE (*approaching*). It's home cooking again, is it?

KATE. Anne's cooked most of it. The soup is my contribution.

EDDIE. You must have a beer can-opener.

Sound of cutlery being sorted.

KATE. Brilliant.

Sound of tins being pierced and poured into a saucepan.

EDDIE. Has he rung?

KATE. No.

EDDIE. Thought maybe that's why you were edgy.

KATE. I'm not. But it wouldn't be fair on Sally — her loyalties are divided enough already.

EDDIE. Think David cross questions her?

KATE. I don't know. But you can't ask a child to lie. Not to her father.

EDDIE. Ugh! Who's this for?

KATE. Oxtail soup, steak and kidney pie and trifle. Americans of course.

EDDIE. What's their name?

KATE. Boy Kruschefski Senior is one. . .

EDDIE. I'd better stay.

KATE. And the other is a partner, I think he said, from the Bahamas.

EDDIE. In case they're kosher.

KATE. Oh, Eddie, I hadn't thought of that.

EDDIE. I'll go out for the fish and chips.

KATE. Anne's coming anyway.

EDDIE. Why?

KATE. Man, woman, man, woman. Americans are very conservative.

EDDIE. Then my presence will unsettle them just enough to tilt the business discussions in your favour. What business is it?

KATE. Art by the yard.

EDDIE. What? What?

KATE. His clients are all interior decorators.

EDDIE. You don't mean a pale green picture for a pale green wall?

KATE. I've got plently for him to look at all laid out upstairs. I've got two of your illustrations up there.

EDDIE. How disgusting! Oh, no thanks!

KATE. What makes you think your pictures are more important than tasselled lampshades?

EDDIE. And to think you are posing as the innocent party!

KATE. What?

EDDIE. With David.

KATE. I want his half of the house, no arguments, so far he isn't contesting anything. Oh, I know that he is formally contesting my claim for custody of Sally but that's just to annoy me. He more or less admits he doesn't stand a chance.

EDDIE. Unless you give him the chance.

KATE. Exactly.

EDDIE. Unless you make a sacrifice of Sally to pay off your guilt.

KATE (*amused*). You are so young, Eddie, and the young are so old-fashioned. Using words like 'guilt' and 'sacrifice' and 'saint' without even blinking.

EDDIE. Oh, and let's see — 'fallen woman' and 'woman of easy virtue'! Oh, I could tell David how you prostitute yourself and now my paintings.

KATE. It's time you stopped behaving as though you were still cocooned by a grant at Art School.

EDDIE. Bloody tart!

KATE. Sally wants me to get a pair of scarlet shoes with very high heels.

EDDIE. You should be made to wear them. And a bracelet round your ankle.

KATE (*softly*). Eddie?

EDDIE. How much will the American pay?

KATE. Ah! He's not really after illustrations anyway, he's after marine art. Because that's what Britain is noted for in the New York decor trade. And I don't have too many of those.

EDDIE. I'll paint him a hundred sailing ships in a hundred storms.

KATE. Can I really corrupt you so easily?

EDDIE. Oh, yes.

KATE. But having corrupted you — can I keep you?

EDDIE. Are you talking about money, art, your half of the house or what?

KATE. I just mean if you're going to leave me, Eddie, I want to know.

EDDIE. I'm asking to stay this evening because I don't want you to have to seduce this Boy Senior.

KATE. D'you think I can only do deals with my legs open?

EDDIE. It's how you do deals with me. Suddenly weaken. And I come tumbling down on top of you. (*He kisses her.*) This evening . . . Sally'll be in bed. . . Anne knows me anyway.

KATE. Ah, well. . . she did.

EDDIE. You mean she doesn't know that we still. . . as a continuing thing.

KATE. No.

EDDIE. But she's your closest friend. You confide in her.

KATE. Oh, yes, everything. . . except. . . she knows David.

EDDIE. But she's your friend.

KATE. Oh, yes. But I think she has slept with him.

EDDIE. She told you?

KATE. No. But she'll get round to it.

EDDIE. You can't have a friend like that.

KATE. I expect she'll be wearing something pretty fancy for tonight. I must get changed.

EDDIE. I'll help you.

KATE. No, thanks. Americans like things bright and direct. Comes from years of technicolour.

EDDIE. Then wear black.

KATE. But I wonder if I should ring him first?

EDDIE. David?

KATE. How right you are. It'd be a waste of time. The correspondent'd answer anyway. He'd come to the phone coughing. And she'd listen.

EDDIE. Well, what'd you say if she wasn't listening?

KATE. She came round the other day.

EDDIE. Here? What for?

KATE. As though she was looking for something. I was glad Sally wasn't in.

EDDIE. The nosey cow!

KATE. Said she'd come to apologise for David.

EDDIE. Big of her.

KATE. She is big. Said he wanted to say 'sorry' for smashing the conservatory window last week, but couldn't quite bring himself to.

EDDIE. I saw you'd had it fixed.

KATE. Wanted me to know, I suppose, that she didn't condone his behaviour.

EDDIE. What's she like then?

KATE. If Sally comes in — we'll hear the front door. You will go?

EDDIE. Instantly. Apart from big?

KATE. Big? Oh, well, with feet, toenails a bit dirty in those old men's sandals.

EDDIE. Didn't you look higher than her feet?

KATE. Above that she was, well, lumpy. Big shoulders and arse, small hands and something on her mouth.

EDDIE (*beginning to laugh*). Like what?

KATE. Well, maybe. . . had been a harelip. . . (*Beginning to get angry.*) I don't know.

EDDIE (*laughing*). Why would anyone want to live with someone like that?

KATE. Sally says she makes very good bread — wholemeal.

EDDIE (*laughing*). What's her name?

KATE (*furious*). How should I know?

EDDIE. Well, you must even if you didn't before. I mean, when she stampeded your front door she surely must've said, 'Hello! I am di-da-di-da-di-da'. Or with her cleft palate, 'Ti-ta-ti-ta-ti-ta'.

KATE. I'm not wasting any more time on this ludicrous conversation.

EDDIE (*furious, shouts*). Tell me.

KATE. She still lactates.

EDDIE. What? I know she's got kids of her own but they're both older than Sally.

KATE. If she squeezes, or presumably someone else squeezes — there's milk.

EDDIE. How do you know?

KATE. Anne told me.

EDDIE. Anne?

KATE. Apparently David told her.

EDDIE. Why would he tell Anne?

KATE. That's how I know he's slept with her.

EDDIE. How?

KATE. Because why else would he boast to her of such a thing?

EDDIE. But why should Anne tell you?

KATE. How could she not? When we tell each other everything.

EDDIE. But you don't.

KATE. Mainly we do.

EDDIE. Oh, give me patience! It's lucky I adore you.

KATE. Oh, yes, when this is all over, darling. . . oh, but I must set the table first.

EDDIE. We'll go somewhere that's got a funfair.

Sound of cutlery, china, glass being set on table.

KATE. We'll stay at the seaside.

EDDIE. We'll abandon ourselves.

KATE. It won't be easy for Sally.

EDDIE. I'll make it easy. I'll make her laugh. I'll be ridiculous. I'll stand on my head. I'll take calculated risks balancing on the sea wall. Lots of candy floss.

KATE. I don't want to end up with two children.

EDDIE. I'll be very grave. And I'll grow a beard and only tell stories that have some moral point.

KATE. You will have to be strong and responsible. You'll have to apologise to the other hotel guests for me. When I cry instead of laughing, when I try to say a casual 'Good morning' and burst into song. And in the dining room when Sally's tucked up in bed I shall refuse to eat unless you feed me off your plate.

EDDIE. I'll take you across the road and duck you in the sea.

KATE. I ache in bed without you. I have such a pain.

EDDIE. I knew really, I mean, that it must be the same for you. Tasteless jokes I make. I tell you, even if the blonde upstairs did bounce her tits like big dumb bells on my ceiling — I wouldn't hear. My ears are too full of imaginary telephone bells, you calling, and my own heart. So! Have a lovely evening.

KATE. Eddie. . . ?

EDDIE (*moving off*). And then a pain in bed.

KATE. You could stay.

EDDIE. You better go and change.

KATE. Then take the key with you.

EDDIE. No.

KATE. Yes. I must have the possibility. . . of your return.

Fade.

Fade up MRS KERSHAW's *office as before.*

MRS KERSHAW. You feel better now, Mrs Lister?

KATE. I felt all right anyway.

MRS KERSHAW. Nothing like a cup of tea though, is there?

KATE. No.

MRS KERSHAW. Now — where were we? Ah, yes, still with the Petitioner but a new heading. . . (*She reads.*) 'Plans. The petitioner intends to remain living with the child in the same house which is sited in a pleasant area of similar private dwellings. This will ensure that the child will retain her social contacts in the area and attend the same school. The petitioner plans to alter her work schedule to allow her to be free both to collect the child from school and to spend the greater part of the school holidays with her. This alteration in work schedule is to be facilitated by the petitioner taking a partner into her business — in the person of her friend, Anne Troubridge. Miss Troubridge has also indicated her willingness to collect the child from school when it is impossible for the petitioner to do so.

KATE. Good. Really that's excellent.

MRS KERSHAW (*reads on*). 'Number 5. The Respondent. Employed part-time by the Housing Dept. London Borough of Hammersmith at a salary of £3,500 per annum. David Lister is at present living with the co-respondent in her house in Putney. My impression has been that the respondent's counter petition for custody of the child has been less well thought out than his wife's application. And during the course of my investigations I have wondered if the respondent's antagonistic feelings towards his wife have over-ridden his perceptions of the child's best interests. However the respondent states he has some reservations about his wife's ability to care adequately for the child and wishes to make the court aware of his anxiety.

SALLY (*calls, off, distant*). Mummy?

MRS KERSHAW (*ploughs on*). He says she is moody, neurotic, easily depressed and a hypochondriac. My impressions on this count do seem to contradict this. However as I felt a certain degree of uncertainty I spoke to the petitioner's Doctor who does not know of anything to confirm this although he did treat her for depression two years ago (*Fading.*) it lifted quickly and the valium he prescribed. . .

Fade.

Fade up KATE's *house as before. A meal in progress.* BAHAMA, BOY *and* ANNE *are eating pudding.*

BAHAMA. What birth sign is she?

ANNE. I beg your pardon?

Sound of drink being poured.

BOY. She means what star was Kate born under?

ANNE. Oh, you'll have to ask her when she comes back. Oh, but her birthday is this week.

BOY. You don't say.

BAHAMA. I should've known. This whole meal is so imaginative. I mean, like the idea of putting offal into pastry I mean, as a Capricorn the idea of putting offal into pastry'd never occur to me.

ANNE. It's steak and kidney pie actually.

BAHAMA. That's the kind of idea betrays real independence of mind.

ANNE. That is a quality Kate is noted for.

BAHAMA. That's a quality I'd like.

BOY. You can't wear it, you can't sleep with it, you can't drink it.

ANNE. I learn something every time I see Kate. I always leave her feeling I've gained some insight. About how to survive on one's own, I mean.

BOY. And about how to cook I'll bet.

ANNE (*laughs*). Oh, no, not that.

BAHAMA. You mean you didn't like the pie either?

ANNE. Oh, no, I mean. . . well, to be honest I cooked it and this trifle.

BOY. Now I know why Kate's got a reputation . . . for being a smooth operator.

BAHAMA. I'd like a reputation — I mean, different to the one I got. I'd like what she's got — this house and everything her own up to and including a child of ten.

ANNE. She could lose everything — even the child.

BAHAMA. Oh, come on!

ANNE. She can't count on anything being her own yet — till the divorce is through. Though I agree she does seem confident of the outcome.

BAHAMA. And why not?

ANNE. I think it's unwise to take anything for granted, that's all. Tempting fate — I wouldn't dare.

BAHAMA. Fate in the shape of her husband dealt her a cruel blow, right? So in that situation what does a woman do? She screws him for all he's got. And get it — right, Boysie?

KATE (*approaching*). I am sorry.

Sound of door closing.

ANNE. Sally all right?

KATE. Yes. Not really awake.

BAHAMA. Does she often call out like that?

KATE. Sometimes when she's dreaming.

BAHAMA. I could maybe interpret her dreams.

KATE. Thanks, Bahama, but I'm afraid she doesn't remember them. Now! Coffee, Boy?

ANNE. You sit down, Kate.

KATE. Thanks. Oh, and yes, Bahama, do help yourself to scotch.

Sound of drink being poured.

BOY. Ba, honey, you had enough.

BAHAMA. I want you to know I feel really moved to have received this invitation to your home in England where there's such peace and love and mellowness. And I sure wish there was something I could do for you.

BOY (*threatening*). Sit down, Bahama.

BAHAMA (*threatening him back*). I feel a genuine urge to repay my hostess.

BOY. Sit down.

BAHAMA. And as to the idea of putting offal into pastry well — I have to say it was a whole new experience for us and like a total revelation to me.

KATE. I am sorry you didn't like it.

BAHAMA. Hell, no, don't apologise. It's not as though you even cooked it.

Sound of coffee cups being handed round.

ANNE. Sorry, Kate, I had to own up. . . if only to save you from the responsibility of the mistake.

KATE. Oh, dear, then I shall have to own up too. It was a mistake for Anne to come to dinner with us in the first place.

BOY. How come?

ANNE. Kate!

KATE. You know it was. The idea was to make up a foursome. You see, I thought Bahama was a man. Let's move to comfy seats, shall we? (*Moving off slightly*.) I thought you said you were bringing a partner from the Bahamas.

BOY (*approaching*). Two things I'm sure of. She's a woman. And it was very prophetic of her parents to call her after a tax haven.

BAHAMA (*approaching*). That's where they went for their honeymoon — where I was conceived.

BOY. Which reminds me while we're still upstanding I'd like us to raise our glasses and (*He clears his throat and sings solemnly*.) 'Happy Birthday to you. Happy Birthday to you. Happy Birthday, dear Kate, Happy Birthday to you.'

Silence. They all sit.

BAHAMA (*sadly*). I sure wish I'd thought of doing that.

ANNE. I didn't mean to tell them anything about. . .

KATE. Thank-you, Boy, very sweet of you. And Anne you mustn't think I didn't want you to come to dinner. I simply meant. . .

ANNE. I know. I know.

BAHAMA. Who would you have asked for me — knowing I was a woman?

KATE. Oh, Bahama, someone very special.

BAHAMA. Virile, young, blue-eyed, intelligent.

KATE. That's him!

BOY. She could've left off the intelligent.

BAHAMA (*furious*). There's something about England makes me see you in a different light, Boysie.

BOY. You're out of your depth here, that's all.

BAHAMA. You end up looking like a real screwball. Well, doesn't he?

KATE. I keep trying to imagine how you two met. I see Bahama sitting in a cool green room in a corn coloured dress. Her silver mink tinged green by reflection from the walls, and her lovely green eyes.

BOY. She was a picture.

BAHAMA. A goddam wholesale picture.

BOY. But the coat then was racoon not mink.

BAHAMA. So he gets me framed and puts me down on his expense sheet for the gallery. You better watch out, Boysie, because I might not have girl friends, like Kate got Anne, willing to give me moral support but I got men friends who know a thing or two about income tax that could blow the whole thing. . .

BOY. Shut up, will you? There's someone trying to break in the side door.

Sound of door opening.

EDDIE. Good evening.

KATE. Eddie!

BAHAMA. Is this the one you would've invited for me?

EDDIE. I heard Mr Kruschefski was here. And as a connoisseur of marine art I thought he might appreciate this picture I painted.

Back door closes.

I copied it off a postcard of the QE 2 but I've done it after the style of Turner.

KATE. May I introduce you? Bahama — Eddie Marchant — Bahama Kelly. And this is. . .

EDDIE. Don't touch, Mr Kruschefski, it's still wet.

KATE. And I think Anne and Eddie, you have met. . . ?

ANNE. Yes but. . . what a surprise!

KATE. Isn't it? I thought we might need one at some point in the evening.

ANNE. And how right you were!

BOY. How much?

EDDIE. For the picture? Oh, I was going to say sixty. . .

KATE. I'm his agent, Boy, we'll view this picture as a sample — so if you want it have it free.

BOY. Oh, hey, but what's this?

EDDIE. Oh, the man drowning.

BAHAMA. That's just beautiful. So. . . creative.

BOY. An arm sticking out like that isn't for me.

BAHAMA. I just love a picture that tells a story.

KATE. Boy, there are plenty more for you to see.

BAHAMA. An arm like that makes for a real talking point.

BOY. Oh, ignore her!

EDDIE. Sorry, I'd find that impossible. Miss Kelly, I wonder if you'd accept this picture as a gift?

BAHAMA (*suddenly close to tears*). I'd be delighted. (*Hardening again.*) You see, Boysie, what a crud you turned out to look among all these open-hearted people? You see how they don't even lock the back door in case someone wants to walk in . . . with a present?

EDDIE. I had a key actually.

BAHAMA (*ignoring this*). So much inner peace and harmony and all I can't take sitting down. But, hey, that's what I could do — I could do a little entertainment.

BOY (*shouting*). Who needs it? None of us needs it.

BAHAMA. Don't you need anything either, Kate? No. I'll bet you don't even need Gestalt, nor Tai Chi, nor even Yoga.

KATE. I tried Yoga but it hurt.

BAHAMA. Oh, isn't nature wonderful? You've got the natural rhythms anyway, you don't need that type of inner discipline so the body rejects it.

EDDIE. How would you entertain us?

BOY. I'm warning you, Bahama.

BAHAMA. With music — I can always do an exotic dance.

KATE. It's a lovely idea.

BAHAMA. With a cobra.

KATE. But Boy and I must steal ourselves a little time for business.

ANNE. Not with a live snake?

BOY. She's not that much of a fool.

BAHAMA. I've got a rubber one at home. But I'm sure there'd be something here I could utilize.

KATE (*moving off to record player*). Used to be a dancer?

BAHAMA. Yes. Exotic.

EDDIE. I could tell. There was something about you. . .

Sound of music very faint.

KATE. Eddie would love to be entertained. I'm switching the music through to the conservatory. There's a speaker there, a swing seat, a length of garden hose you could utilize and even a few exotic plants.

EDDIE. Come on, Bahama!

BAHAMA. But Kate, are you going to closet yourself with Boy the rest of the evening?

KATE. There are other days.

BAHAMA. Tomorrow is my day at Harrods.

KATE. I might not see you there. . . but somewhere. . .

BAHAMA. You wouldn't recognise me. I have a different wig for every day of the week.

KATE. I'd always recognise you.

BAHAMA (*moving off*). No-one ever does.

EDDIE (*moving off*). The music's started.

BAHAMA. OK.

Sound of door closing.

KATE. Anne, you go in with them, keep them company.

ANNE (*moving off*). Well, I. . . I'm just going to pop up and make sure Sal's all right for you.

KATE. Oh, thanks.

Sound of door closing.

BOY. Bahama had a quarrel with the guy who did her hair.

KATE. Bahama? Oh, so she went out and got the wigs.

BOY. Now every week she goes to the photographer instead.

KATE. Why?

BOY. To have her picture taken. Don't ask me.

KATE. Have you ever thought of illustrations.

BOY. You mean hire an artist to draw her instead?

KATE. No, I mean, selling artists originals in your gallery. The originals for illustrations in books.

BOY. You see how she throws me? No, I don't see illustrations as having the requisite weight.

KATE. When you think of all those originals lying around. . . unexploited. . . well, it's the rage here.

BOY. Here people have more time to look close at things.

KATE. If someone else promotes the idea over there. . . well, I just don't want you to blame me for not prompting you. Someone else will promote the idea, you see, but without your flair and without the right set up.

BOY. I'll look at a few.

KATE. No, no, if you feel they're beneath your interest — and you're right — they are cheap.

BOY. No wonder you've got a reputation! I mean, what sort of an excuse is that? When even artists are getting inflation conscious? I tell them — come the next depression you'll be queuing up to join a team with me for a few dollars a week.

KATE. What team?

Sound of door opening.

Anne? Sally O.K.?

ANNE. Like an angel.

Front door bell rings off.

KATE. Oh, dear.

ANNE. You stay there. I'll go.

BOY. Well, take an angel.

Sound of door closing.

Some kind of gothic type scene. One artist takes the faces, one the wings, one the haloes, one the bows and arrows in their hands.

KATE. Do angels have bows and arrows though?

BOY. My responsibility is limited to the commercial viability of the production line.

Sound of door opening.

ANNE. Kate?

BOY. And a team like this is one hell of a way to step up production.

ANNE (*approaching close*). It was David.

KATE (*approaching close*). Oh! Oh, well.

BOY (*in background*). Provided you got the regular outlet.

ANNE. I said you were entertaining. He promised to go. What are you. . . ?

KATE. Locking the back door.

Sound of door locked and bolted.

BOY (*in background*). They do it all the time with plates.

KATE. Put the key in your pocket.

ANNE. But you surely don't think he'll try anything. . . ?

KATE. After what happened last week?

BOY. I mean, hand painted ceramics.

KATE. You're right, Boy, let's go.

BOY. What?

KATE. We'll leave the plates to Anne. We're going to look at the pictures.

BOY (*moving off*). Oh. Great idea, I'm with you.

Sound of door closing. Sound of crockery etc. in sink. Sound of back door being thumped, handle rattled.

ANNE (*gasps*). David? (*Calls.*) You promised . . . ! No use trying this door. It's locked. (*Pause. Calls.*) Eddie? (*Pause. Sound of door to conservatory opening. Music.*) Eddie! I think you better come out of the conservatory.

EDDIE (*shouts over music*). Please! Not now! We're busy.

BAHAMA (*shouts*). Eddie!

Door to conservatory closes. Cut music.

ANNE (*moving off, calls*). Kate? Kate you'll have to come down again.

Pause. A crash off of glass breaking. A scream off from BAHAMA. A distant cry from SALLY of 'Mummy?'. Pause. Conservatory door opens. Music.

EDDIE (*approaching*). Don't panic. A tile must've fallen.

BAHAMA (*approaching*). So maybe you got used to the blitz. (*Struggling.*) Oh, where's my armhole gone?

EDDIE (*trying to help*). Caught up in the garden hose. Let me . . .

BAHAMA. I don't want to die here. I feel so exposed here. I want to go home. Oh, my god, where's Boysie?

EDDIE. Don't go without your picture — the one I gave you.

BAHAMA (*moving off*). To tell the truth I'm already carrying too much excess and if I go to Harrods tomorrow. . . (*Shouts.*) Boy?

EDDIE (*shouts after her*). Just let me turn this music off. . .

Cut to: the hallway. Music distant.

KATE. Boy's upstairs.

BAHAMA. Thanks. (*She runs fast and upstairs.*)

ANNE. What are you going to do?

KATE. Lock the living room door.

Sound of key being turned in lock. Cut music.

Now at least David can't get out to the hall.

ANNE. But Eddie's still in there.

KATE. He can get out through the side door.

ANNE. No, you locked it and I've got the key so he's trapped.

Cut to: the sitting room.

EDDIE. You er. . . you play golf.

DAVID (*approaching. A bit drunk*). Who told you?

EDDIE. I notice you're carrying a golf putter so I thought . . . Please don't swing it around like that.

DAVID. Don't play at night.

EDDIE. No, and important to be sober.

Sound of drink being poured.

DAVID. Yes. Who chipped my decanter?

EDDIE. I don't know.

DAVID. It's my decanter.

EDDIE. I didn't know.

DAVID. Books on the top shelf are mine too. Borrow one.

EDDIE. I don't want to.

DAVID. You haven't looked at them.

EDDIE. Well, if you'd put that golf club down.

DAVID. It's a putter.

EDDIE. You like Westerns.

DAVID. I like books that don't improve me.

EDDIE. Would prefer to borrow a drink.

DAVID. Good.

Sound of drink being poured.

I never lend books anyway.

EDDIE. I'd like to play golf.

DAVID. Who the hell are you anyway?

EDDIE. Eddie Marchant.

DAVID. What are you doing in my house?

EDDIE. It's not only yours.

DAVID. Half of it is and you're standing in my half. (*Moving off.*) Oh, look — meat! Steak and kidney pie, is it? D'you think anyone'd mind? Where I'm living now. . . we don't eat meat. . . (*Mouth full.*) it's too near the end of the food chain.

EDDIE (*approaching*). I only came to mend the tin opener anyway.

DAVID (*Mouth full*). Doesn't look broken to me.

EDDIE. Must be.

DAVID. Try it.

EDDIE. O.K.

Sound of tin being opened. DAVID *continues to eat.*

Fancy — I must've mended it!

DAVID. You're Kate's lover.

EDDIE. I'd like to play golf but. . .

DAVID. And you've opened a tin of pineapple chunks.

EDDIE. Oh, dear.

DAVID. Never mind. Give them to me.

EDDIE. Aren't you allowed pineapple chunks either?

DAVID (*mouth full*). Sugar content.

EDDIE. What's she like?

DAVID. Who?

EDDIE. The woman you're living with.

DAVID. She's only trying to protect me — my health, see? I love her. She's lovely.

EDDIE *laughs.*

Don't you believe me? I've a photo somewhere. . . oh, yes, next to my heart. See.

EDDIE (*pause*). This can't be her.

DAVID. You've got a bloody nerve standing in my half of the house and. . .

EDDIE. She's lovely. . . she looks. . . really.

DAVID (*snatching photo back*). Don't make a pig of yourself.

EDDIE. I was just trying to make out. . .

DAVID. What?

EDDIE. Well, if she had a harelip or. . .

DAVID (*thumping the table with his fist*). Get out!

EDDIE. I'm sorry but I thought. . . something on her lip. . . sorry.

DAVID. There is — how d'you know? — a little scar. A road accident years ago. It's like a little star and turns white when she smiles. Beautiful. (*He swallows hard a couple of times.*) I don't look in her eyes that often because I have to watch this. . . (*he gags, realising he's going to be sick, moving off.*) little star. I'm going to be. . .

EDDIE. Sick, no, both doors are locked. No, the sinks full. The conservatory. There's a bucket.

DAVID *is sick off. Sound of kettle being filled.*

And I'm going to make you a coffee.

DAVID (*off*). She's right. It's worse than poison, all that junk I just ate.

EDDIE. You'll feel better now.

DAVID (*approaching*). Thanks. I'm David.

EDDIE. Yes.

DAVID. Don't let her poison you.

EDDIE. Who?

DAVID. Kate.

EDDIE. Don't you think our impressions of each other's women are a bit distorted?

DAVID. Why not play golf then if you'd like to?

EDDIE. Oh, I have done but it's. . . well, mainly the green fees.

DAVID. My lady's ex. is the pro. at a club in Hertfordshire — I get there for nothing.

EDDIE. That's friendly. Sugar?

DAVID. Oh, thanks. (*Sound of cup being stirred.*)

EDDIE. Trouble was my swing pulled to the left. A good swing — pretty classical so I've been told but. . .

DAVID. You move the back foot.

EDDIE. No, no, I think it's in the arm.

DAVID. Tension in the right shoulder. Show me.

EDDIE. What?

DAVID. Use my putter. We need an air ball though. I know! (*Moving off slightly.*) If I screw this up and. . . (*Sound of paper being screwed up.*) place it so. Now — take a swing. (*Laughs.*) Ha! Missed!

EDDIE. Tell you what I am good at though — a chip out of the bunker.

DAVID. That's useful.

EDDIE. Yes.

DAVID. So! Let's set this thing up properly. This rug's the green.

EDDIE. There's no hole.

DAVID. Use your imagination.

EDDIE. I need a hole.

DAVID. I usually play golf with people my own age of course. They don't go round grizzling 'I need a hole' like a kid does 'I need a sweetie'. (*Shouts.*) If you need a hole find one.

EDDIE. Well, can I use your coffee cup?

DAVID. How's Sally?

EDDIE. I don't know really.

DAVID. You're not interested. O.K. so the rug's the green. The cup's the hole. And this armchair is the bunker and I'm putting the ball in here.

EDDIE. Where?

DAVID. Between the seat cushion and the arm.

EDDIE. That's too difficult.

DAVID. Not if you straddle the armchair.

EDDIE. I'll have to climb up on it.

DAVID. One foot on this arm, one on that — there!

BOY (*off, distant*). 'Happy Birthday to you, Happy Birthday to you, Happy Birthday dear Kate. . . '

Sound of front door closing off.

DAVID. Keep your eye on the ball. Who was that?

EDDIE. They've gone. Friends.

DAVID. I'm glad she's got friends. I was afraid she'd close in on herself. It's a relief. Now swing hard and chip up but mind that lamp. . . I said mind. . .

Crash of lamp as EDDIE *loses balance.*

Clumsy!

EDDIE. I overbalanced.

DAVID. What a mess!

Sound of door to hall being unlocked.

ANNE (*keeping her distance*). Kate wanted to know. . .

DAVID. Hello, Anne, dear. So she sent you in, did she?

ANNE. I offered.

DAVID. I'll bet.

ANNE. Eddie, are you all right?

DAVID. He's fine.

ANNE. O.K.?

Eddie. I'm fine.

ANNE (*going*). Good then that's all right.

Sound of door to hall being closed and locked again.

DAVID. They heard the noise. Thought we were battling it out. Bloody conceit. Still, I'm very relieved she's not, you know, cutting herself off.

EDDIE. That's your conceit.

DAVID. What?

EDDIE. Imagining she would — without you.

DAVID. And I'm glad she's got you. And I'm glad it's her birthday. I came to give her something.

EDDIE. Oh, what?

DAVID. A fright.

EDDIE. You're overestimating yourself again.

DAVID. Well, Eddie, there are golf courses and golf courses.

EDDIE. And this isn't one of them.

DAVID. No.

EDDIE. But if you're staying. . .

DAVID. Go out through the conservatory. You'll have to anyway. And if she thinks you're still here she might venture in.

EDDIE. But if you're going to give her a fright. . .

DAVID. Do I look like a monster? I'm too tired anyway. Anyway I still have some sort of right, whereas you. . .

EDDIE. O.K. Well, glad to have met you. It helps.

DAVID. Helps me too. Just keep the back foot steady.

EDDIE (*moving off*). Yes, thanks.

DAVID (*calling after him*). Eye on the ball and don't stiffen the arm.

EDDIE (*off*). 'Bye.

DAVID. My pleasure. (*Calls.*) Kate? (*Pause. To himself.*) No matter. . . I can wait. . .

Fade.

Fade up MRS KERSHAW'S *office as before.*

MRS KERSHAW (*reads*). Plans. The respondent sees his present situation as a permanent one — being already that of a stable family situation in the co-respondent's house with her own two children. The co-respondent's children who are older than Sally have already accepted her and liked her on the visits she has already made to their house. And the co-respondent herself seems very capable of adjusting to and indeed welcoming the child into her home. (*Beat.*) The Co-respondent.

KATE. A new heading?

MRS KERSHAW. Yes.

KATE. Skip it.

MRS KERSHAW. Sorry?

KATE. I can do without.

MRS KERSHAW. Some of the things the co-respondent has to say about her attitude to the child are interesting. Particularly in the light of the Supplementary Welfare Report.

KATE. I don't have to listen?

MRS KERSHAW. Of course not. This is meant to be for your benefit, Mrs Lister, but I don't know, I am beginning to wonder. . .

KATE. It's just this heading.

MRS KERSHAW. I wouldn't dream of forcing the issue. (*With a sigh she turns over page and reads.*) 'The Child Concerned. Female. Sally. Aged ten and a half years. Born May 8th 1967. Her headmistress sees her as an attractive reserved child whose occasional lapses of indiscipline are nothing above the normal. Sally was initially unwilling to discuss her situation with me and in fact towards the end of our first meeting called me 'a nosey cow' — this apparently referring to the fact that I was prying, and damaging a situation in which she has remained totally loyal to both parents. However as soon as I pointed out to her the reality of the situation, which she had not so far accepted, her reserve began to break down. And though she still insisted that one day her parents would be brought together again — seeing herself as the instrument that would effect this reunion — she told me she wished to stay with her mother but was unable to tell me why or how she had reached that decision'.

KATE. I could tell you why.

MRS KERSHAW. It's really too late.

KATE. The report is written, I know.

MRS KERSHAW. For all but a brief comment, Mrs Lister.

KATE. It's too late.

Fade.

Fade up KATE's *house as before.*

KATE (*hissing at him*). David! Wake up. You! Wake up.

DAVID. What? Oh, was I asleep?

KATE. It's half past two. I've been waiting to go to bed. I'm tired, tired. And there's still all this clearing up.

Sound of clearing the table, and washing up during the following.

DAVID. You always are. Always tired.

KATE. Nobody else says that.

DAVID (*yawning*). Nothing new.

KATE. What have you come for?

DAVID. Oh, er. . . my decanter.

KATE. Take it.

DAVID. It's chipped.

KATE. And what about that lamp lying in pieces over there?

DAVID. You mean I should give you my decanter in place of the lamp.

KATE. No.

DAVID. Ah! A broken lamp is equal to a chipped decanter. So now we're quits.

KATE. No.

DAVID. Your friend was nicer to me than you are.

KATE. Eddie?

DAVID. He broke the lamp. I liked him.

KATE. And I'm not paying for that conservatory window again.

DAVID. Send me the bill. I'll treasure it as something to remember you by.

KATE. And for the lamp.

DAVID. There'll be so little else to remember you by.

KATE. And pineapple chunks aren't as cheap as they were either.

DAVID. For pineapple chunks you'll be wasting a stamp.

KATE. You don't realise, do you? I could take you for every penny you've got.

DAVID. What's stopping you?

KATE. Slice your puny income in half.

DAVID. What *can* it be?

KATE. Really cut you down to size from a midget that is to a microdot. I tell you, a little thingie on the carpet like — what is it you call a woman? — a bit of fluff.

They pause for breath.

DAVID. Gosh, I feel better for that! And now the ice is broken, Kate dear. . . why tell Eddie, and I really like Eddie, that the tin opener was broken when it wasn't?

KATE. Mind your own business.

DAVID. I'm not turning you off him, am I?

KATE. You couldn't. Eddie takes care of me.

DAVID. That's good news.

KATE. You mean someone has to?

DAVID. I mean, lucky Eddie to get the chance.

KATE. He doesn't need luck or your approval.

DAVID. But I mean the real chance. Not something manufactured like the odd tin opener. Or does it take a tin opener to open your heart?

KATE. Still minding other people's business? Still standing in kitchen doorways arms akimbo?

DAVID. I never met anyone who needed less looking after than you.

KATE. They used to duck village gossips.

DAVID. You're slipping. You're cheapening yourself.

KATE. Good, oh, good. What a relief.

DAVID. Every time you try to insult me you turn me into a woman. One of you.

KATE. No, the way you imagine a woman to be. What could be more of an insult than that?

DAVID. Haven't you told him then of the way you'll melt into his arms? Depend on him? And cling to him with your weak little hands. Haven't you told him that your oestrogen count is low?

KATE. No.

DAVID. You're deceiving him already. Have you told him how old you are? Or that it's nearly your birthday?

KATE. Thanks for remembering.

DAVID. I know how depressed you get.

KATE. I don't see why you should grudge me Eddie.

DAVID. When you need him. You're beginning to look your age.

KATE. At two o'clock in the morning?

DAVID. I don't want to leave you so. . .

KATE. Oh, don't be silly.

DAVID. So down when really I mean, hell, you're still proving you've got what it takes.

KATE. Why did you come?

DAVID. Kate, I wonder if we should. . . get re-united or something? (KATE *laughs*.) What's so funny?

KATE. Now I know I'm dreaming.

DAVID. Disgusting! I could see all your fillings when you laughed.

KATE. Then go quickly! I'm going to laugh again. I'm going to come very close to your face and go 'ha ha ha'.

DAVID. Have you told him your left eye tooth is false?

KATE. Oh, get out!

DAVID. A person's got to admire you — the way you hold yourself together.

KATE. So you came to see if I mightn't fall apart after all.

DAVID. I suppose I came because I'm feeling a tiny bit panicky.

KATE. Why?

DAVID. Aren't you? Now this whole thing is going to be resolved and well, all this — finished with.

KATE. Funny. I feel calmer with every day that passes.

DAVID. And more certain.

KATE. Oh, yes.

DAVID. And not even a tiny bit. . .

KATE. Oh, no.

DAVID. You missed me a bit last year though? First of all? When you first decided on all this?

KATE. When I decided?

DAVID. I didn't do anything, Kate.

KATE. Of course not.

DAVID. Oh, I know I started. . . with someone else. But as for a divorce. . .

KATE. That just happened to you. Poor ickle David.

DAVID. I let it happen. But I still feel a bit surprised somehow, you know?

KATE. Of course I know. I know you never finally admit responsibility for anything. You just sit there, don't you? A little tin statue, a graven image, waiting for it all — sacrificial offerings — whatever they might be. A bit of steak and kidney, a devotional display, some wholemeal bread, garlands, a hole in one, a firstborn child . . .

DAVID. How is she?

KATE. Go and look at her — if you like.

DAVID. No, I might wake her.

KATE. I don't know how you can resist. It is cheating, of course, but I often stand a full ten minutes. . . and feel more and more surprised to see her sleeping. . . in my house. . . imagine. . . never less.

DAVID. You ought to change her dentist.

KATE. Why?

DAVID. Apparently he doesn't believe in fluoride. Whilst my. . . or most children are having their teeth coated or taking the pills.

KATE. How dare you!

DAVID. And you give her too many sweets.

KATE. In a few years fluoride'll be the same sort of historical joke that chlorophyl turned out to be.

DAVID. And having bought her rubbishy sweets, you buy her a rubbishy dentist to make up.

KATE. Don't you remember? Don't you? Everybody's toothbrush was stained green? Everybody who was anybody had green toothpaste. I'm not saying I don't sympathise with toothpaste manufacturers. They've got to keep what is a dull and totally unnecessary product looking lively.

DAVID. Why get so excited about toothpaste?

KATE. They've got to keep injecting the market with these pseudo-scientific ideas to give their product credibility.

DAVID. And this is what I mean — you go from one extreme to the other. How is a child to calculate what you're really driving at?

KATE. I've got a headache.

DAVID. Naturally.

KATE. You give me a headache.

DAVID. Naturally.

KATE. Nobody else does.

DAVID. The wine couldn't have helped. You're not meant to drink it.

KATE. I know.

DAVID (*almost tenderly*). Kate?

KATE. I just want to lie down. And I can't rest with you here.

DAVID. You must think I've got designs on you.

KATE. What?

DAVID. Afraid to lie down and close your eyes. Afraid I might. . . touch you.

KATE (*disgust*). Don't touch me.

DAVID. Ridiculous!

KATE. I'd be sick.

DAVID. And what about me? The only way I could touch you would be with a very sharp knife.

Pause.

KATE. I'll ring the police.

DAVID. They're not interested in domestic disputes. Anymore than I am in you. (*Moving off slightly.*) But perhaps I will go and look at Sally after all.

KATE. No!

DAVID. Why?

KATE. She's part of me.

DAVID. I'll give her a kiss.

KATE. No.

DAVID. Remember when she was three — that tramp on the beach she kissed?

KATE. We might go to the seaside soon.

DAVID. You thought she'd get foot and mouth.

KATE. You encouraged her.

DAVID. She was very free with her kisses.

KATE. To give you your emotional fix for the day.

DAVID. Who are you going to the seaside with? Eddie?

KATE. And Sally.

DAVID. He's too young.

KATE. What?

DAVID. Oh, I know from your point of view you need the injection of youth's elixir. But Sally. . . no, he's too young.

KATE. For what?

DAVID. Think. When you're fifty Sally will be nineteen. Which one of you d'you think Eddie'll find the most attractive then?

KATE. Still get those soft porn, magazines, do you?

DAVID. Don't need them now.

KATE. You pig.

DAVID. But I don't know about Uncle Eddie.

KATE. Anyway who says I'll still be with him in ten years?

DAVID. Oh, we're going to have a succession of Uncles, are we?

KATE. Have you slept with Anne?

DAVID. Oh, er. . . yes.

KATE. Why?

DAVID. I knew she'd tell you.

KATE. She hasn't. Yet.

DAVID. She is very honest though.

KATE. That's hardly a reason for sleeping with her.

DAVID. But you know what I'm driving at — she's a sympathetic character. And who can resist sympathetic characters? You can't.

KATE. I can get bored with them.

DAVID. Well, you won't get bored with me. 'Specially when I tell you — I'm changing my tactics. I've only discussed it fairly casually with my solicitor so far, but he did imply I could easily build up my case.

KATE. The house.

DAVID. I've decided not to play at it anymore. I mean, I want sole custody.

KATE. What?

DAVID. That's what I came to see you about.

KATE. What?

DAVID. The closer I get to losing her the more I want her. Badly — we want her.

KATE. We?

DAVID. With us.

KATE. You won't stand a chance.

DAVID. Oh, I don't know. Remarkable luck my bumping into your adolescent lover this evening. And as for my own situation — perfect family setting with affection to spare. Oh, I'm sure if Sally were younger the fact that you're her natural mother would seal my fate but. . .

KATE. What about hers?

DAVID. Whose?

KATE (*choking*). Greedy cow. Hasn't she got enough? She's not so old she can't reproduce. . . for herself. . . with you. Stuff her oozing tits into the mouths of her own. But Sally. . . won't drink. . . what does she want. . . to suffocate her. . . or me.

DAVID. It was my idea. I think.

KATE. Yes, only you know how I love her.

DAVID. And I might not get her but. . .

KATE. Have the house.

DAVID. Can I?

KATE. Yes.

DAVID. I don't want it.

KATE. Have it.

DAVID. No.

KATE. I haven't got anything else to give you.

DAVID. I'm not trying to bankrupt you.

KATE. Perhaps if she was a boy. . .

DAVID. I prefer girls.

KATE. Why should you be able to stand there and say that whilst insinuating there'd be something nasty about Eddie liking her.

DAVID. She's my daughter.

KATE. And as I am her mother. . .

DAVID. I was as much a mother as you.

KATE. No, no, no.

DAVID. Ah! Time to disgard the convenient theories of equality between the sexes in favour of the convenient ones about physical bonding between the female and her young as demonstrated throughout the animal kingdom.

KATE. I'll change her dentist. You recommend one.

DAVID. You're pathetic.

KATE. Nobody else thinks so.

DAVID. And what does she think? Have you asked her?

KATE. What?

DAVID. Who she wants to live with.

KATE. Of course not. . . in so many words.

DAVID. Neither have I. . . one just assumed.

KATE. She's too young. It has to be our responsibility.

DAVID. Wrong. The decision will rest with the court.

KATE. David please!

DAVID. Then let's ask her. (*moving off*). We'll wake her up.

KATE (*moving off*.) Don't you disturb her.

DAVID. What are you afraid of?

KATE. Only of hurting her.

DAVID. She's hurt already. Leave go of me.

Sound of a scuffle.

KATE. Ow!

DAVID. All right then.

KATE. What?

DAVID. Tomorrow is Saturday. She comes to see me anyway.

KATE. She won't be coming.

DAVID. You've no right to stop her.

KATE. I'll make it my right.

DAVID. I'll come and collect her.

KATE. I'll make her a ward of court.

DAVID. So will I.

KATE. I'll do it first.

DAVID. Not by Saturday. Then the next day's Sunday — what are you going to do about Sunday. Then a thing like that takes several days.

KATE. You shan't get her.

DAVID (*moving off*). But send me that bill if you like.

KATE. I shall tell her. I shall explain why it has to be.

DAVID (*off, calls back*). For the pineapple too — if you like.

Fade.

Fade up MRS KERSHAW's *office as before.*

MRS KERSHAW (*reads*). 'So to sum up I would say that the child concerned although reserved is popular and has plenty of friends. She is a child surrounded by adults willing to play a supportive role. She is fond of both the petitioner and the respondent and they of her' (*Turns to call.*) Can you er. . . see anything, Mrs Lister, out of the window?

KATE (*off*). Nothing.

MRS KERSHAW. Didn't think you would.

KATE (*approaching*). No.

MRS KERSHAW. I'm sure a child in the street below. . .

KATE. Called out, oh, I know.

MRS KERSHAW (*resuming her reading*). 'However the fact that the child concerned is living with the petitioner at present should be taken into account — as the effect of moving her might prove emotionally disturbing. Therefore, in a case such as this, I would respectfully recommend that the court give special consideration to the child's stated preference to remain with her mother.'

KATE. There!

MRS KERSHAW. Yes, well, of course, that was it — signed, designation and date — but then I had to re-open enquiries, Mrs Lister.

KATE. No, I mean, I heard it again.

MRS KERSHAW. Oh?

KATE. Didn't you?

MRS KERSHAW. No. So now we come to the Supplementary Welfare Report. I really don't think it was anything. A child playing somewhere, calling its mother. . . (*Reads.*) 'Three days after the conclusion of the above report I received an unexpected telephone call from Miss Anne Troubridge — who I had previously interviewed once in her own home in connection with my enquiries — details of which appear on page 6. She seemed upset and requested that I go immediately to the petitioner's house — that being where she was telephoning from.'

KATE (*moving off*). If you don't mind — I'll just check.

MRS KERSHAW. A child playing or something.

KATE (*going*). This time I'll just go to the top of the stairs.

Fade.

Fade up KATE's *house. The living room as before.*

ANNE. Oh, yes! Oh, Kate!

KATE (*approaching*). Really?

ANNE. Lovely shoes.

KATE. Bit high?

ANNE. No.

KATE. Feel.

ANNE. Soft. Or are they agony?

KATE. Not for the first half hour.

Sound of tea being poured.

They're a bit tarty?

ANNE. They're you. I mean, you can't ignore them. . . that red colour. . . a positive statement. . . like you.

KATE. They wouldn't suit you then.

ANNE. Kate, if I'm not welcome. . . ?

KATE. Here's your tea.

ANNE. But I would've thought that today. . . I mean, the idea that he should've come and taken Sally by force is abominable. Surely you. . . or don't you want to talk?

KATE. Isn't it you who needs to talk?

ANNE. I mean, it's a moment of truth really, isn't it?

KATE. So what is it you wanted to say to me, Anne?

ANNE. Me? What about? I only ever say things I've heard other people say. I never have the courage to form opinions. Never have the courage for a pair of shoes like that.

KATE. Never mind the shoes.

ANNE. I do mind them. I want some. I envy you. Feel desperate sometimes — trailing along behind you in my comfy boots.

KATE. I knew it — it's you who's desperate.

ANNE. No, it's just that it's your birthday, Kate.

KATE. We're both desperate then.

ANNE. And I didn't want you to be on your own.

KATE. I'm surprised Eddie hasn't come.

ANNE. Perhaps he's just being discreet. Knowing you'd like to forget.

KATE. I'm sure I don't take it as badly as Miss Ba must.

ANNE. Who?

KATE. Bahama Kelly.

ANNE. Oh, much worse for a woman like that.

KATE. Miss Ba the Living Bras.

ANNE. Wasn't it awful?

KATE. That evening? I thought it was a wild success.

ANNE. The 'offal in pastry'.

KATE. He bought twenty paintings and two illustrations. Bahama practised freedom of expression in the conservatory and found new insight into her relationship with Boy.

ANNE. I felt upset.

KATE. I'm surprised Eddie hasn't sent a card. Perhaps I insulted him.

ANNE. Oh?

KATE. You know — how creepy my skin goes at displays of sentiment.

ANNE. But why shouldn't he. . . ?

KATE. Go all soft on me? Send me a card in a box addressed to 'The Girl of my Dreams'. We all know how easily dreams get squashed in the post. So I said to him, vis-a-vis the card with the pink satin heart, 'Don't you go all esoteric on me, ducky, I only shacked up with you for the laughs.'

ANNE (*shocked*). Did you say that? You don't talk like that.

KATE. Oh?

ANNE. I've never heard you call anyone 'ducky'.

KATE. Oh, often — when I'm drunk.

ANNE. You don't drink.

KATE. How well you know me, Anne.

ANNE. I'm very fond of you.

KATE. I used to look in the mirror to drink my image in — got drunk then. Then one day, one year I looked in the mirror and tried not to notice. . .

ANNE. And then the next year. . .

KATE. You look and see you've been involved in a dreadful accident.

ANNE. You haven't lost Sally. You'll get her back.

KATE. Age. Photos, of course, you can have retouched.

ANNE. What?

KATE. Bahama had her photo taken every week.

ANNE. She told you?

KATE. No, Boy did. But he doesn't understand. You can't retouch the image in the mirror.

ANNE. But you have so much else to draw on, Kate. . . inner strengths.

KATE. And I shall be much freer.

ANNE. Oh, yes.

KATE. Without a child.

ANNE. But you won't be without.

KATE. Best to be prepared, isn't it? On the defensive. I always went round before exams at school saying I'd fail, didn't you? Saying I had to fail because I hadn't worked at it.

ANNE. The thought of exams struck me dumb.

KATE. Your driving test! Oh, I'll never forget that. And the lead up to it. And then I practically carried you there.

ANNE. I'm grateful to you in all sorts of ways.

KATE. Oh, and me to you.

ANNE. I should never have put that red rinse on my hair.

KATE. That wasn't the reason you failed your test, Anne.

ANNE. But you said it'd give me confidence.

KATE. Years ago. Remember how we sometimes chose the same moment to ring each other and got the engaged signal?

ANNE. I know — I could ring David now. Find out how she is.

KATE. Why? What are you talking about?

ANNE. David. How was it after I left? After the dinner party?

KATE. In fact I haven't heard from Eddie since then.

ANNE. Did he stay long?

KATE. David did. Well, it was time we had a chat.

ANNE. It was friendly then.

KATE. I can understand that he wants her. And he doesn't want the house.

ANNE. It seems almost as though she has become a thing.

KATE. A house has much less potential — as a giver and receiver of love — a house is a passive thing. But then children have their own front doors, Anne, and they must be allowed to shut them and retire to their own privacy beyond.

ANNE. You mean, she'd shut you out? I don't believe it.

KATE. Of course I never saw her as a thing. But as a visitor to my house, yes. That's the only way to regard one's children. Otherwise the shock of parting would be too great. No, best to keep in mind the fact of their leaving just as its best to keep in mind the fact of one's own death.

ANNE. I knew you'd be feeling awful.

KATE. I thought I was explaining that I'm not.

ANNE. Only trying to help.

KATE. Well, that's always been your problem, hasn't it?

ANNE. What d'you mean?

KATE. But I feel freer already — quite light headed with it.

ANNE. Free for what?

KATE. Sally bought me a pair of slippers for my birthday. They must be here somewhere but I can't find them.

ANNE. She told you.

KATE. Not exactly.

ANNE. Clever of her.

KATE. What?

ANNE. To have known your size.

KATE. Yes. I asked her how she knew but she wouldn't tell me. Shame — I could've been wearing them now instead of these.

ANNE. But those are lovely.

KATE. You don't have to say things just to please me.

ANNE. Kate — I slept with David once.

KATE. Ah.

ANNE. I had to tell you.

KATE. I'm glad.

ANNE (*pausing*). You're too disgusted to speak, aren't you?

KATE. I'm delighted — really.

ANNE. I knew it was something you could never like me for. I mean, even though you don't like David. I mean, it was such a deceitful thing to do.

KATE. That means he's been unfaithful to her too.

ANNE. I knew I had to tell you. I agonised over when. But I've such a conscience. . . and yet I knew if I told you I risked losing your respect and friendship and everything.

KATE. That cuts her down to size. He always pretended his love was so pure, so incorruptable — first to me and then to her.

ANNE. I'm vile. I feel unclean and filled with self-disgust.

KATE. Oh, why?

ANNE. What?

KATE. Why now? Why tell me now?

ANNE. Oh, I don't know. Everybody seems to be, well, pushing you around and deceiving you. Suddenly I felt I couldn't leave you without. . . Oh, I know you can be polite about it now. People are polite about these things. But in a few days when you've really grasped the implications of what I've said. . . had time to absorb the nasty. . . oh, and your imagination has supplied the details.

KATE. Tell me the details.

ANNE. Oh, God, well, I suppose that serves me right. It was two years ago one evening in early September and. . . oh, in a few days time you're going to hate me for this.

KATE. This is a few days time, Anne. I've known about it for several days.

ANNE. Who told you?

KATE. David.

ANNE. The pig!

KATE. Yes.

ANNE. D'you know once when he came to me and afterwards, you know, had a bath. In my bathroom. . . he cut his toenails.

KATE. He enjoys doing things like that.

ANNE. I could hear them shooting off and clunking against the tiles.

KATE. He was sick all over the place when he came here.

ANNE. What got me was he'd brought his own nail clippers with him. D'you see what that implies?

KATE. He says he's come for one thing when all the time. . .

ANNE. And my hoover doesn't reach the bathroom.

KATE. So you had to go down on hands and knees. . .

ANNE. And pick them up one at a time.

KATE. Poor Anne.

ANNE. My fault.

KATE. He's a pig.

ANNE. He'll have to give her back, Kate. He can't just steal a child. It'll go against him.

KATE. He'll tell them about Ed.

ANNE. Eddie? Oh, that won't count for much. I mean, how could that compare. . . Kate, if one day you could forgive me?

KATE. Nothing to forgive.

ANNE. It was one evening early in September there was this ring at the door. . .

KATE. I need you, Anne. I'm glad you came. I was feeling lonely. The house was feeling very full of space.

ANNE. Oh, I wish there was something. . . Oh, I know! Look — what I came for!

KATE. A present! Oh, you shouldn't have. . . (*Sound of paper tearing.*) Oh, it looks so expensive!

ANNE. I kept the bill. Eleven pounds ninety-nine. In case you don't like it.

KATE. I wanted a shawl! With poppies on it! And talking of flowers I lost two geraniums and a spider plant through there as a result.

ANNE. Of David?

KATE. Shrivelled over night. I used an old pair of coal tongs to carry them out at arm's length and lock them in the shed.

ANNE. Well, if they're dead. . .

KATE. I haven't looked.

ANNE. Plants like animals do have an amazing resilience.

KATE. I'd nurtured them from cuttings.

ANNE. Like people.

KATE. There's so little left, Anne.

ANNE. She won't be staying there. He'll have to return what is rightfully yours.

KATE. You don't understand.

ANNE. I do. I've always wanted a baby.

KATE. I've been heavy with child for eleven years. It's not just the nine months before they're born.

ANNE. I could stay with you.

KATE. But now — with nothing to weight me down — I'm drifting away, Anne.

ANNE. I could — just go and get my things.

KATE. Why?

ANNE. I've stayed before.

KATE. I'm frightened.

ANNE. I'll move into the spare room.

KATE. I'm too frightened.

ANNE. It's only temporary.

KATE. To stay here. I want to go away.

ANNE. You mustn't — not yet, you must see it through.

KATE. Come with me. Somewhere soft, misty, undemanding. We'll take our boots, I'll wear my shawl.

ANNE. No. Out of the question.

KATE (*voice hardening*). Take it back then.

ANNE. What?

KATE. The shawl. I've no use for it.

ANNE. You're being very short-sighted, you know you are. (*Moving off.*) I'll only be half an hour and I'll be back with a suitcase.

KATE. It'd be most unwise.

ANNE. What would?

KATE. For you to stay here. I don't want you here. I don't want anyone here. Thanks all the same.

ANNE (*approaching*). There! I knew, I knew you'd punish me.

KATE. Oh, have it your own way. I don't care.

The telephone rings.

ANNE. Oh! Might be David. . . if it is you could say. . . I know. . . I'll go and collect her. . . if he's not. . . you know. . . wanting to see you.

Ringing ceases. The receiver has been lifted.

KATE (*to phone*). Hello? (*Pause.*) Yes, of course it's me. (*Voice softening.*) A bit fraught but nothing. . . (*Pause.*) What for? (*Whispering to* ANNE.) It's Eddie! (*To phone.*) Yes, why not? in fact I was just thinking it'd be nice to get out of the house for a bit. O.K. Darling. . . Till five minutes. 'Bye! (*The receiver is replaced.*) He wants me to go round. Sounded quite urgent. And as he's never asked me to go before but always ambled round here when it suited. . . (*Moving off.*) well, I must go to him, Anne.

ANNE. I'll just wash the tea things and then. . .

KATE (*calls*). I must fly. You'll see yourself out?

ANNE. I went to see him the other night.

KATE (*approaching*). Who? Eddie? What for?

ANNE. Oh, only to talk about you. I was worried about you. We both were.

KATE (*moving off*). I do feel, Anne, that you and I are beginning to enact the memory of a friendship (*Calling back.*) rather than just be friends, don't you?

The front door slams off.

ANNE. Kate, the shawl. . . I . . . oh. (*She sighs.*)

Sound of cups and saucers being cleared.

SALLY (*off, calls, distant*). Mummy?

Sound of a cup being dropped.

ANNE (*gasps*). No! (*Pause, reassuring herself.*) No.

SALLY (*off, calls, distant but very insistent*). Mummy?

ANNE (*moving off fast*). Sally? Where? Coming. . .

Fade.

Fade up MRS KERSHAW's *office as before.*

MRS KERSHAW (*reads*). 'On my arrival at the house approximately twenty minutes later Miss Anne Troubridge reported that she had released the child from an upstairs attic room which had been locked from the outside.

KATE. Did I tell you she went off with Eddie?

MRS KERSHAW. Who?

KATE. My friend Anne.

MRS KERSHAW. Oh? I'm sorry but unless that has some bearing on the Supplementary Welfare Report. . . ?

KATE. None.

MRS KERSHAW (*reads*). 'Miss Troubridge reported that the child had spoken in a disturbed fashion of a man who had threatened her mother with a plant and stolen the backdoor key, of agreeing with her mother that she be locked in an upstairs attic room to hide from her father. Part of the agreement had been that she was not to call out — if she called out she would not get any food. This latter part of the agreement the petitioner had not kept. Miss Troubridge had given her some baked beans which the child had eaten so quickly she had been sick. Since the child was naturally much distressed it was impossible to ascertain how long she had been imprisoned. My impression that it must have been for at least two days seemed to be supported by information given me by Miss Troubridge. It should be noted that the child concerned insisted that her distress was due to the fact that her mother was not there, that her mother had forgotten the terms of their agreement with regard to food, and that she loved her mother and only wanted to be with her. In fact when I suggested that she live with her father she replied, 'I'll run away and come back here always.' However I feel it my duty to stress the understandably hysterical nature of the child's talk. For example, she kept repeating the sentence, 'Tell Mummy I looked in her shoe and saw it was size 6'. In respect of the petitioner's cruelty in locking the child up perhaps the court might like to investigate further this reference to a shoe. I would further respectfully recommend the court that for the future safety of the child concerned custody of her should be given solely to the father with whom the child is now staying'. I've signed it. Have you any comment to make, Mrs Lister?

KATE. She didn't mention a parcel or . . . ? She told me the paper cost 12p.

MRS KERSHAW. Forgive me, yes. (*Sound of paper crackling.*) She entrusted me with this.

KATE. Oh! Thank you!

MRS KERSHAW. Have you any comment to make?

KATE. Thank you!

MRS KERSHAW. With regard to the report. Any comment?

KATE. None.

Fade.

The End.

SATURDAY NIGHT THEATRE

REMEMBER ME

by Jill Hyem

Remember Me was first broadcast on BBC Radio 4 on 20th
May 1978. The cast was as follows:

THELMA WEADON	Jill Balcon
PAUL SUTTON	Julian Glover
MARGOT SUTTON	Sarah Badel
EDGAR PARSONS	Peter Tuddenham
HESTER DREW	Pauline Letts
ENID GOSLER	Margot Boyd
NANCY	Rowena Roberts

Director: Kay Patrick

Jill Hyem was born in London. She trained at the Webber-
Douglas Academy of Dramatic Art and worked as an actress on
stage and in films, radio and television. While in repertory in
High Wycombe she wrote a revue in which she also appeared.
She sold her first play to radio while acting in a long run in the
West End. She has subsequently written many radio plays
including *A Shape Like Piccadilly*, *Equal Terms* and *Thank You*,
all of which were later produced on television. She was also one
of the originators of the radio serial *Waggoner's Walk*, to which
she still contributes. She has written for the cinema (*Leopard
in the Snow*), for television (the *Angels* series as well as plays)
and has published two stage plays. But radio remains her favourite
medium. Married to a social worker, her plays often have social
themes and have been used by various organisations such as the
Samaritans as part of their training course. *Remember Me* is her
first excursion into the realms of horror.

Fade in. Interior. THELMA's *sitting room at 'Larksmoor', a guest house in a remote part of the Peak District. In the foreground a musical box plays a haunting sinister little melody.*

NANCY (*after a moment, off. She is about twenty, on the slow side with a local accent*). Mrs Weadon? Mrs Weadon? (*Sound of her opening the door.*)

THELMA (*turning, preoccupied*). Yes? What is it, Nancy? (*She is a woman of about forty although she is taken to be a good deal older. She presents a warm and charming manner on the surface. Only later do we start to catch glimpses of the deeply disturbed personality that will emerge as the play develops.*)

NANCY (*joining her*). There's someone on the phone. Long distance. Wants to know if we've got a double room for the coming week.

THELMA. You know we haven't. We're booked solid over the Easter holidays.

NANCY. Thought I'd better check. Only he said they were acquainted with you.

THELMA. Oh? (*Beat.*) What was the name?

NANCY. I think he said 'Sutton'.

Sound of THELMA *closing the musical box sharply. Cut music.*

NANCY. Would that be right?

THELMA. Yes, Nancy. That's right. Good girl. (*Moving off.*) Leave it to me. I'll deal with it.

Over to telephone in reception area.

THELMA (*picks receiver up*). Good afternoon. Thelma Weadon speaking.

PAUL (*on distort, about forty with a great deal of charm*). Hello, Mrs Weadon. This is Paul Sutton. I don't know if you remember me. We met on several occasions when you were staying with Barbara and Alec Trent.

THELMA. Oh yes, Mr Sutton. I remember you well. And your charming wife. How is she?

PAUL. Not been too good as a matter of fact. A bout of flu that seems to've hung on. That's really why I'm ringing. The boys are spending the holidays with their maternal grandparents in France, and Margot and I thought we'd like a recuperative break. Somewhere remote. Away from all the pressures.

THELMA. And you thought of me?

PAUL. You made it all sound so idyllic. And we've never been to the Peak District. But it's only a long shot. You're probably booked up at this time of year.

THELMA. When was it you wanted to come?

PAUL. Saturday for a week.

THELMA. You're in luck. We've just had a cancellation.

PAUL. No. That's marvellous. Must be fate.

THELMA (*slight double edge*). Yes indeed.

PAUL. Will you need a letter of confirmation?

THELMA. No, no. Nothing like that. You'll be driving up I take it?

PAUL. Yes.

THELMA. Then I'll put a direction sheet in the post. I've got your address.

PAUL. Please don't trouble.

THELMA. No trouble. Larksmoor's a bit off the beaten track. I'll look forward to seeing you on Saturday then.

PAUL. We'll look forward to seeing you too. Goodbye for now.

THELMA. Goodbye. (*Sound of her hanging up.*)

THELMA (*beat*). Nancy?

NANCY (*approaching*). Yes, Mrs Weadon?

THELMA. Fetch me the diary would you? I shall have to put off one of the other couples.

NANCY. What a shame.

THELMA. I'm afraid it can't be helped. The Suttons are rather special.

Clean cut.

RECORDED ANNOUNCER. 'Remember Me' A play for radio by Jill Hyem.
Credits.

Bring in atmospheric music. Then fade. Fade in. Interior. Car. Windows open. Bird song in background. Sheep bleating.

MARGOT (*she is in her mid-thirties, French, but only a slight accent*). Slow down a bit, Paul. There's another sign post.

PAUL. Castleton and Hope that way. Hathersage the other. You're the map-reader, which do we take?

MARGOT. Castleton I think. (*Sound of her consulting instruction sheet.*) Yes. She says 'Follow the Castleton Road until you come to a cattle grid, then take the next lane on the left for about a mile.'

PAUL. See what she means about being off the beaten track.

MARGOT (*luxuriantly*). It is beautiful though, isn't it? Look at those hills. And I love the old stone walls.

PAUL. Glad we came?

MARGOT. I feel better already. I wonder what the hotel will be like.

PAUL. Hardly the Hilton. It's more of a guest house. She only takes a handful of people.

MARGOT. At least we know it'll be clean.

PAUL. And cheap.

MARGOT. Yes. Nice of her to offer us a reduction like that. We're only friends of friends.

PAUL. I think the old girl rather took to us.

MARGOT. She is not that old, Paul.

PAUL. Hardly in her first flush. Her hair's virtually white.

MARGOT. Whose wouldn't be if they let it go!

PAUL. She could give us a good few years.

MARGOT. Let's face it, we aren't so young anymore.

PAUL. You look as young as you did the first day I saw you.

MARGOT. Oh yes! After eighteen years!

PAUL. Any changes are only for the better.

MARGOT. You are very sweet.

PAUL. Remember the day we first met? You clutching your A-Z and asking me the way to St Paul's Cathedral.

MARGOT. That was only an excuse. I knew perfectly well where it was. Map-reading expert that I am!

PAUL. And I knew that you knew, but that didn't stop me taking you there.

They share an intimate laugh.

PAUL. And we've never looked back. (*He leans across to kiss her.*)

MARGOT. Hey, keep your eyes on the road, or we'll miss the cattle grid.

PAUL (*sexily*). You wait till we get there.

MARGOT (*happily*). Oh Paul, isn't this good? I love the boys very much, but it is wonderful to be on our own.

Edge out.

Fade in. Interior. Hallway. 'Larksmoor'. Sound of EDGAR *coming through outer door followed by his dog. He is a man of about fifty, with a Northern accent. A lonely person under his rather bluff manner.*

EDGAR (*as he comes through the front door*). Come on, Rags. Time to go in now. We've had enough walking for one day. That's the fellow. Now let's have look at your paws, make sure they're not muddy.

NANCY (*approaching*). 'Evening, Mr Parsons.

EDGAR. Hello, Nancy.

NANCY. Hello, Rags. Been out walking have you?

EDGAR. Up on Derwent Edge. Had a rare time didn't we, Rags?

RAGS *whines off.*

EDGAR. That packed lunch was a treat too.

NANCY. Good. Hope you've left some room for supper.

EDGAR. Oh ay. Nothing like a day's walking to work up an appetite. (*Turning off.*) Hey, Rags, what're you up to? (*Moving off.*) That dog gets his nose into everything.

NANCY. He's a lovely old fellow.

EDGAR (*off*). Looks like he's gone down the cellars.

NANCY (*beat*). What was that?

Over to cellar door area.

NANCY (*fake approach*). What did you say?

EDGAR. Looks like he's gone down there. Cellars is it?

NANCY (*quickly*). Oh no. He mustn't do that.

EDGAR. It's all right.

RAGS *can be heard whining below.*

NANCY. Mrs Weadon don't allow no one down there. Not even me.

EDGAR. He won't do any harm. (*Calls down, slight echo.*) Come here, Rags. Rags! No use. I'd best go and fetch him.

THELMA (*slightly off, she has approached unnoticed*). No please, Mr Parsons!

EDGAR (*turns, warmly*). Oh hello. Thelma. And I thought it was going to be 'Edgar'.

THELMA. Sorry.

EDGAR. Trouble with you Southerners, you're too formal.

THELMA. I'll fetch Rags. The steps aren't too safe.

EDGAR. All the more reason to let me. Rags!

THELMA (*stopping him, but pleasantly*). No I'd rather you didn't. If you don't mind . . . Edgar.

EDGAR. All right. As you wish.

THELMA (*going down steps, echo*). Rags!

EDGAR (*lightly*). What's she got down there anyway? A dead body?

NANCY. Lor' no. Just wine and such.

THELMA (*from cellar*). Rags. Here, boy. Come here. I said come here. I've got a lovely bone for you in the kitchen.

EDGAR (*amused*). Bribery and corruption.

NANCY. She had an' all. Kept it back from lunch.

EDGAR. That was nice of her.

THELMA (*off*). There's a good dog. Got him.

EDGAR (*as she returns*). Here, Rags.

THELMA. Go to your master.

EDGAR. Let's have you. (*Taking him.*) You're in disgrace you are.

THELMA (*charmingly*). Sorry to make such a fuss. All right, Nancy. But I don't want any of my guests having an accident. It's the oldest part of the house you see.

EDGAR. Ah.

THELMA. The one bit I haven't had renovated yet. I usually keep the door bolted, but I went down earlier to fetch some wine and must've left it open.

EDGAR (*to dog*). You hear that, Rags? That's private property down there. So no more exploring, eh?

THELMA. It was my fault. I'll make sure I keep the door shut in future. (*Sound of her pulling door to. It makes a creaking sound.*)

EDGAR. That could do with an oiling.

Sound of her drawing bolts across.

EDGAR. You know what you need? You need a man about the place.

A moment's pause, then we hear a bell ring off.

THELMA. Sounds like the new arrivals.

EDGAR. That's your friends from London.

THELMA. They're just acquaintances really. Come and meet them.

Over to hall area.

MARGOT. Oh look, Paul. At this fireplace.

PAUL (*as he joins her*). Oops. I'm going to have to watch those beams. Magnificent isn't it?

MARGOT. How old did Mrs Weadon say the house was?

THELMA (*as she comes in*). It's sixteenth-century. The original part anyway.

PAUL (*turning*). Hello there.

MARGOT (*simultaneously*). Oh hello.

THELMA (*joining them*). But of course other bits have been added at various stages. (*Warmly.*) How lovely to see you again.

MARGOT. And you.

PAUL. This is a far cry from Wimbledon, isn't it?

MARGOT. It's even better than we imagined.

PAUL. Just what the doctor ordered.

THELMA. Yes I'm sorry you've been unwell.

MARGOT. It's left me a bit shaky, that's all.

THELMA. Let's hope the weather stays fine for you.

Sound of RAGS *bounding up to greet them.*

PAUL. Hello, old chap. Is he yours?

EDGAR (*approaching*). No, mine. Steady, Rags.

THELMA. Let me introduce one of my other guests. Mr Parsons from Hull. Mr and Mrs Sutton.

PAUL. How do you do?

MARGOT. Hello.

EDGAR. Glad to meet you. You've chosen the right spot for a holiday. Especially if you like walking.

MARGOT. Paul does. I'm afraid I am less hardy.

PAUL. You didn't go to an English public school!

They all laugh. The front door opens and we hear HESTER DREW *and* ENID GOSLER'*s voices as they return from a day out. They are both teachers in their fifties.*

THELMA. Oh and here are some of the others. Good evening, Miss Drew. Miss Gosler.

HESTER (*the more dominant of the two*). Hello, Mrs Weadon.

THELMA. Had a good day?

HESTER. Lovely thanks, didn't we, Enid?

ENID. Most enjoyable.

HESTER. We drove into Buxton.

THELMA. Did you see the famous Crescent?

ENID. Oh yes, and the Baths and the museums —

HESTER. As well as buying up half the bookshop.

ENID. You know what avid readers we are.

HESTER (*as they move to the stairs*). She should by now.

THELMA (*going with them to foot of stairs*). By the way do feel free to borrow anything you see on my book shelves. I meant to say before.

HESTER (*off*). We may take you up on that.

They exchange a few more pleasantries in background before they go upstairs.

EDGAR (*aside to the* SUTTONS, *explanatorily*). School teachers. You'd think they'd want to get away from books on holiday. But they even read through meals.

MARGOT. How long have you been here, Mr Parsons?

EDGAR. A week now. I'm staying a full fortnight. I had intended moving on the second week, try the other side. But we've taken to this place, haven't we, Rags?

PAUL. I don't suppose it's everyone'll accommodate dogs either.

EDGAR. Right. And I couldn't come away without old Rags. He's all I've had for company since my wife died. Anyway Thelma was good enough to squeeze us in for another week.

Sound of another guest coming in through outer door.

EDGAR (*turns off*). 'Evening, Mr Lumley. (*Flippantly.*) Seen any good rocks lately? (*Turns back to* SUTTONS, *aside.*) He's a geologist. Studying at the University.

PAUL. Ah.

EDGAR. This area's a gift for them of course, with all the caves and rock formations. You've heard of the Blue John Caverns?

PAUL. We saw a sign on the way here.

MARGOT. What is Blue John?

EDGAR. A local stone. Found nowhere else in the world.

PAUL. Good Lord.

EDGAR. That bowl on the side there is Blue John.

MARGOT (*moving to it*). Oh yes. More mauve then blue.

EDGAR. Hold it up to the light.

MARGOT. Oh, It's beautiful isn't it, Paul?

EDGAR. You'll have to go and see it in its natural state. The Caverns are over Castleton way. These long caves that run for miles under the hills.

MARGOT. I'm not sure I should like that.

EDGAR. Don't worry they're all floodlit now. For the tourists' benefit. And there are cheery guides to give you all the gen. They're well worth a visit.

THELMA (*returning*). Sorry about that. Now let me show you to your room.

MARGOT. Thank you.

EDGAR. See you at supper.

THELMA (*leading them off*). I hope you'll like it. You get a marvellous view of Hannah's Tor from the window.

They move off up the stairs. RAGS *starts whining off by door.*

EDGAR. Now Rags, stop that. You heard what she said. You can't go down there. What *was* it you were after, eh?

Clean cut.

Fade in. Interior. Bedroom. 'Larksmoor'.

PAUL. That's what I call a bed.

MARGOT (*at window, preoccupied*). Mm?

PAUL. If someone told me Queen Elizabeth slept there, I'd believe it.

MARGOT. Sorry, darling, I was looking at the view.

PAUL (*joining her*). Quite something isn't it?

MARGOT. That must be the peak she mentioned. The high one there with the shadow across it.

PAUL. Hannah's Tor. Whoever Hannah was.

MARGOT. I don't much like it.

PAUL. It'll look different in the morning when the sun's shining on it.

MARGOT. Probably. (*She continues to look out, then shivers involuntarily.*)

PAUL. What's the matter?

MARGOT. Nothing. I just shivered.

PAUL. I hope your flu's not starting up again.

MARGOT. No, it was not that sort of shiver. It was as if — (*She breaks off.*) What is that saying?

PAUL. 'As if someone had walked across your grave?'

MARGOT. Yes. . . .

Clean cut.

Bring in. Interior. THELMA's *sitting room. The music box is playing its haunting tune.*

THELMA (*coming in and hearing music, sharply*). Who's that? Nancy?

EDGAR. No, it's me. (*Sound of him closing box. Lose music.*)

THELMA. Oh. Hello Edgar.

EDGAR. Came to look for you. I did call. Wanted to order another packed lunch for tomorrow. Sorry if I startled you.

THELMA (*regaining her composure*). It was hearing the music box.

EDGAR. It caught my eye. Lovely old thing.

THELMA. Yes . . . it was a present from someone. A long time ago.

EDGAR (*drawing the obvious, but wrong, conclusion*). Your husband?

No reply.

EDGAR (*sympathetically*). Ay, it was, wasn't it? I couldn't help noticing the trinkets inside. The ring, the lock of hair, the wad of letters.

THELMA (*with quiet intensity*). You saw them.

EDGAR. I'm sorry. I didn't mean to pry. (*Gently.*) I do the same with Evie's things. Hoard them. It's all you've got isn't it? Once they've gone. Memories. (*He opens the box again. And we hear the little tune again during the following.*)

EDGAR. Tell me about him. It helps to talk.

THELMA (*bitterly*). That's what they all say.

EDGAR. They?

THELMA (*covering up*). In women's magazines and such. They're always writing articles about it. Well I don't believe them. You can talk till you're blue in the face, but you've still lost the person you loved.

EDGAR (*gently*). Yes. And you have to accept the fact.

THELMA. *Why* do you?

EDGAR. Because it's all there is you *can* do.

THELMA (*quietly*). Is it?

Edge out.

Fade in. Interior. SUTTON's *bedroom. An owl hooting off somehwere.*

MARGOT (*after a moment*). Paul?

PAUL. Mm?

MARGOT. Can't you sleep either?

PAUL. Not very easy with you tossing about beside me.

MARGOT. Sorry. I can't seem to settle.

PAUL. The bed is a bit eccentric isn't it? (*Suggestively.*) I like the dip in the middle though.

MARGOT. You would!

PAUL. Since we can't get to sleep we might as well pass the time constructively.

MARGOT. What do you suggest? Letter-writing?

PAUL. You know what I suggest.

MARGOT. Anyone ever tell you you've got a one-track mind?

PAUL. Where you're concerned I have.

MARGOT (*as he takes her in his arms*). Oh Paul.

PAUL. I want you.

MARGOT. Again?

PAUL (*with passion*). Again and again and again. How can it be so good still?

MARGOT. I know.

PAUL. I've never stopped fancying you from the first moment I saw you. Or loving you.

They start to make love. Then suddenly.

MARGOT. No Paul —

PAUL. What's the matter?

MARGOT. I don't know. It's no use, I can't.

PAUL. Why? You were keen enough a moment ago.

MARGOT. Yes but I — it's stupid I know but —

PAUL. What?

MARGOT. I feel as if we weren't alone.

PAUL. Eh?

MARGOT. As if — someone was watching us —

PAUL. Margot! Like who? One of the schoolmarms or the horn-rimmed geologist? I thought he was giving you strange looks at supper!

MARGOT. Don't laugh, please.

PAUL. Or maybe it's the ghost of some previous owner. The one who caused the original dip perhaps.

MARGOT. Please, Paul!

PAUL. Love, you're letting your imagination run away with you.

MARGOT (*without conviction*). I suppose so.

PAUL. You've had a long day. You're over-tired. (*Getting out of bed.*) Look I'll go and open the door so you can see for yourself. (*Sound of him opening door.*) There. Not a Peeping Tom in sight.

MARGOT. Quiet. What's that?

PAUL. Can't hear anything.

MARGOT. Listen.

We hear RAGS *whining off in distance.*

PAUL (*deliberately*). Oh my God.

MARGOT. What?

PAUL. It's a banshee. Wailing his death warning.

MARGOT' Stop it!

PAUL (*anti-climatically*). It's only that dog of old Parson's whining away downstairs somewhere. All right? Happy now?

Sound of him closing door. Clean cut.

Fade in. Sound of RAGS *whining and scratching at cellar door. Sound of footsteps approaching. Dog stops whining then yelps suddenly. Clean cut.*

Fade in. Interior. Dining room. Breakfast time. Breakfast noises in background.

HESTER (*as she and* ENID *pass the* SUTTONS' *table*). Good morning.

ENID. Beautiful day.

PAUL. Yes indeed.

MARGOT. Good morning.

HESTER (*off*). Good morning Mr Lumley. And where are you off to today?

PAUL (*aside to* MARGOT *as general chat continues off in background*). I see what Mr Parsons meant. Each with her little book clasped in her hand.

MARGOT. I wonder what they read.

PAUL. High romance I expect. Of the Barbara Cartland variety. Or maybe they go for the other extrene. An orgy of Harold Robbins.

MARGOT. It's sad isn't it? I expect that's the nearest they ever get to it.

PAUL. Sex?

MARGOT. Or romance. Or marriage. Or children. There must be thousands of women like that who never have the chance to have — well, what I've got.

PAUL. What *we've* got.

   A moment of intimacy.

THELMA (*who has approached unnoticed*). Good morning.

PAUL. Oh good morning.

MARGOT. Hello. This is a marvellous breakfast.

THELMA. Good. Is Nancy looking after you all right? She's a bit on the slow side but it's not easy to get staff up here.

MARGOT. She lives in the village does she?

THELMA. Yes. Comes in daily.

EDGAR (*approaching, in a state of some anxiety*). Thelma? (*To* SUTTONS.) Excuse me.

PAUL. 'Morning, Mr Parsons.

EDGAR. Good morning. (*To* THELMA.) I'm sorry to barge in but have you see Rags this morning?

THELMA. No, I don't think I have.

EDGAR. I can't find him anywhere.

THELMA (*sympathetic*). Oh dear. Maybe he slipped out when Nancy arrived this morning.

EDGAR. I've looked all round the garden and walked up to the top of the lane.

THELMA (*turns off*). Nancy!

EDGAR (*to* SUTTONS). Sorry about that but I'm beginning to get a bit worried. We've got into this routine here you see. I come down first thing and he's waiting there by the front door. Then we go for a little stroll before breakfast.

NANCY (*approaches*). Yes, Mrs Weadon?

THELMA. Have you seen Mr Parsons' dog this morning?

NANCY. No. I missed him. He usually gives me a nice greeting of a morning.

THELMA. I suppose he couldn't have got out last night. When I locked up.

EDGAR. It's a possibility.

PAUL. No. He was here last night. We heard him whining in the early hours didn't we, Margot?

THELMA. Really? I didn't hear anything.

EDGAR (*concernedly*). I don't know what can've happened.

MARGOT. Perhaps he's got himself shut in somewhere.

THELMA. We'd've heard him barking now.

EDGAR (*as it occurs to him*). What about the cellar, Thelma? You know how intrigued he was with that yesterday.

THELMA. No. He couldn't possibly have got down there again. It's been locked ever since. I'm sure he'll turn up, Edgar.

NANCY. Yes he'll turn up soon as he's hungry.

EDGAR. I hope so. It's not like Rags to go off. Not like him at all.

Edge out.

Fade in. Exterior. Moors at the back of the house. A stream can be heard. Lambs bleating off. A sheep ma-as protectively on mike.

MARGOT. It's all right, sheep, I am not going to hurt your baby. Oh look, Paul, isn't it adorable? The one with the little black face.

PAUL. Cant've been born that long. It's still a bit shaky on its pins.

MARGOT. And look at those two over there, leaping about like Russian ballet dancers.

PAUL. We certainly chose the right time to come away. Spring with a capital S.

MARGOT. It's beautiful.

PAUL. Say when you want to turn back.

MARGOT. Let's go a bit further.

PAUL. 'Long as you're not tired.

MARGOT. We haven't come far. You can still see the house down there.

PAUL. Oh yes. Funny old place isn't it? I wonder how Thelma Weadon came by it.

MARGOT. She was left it by some relative. I remember Barbara Trent telling me.

PAUL. And she decided to come and live up here. I can see the appeal, mind.

MARGOT. I don't know. It'd be very cut off in winter. I don't suppose she has any guests then either. I wouldn't like to live on my own there.

PAUL. But then you, my darling, are a touch squeamish. Look at you last night. Strange feelings. Spooks watching us in bed.

MARGOT (*smiling*). All right I was stupid. Right now even that old peak up there looks friendly.

PAUL. I told you it would in the sunlight. Let's cross over the stream. There's some stepping stones.

MARGOT. Okay.

PAUL (*as they cross*). That one's a bit slippery. Can you manage?

MARGOT. Yes. (*Then stopping on stone.*) Oh Paul, isn't this perfect? Listen! No cars. No aeroplanes. No transistors. Just the sound of the stream and the sheep.

Pause as they listen for a moment. As well as the sheep and stream we gradually become aware of some kestrels cawing persistently.

PAUL. And those birds. What's all that about I wonder?

Peak birds.

MARGOT. They must've seen something. Look at the way they're hovering.

PAUL. A dead lamb perhaps.

MARGOT. Oh no!

PAUL. It's not uncommon, this time of year.

MARGOT (*looking up at birds*). How cruel they look.

PAUL (*moving off a bit*). Yes they've spotted something all right. Something white in the water there. Already having a go at it too.

MARGOT. Horrible things.

PAUL (*suddenly*). No! Stay there, Margot. Don't come any further. It's not a very pretty sight.

MARGOT. Is it a lamb?

PAUL (*beat*). No it isn't . . . it's Mr Parsons' dog.

Clean cut.

Fade in. Interior. THELMA's *sitting room.*

EDGAR (*upset*). I can't understand it . . .

THELMA (*all sympathy and understanding*). Drink some more brandy, Edgar.

EDGAR. How could he drown in a stream that shallow?

THELMA. I expect Paul Sutton's right. He must've lost his footing somehow. Hit his head against a rock.

EDGAR. Not Rags. That dog was sure-footed as a goat.

THELMA. Accidents happen.

EDGAR. And how did he get out in the first place? I'm still flummoxed by that.

THELMA. I'm afraid he must've slipped past Nancy. Whatever she says. It's the only explanation.

EDGAR. You don't miss a dog like my Rags.

THELMA. She's not the most astute of girls.

EDGAR (*introspectively*). That dog was my life. We never had any children. Evie and me. She couldn't have them. After she'd gone Rags was everything.

THELMA.(*sympathetically*). You'd've had to lose him sooner or later.

EDGAR. But not this way. Not violently. (*Then apologetic.*) I'm sorry, lass. I shouldn't take it out on you.

THELMA. Please. I only wish there was something I could do.

EDGAR. You've been wonderful.

THELMA. I feel responsible in a way.

EDGAR. It was my fault. I should've kept him up in the room with me. But I've never known him roam off like that. I'd better go upstairs now.

THELMA. If you want to. But you're welcome to stay down here with me.

EDGAR. Best not. I'm no sort of company. Thanks though. I'll say goodnight.

THELMA. Good night. And Edgar — I'll quite understand if you want to leave 'Larksmoor' after this. I won't charge for the extra days.

EDGAR. No. I'd sooner stay on. What's there to go home for?

Clean cut.

Fade in. Interior. Bedroom. Sound of MARGOT *writing letter.*

PAUL. How much longer will you be, darling?

MARGOT. Don't rush me. I am thinking what to put.

PAUL. 'Having a lovely holiday. Wish you were here. Love Mum and Dad.'

MARGOT. I must say more than that.

PAUL. Why? It's all *they* ever say.

MARGOT. No. That was quite a newsy letter we had yesterday. Can you pass it over? I'd better see if there is anything I should answer.

PAUL. Where is it?

MARGOT. On the bedside table.

PAUL (*slightly off*). I can't see it.

MARGOT. By my book.

PAUL. No.

MARGOT (*goes to bedside table*). That's funny. It *was* last night.

PAUL. Perhaps Nancy tidied it away.

MARGOT. Oh and I like to keep their letters.

PAUL (*sending her up affectionately*). For the Baby Book?

MARGOT (*indignant*). Well I am proud of our sons.

PAUL. So am I. *And* of my wife.

He kisses her. MARGOT *shivers.*

PAUL. What is it? The shivers again?

MARGOT. That same feeling I had before, as if we were not alone.

PAUL (*lightly*). Want me to look under the bed?

MARGOT (*not amused*). Don't tease me.

PAUL. Darling, how could there be anyone?

MARGOT. I don't know. . .

PAUL (*moving to door*). Perhaps Nancy's outside doing the landing. (*Sound of him opening the door.*)

Over to landing.

PAUL. No.

MARGOT (*joining him*). It wasn't that sort of thing. (*Then.*) Listen.

PAUL. Mm?

MARGOT. I can hear something.

PAUL. Can't be Mr Parsons' dog this time.

MARGOT. Music. . .

PAUL. No law against playing the radio at 10.00 a.m. in the morning. Anyway I can't hear it.

MARGOT. It's stopped now. (*With an apologetic smile.*) I'm sorry. I must be going crazy.

PAUL. Flu often leaves people a bit jumpy.

Door off below.

THELMA (*coming upstairs*). Good morning, you two.

PAUL. Hello, Thelma.

THELMA. Just who I wanted to see. I was hoping to catch you before you went out.

PAUL. We're not going yet.

THELMA. Can you spare a moment?

MARGOT (*moving back into the room*). Of course.

Over to room.

PAUL (*fake approach*). Come on in.

THELMA (*approaching*). Thanks. I want to ask a favour of you. I wouldn't if you weren't friends.

PAUL. Fire away.

THELMA. I'll just shut the door. (*Sound of her closing door.*) It's about Edgar. Mr Parsons.

PAUL. Yes?

THELMA. He's still feeling very depressed about his dog.

MARGOT. Poor man.

THELMA. And I can see him sitting up in his room all day again if we don't do something.

MARGOT. You'd like us to take him out?

THELMA. Would it be an awful imposition?

MARGOT. Not at all.

THELMA. Only I'm busy myself. The shopping, meals and so forth.

PAUL. Leave it to us.

THELMA. If you could do it tactfully though. Make it sound as if you need his help. Ask him to show you the walk up Hannah's Tor this afternoon perhaps.

PAUL. That's an idea. I wouldn't mind getting a closer look at that.

THELMA. The view from the top is unbelievable. I often go up there when I'm less busy. Oh but it might be a bit arduous for *you*, Margot. How thoughtless of me. It's quite a haul up.

MARGOT. I must admit I can't see myself making the top. But that needn't stop you going, Paul.

PAUL. No we'll think of something else to do.

MARGOT. You'd enjoy it though.

THELMA. The last thing I want is to split you up.

MARGOT. It's only for an afternoon. We can survive without each other for that long. Can't we, darling?

PAUL. At a pinch!

MARGOT. And I'd be quite happy pottering about here. Finish my letters in peace. Put my feet up in the garden.

THELMA. There's a marvellous suntrap out the back.

MARGOT. I noticed. Yes, you go off for a nice climb with Mr Parsons, Paul. You can always wave to me from the top.

THELMA (*turning to go*). I'll leave it with you then. I'm most grateful.

PAUL. Not at all.

MARGOT. Oh — Thelma? (*As she turns.*) Was someone playing the radio downstairs just now?

THELMA. No. Not that I heard. Why?

MARGOT. It's not important.

Clean cut.

Fade in. Interior. Kitchen. 'Larksmoor'. Washing-up sounds.
NANCY *sings tonelessly to herself as she washes up.*

THELMA (*coming in*). Have you nearly finished that, Nancy?

NANCY. Yes, Mrs Weadon. 'Cept for the coffee things. I'll lay up the tables for supper next shall I?

THELMA. No leave that. (*deliberately*). You can take the rest of the afternoon off.

NANCY (*surprised*). It's not my half day.

THELMA. Not but you've worked hard the last week. You deserve a bit of extra free time.

NANCY. Thank you, Mrs Weadon.

THELMA. And didn't you say your brother was home on leave?

NANCY. That's right.

THELMA. Then you'll be wanting to see as much of him as you can. So off you go as soon as you've finished the washing-up.

NANCY. What about teas?

THELMA. Everyone's out this afternoon, except Mrs Sutton. And I can see to her.

Edge out.

Fade in. Exterior. Garden. 'Larksmoor'. A bee buzzes around.
Birdsong. The occasional bleat of a sheep in the distance.
MARGOT *gives a sleepy contented grunt as she rearranges herself in the deck-chair.*

THELMA. Ready for a cup of tea.

MARGOT. Oh — Thelma — I didn't see you.

THELMA. I'll put the tray down here. (*Sound of her putting down tray.*)

MARGOT. Thank you. What a lovely lazy afternoon I am having.

THELMA. Why not? You're on holiday.

MARGOT. I do love your garden.

THELMA. I'm afraid I've let it run wild. I've put all my energy into the house so far.

MARGOT. I expect it needed a lot of work on it.

THELMA. You should've seen it eighteen months ago. When I first came up here. The old lady hadn't done a thing to it in years. Everything riddled with damp and woodworm. A lot of the original parts blocked up. You'd be amazed at some of the discoveries I've made.

MARGOT (*thinking of her uneasy feelings*). Yes. One can sense it's a house with a past. It was a cousin of yours left it to you?

THELMA. A very distant one. On my mother's side. I'd been here a couple of times as a child and I always remembered the place. But I hadn't seen Cousin Emily since I was about twelve. The bequest came as a complete surprise.

MARGOT. How exciting.

THELMA. It was. It provided me with everything I was looking for. (*Deflecting her back again.*) I'll show you round later if you're interested.

MARGOT. That would be nice.

THELMA. Then come and find me when you've finished your tea. I'll be in my sitting room.

Fade.
Creep in music box as heard from MARGOT's *point of view as she stands in the hall.*

MARGOT (*approaching*). Thelma? Thelma. I'm rea — (*She breaks off, hearing the music.*)

Pause as she listens. Then she knocks on the door.

MARGOT (*as she knocks*). Thelma?

The door opens. Music continues in background.

THELMA. Ah good, you're ready.

MARGOT. That was the sound I heard this morning. When I asked you about the radio.

THELMA (*moving off*). Oh my music box. You like the tune?

MARGOT. 'Like' is not the word exactly.

THELMA. Mm, it's a haunting little melody isn't it?

Hold music for a moment. Then cut as she closes the box.

THELMA. Well now where shall we start? Upstairs or down? Down here I think. There's one thing especially I want you to see. . .

Fade out.

Edge in. Interior. Cellar as the door creaks open.

THELMA. Careful down the steps now.

Their footsteps on the steps.

MARGOT (*as she descends, a little uneasily*). You have no electricity down here?

THELMA. No. I make do with the old oil lamps. You eyes'll soon get used to it.

MARGOT. It's coming in out of the sun.

THELMA. Here we are then. The cellars.

MARGOT (*as if looking round*). They are big aren't they?

THELMA. Yes. They run the whole length of the house. When I stayed at 'Larksmoor' as a child I spent my whole time playing down here.

MARGOT. Not my idea of fun.

THELMA. That's what my mother used to say. But then she didn't know what I'd discovered.

MARGOT. What was that?

THELMA. I'll show you. See round the corner here. In that wall. Look.

MARGOT. A door?

THELMA. Yes. It was hidden behind a lot of old boxes and so forth, and boarded over. That's why the old lady never knew about it. Or anyone else.

MARGOT. Where does it lead to?

THELMA. Ah. That's my surprise. Come and I'll show you.

Sound of her opening door. Slight echo.

THELMA (*as* MARGOT *hangs back*). It's all right, there are lamps down here too.

MARGOT (*surprise*). You keep them lit all the time?

THELMA. No. I lit them just now. For you. I thought you might like to see down here.

Sound of water lapping below them.

MARGOT. Water.

THELMA. Yes.

MARGOT (*as they go nearer*). A tunnel.

THELMA. That's right.

MARGOT. What is it?

THELMA. An old channel way carved out by miners over two hundred years ago. It's similar to the one in Speedwell Cavern, except this isn't open to tourists. (*Pointedly.*) Except specially chosen ones.

MARGOT. How far does it go?

THELMA. Nearly half a mile. The entrance was up by the Tor. But of course it was blocked up once the mine went out of use. Now it's all overgrown. No one knows of its existence.

MARGOT. It's incredible.

THELMA. Even more incredible when you go along it by boat.

MARGOT. Boat?

THELMA. There, under the canvas. It was the only means I had of exploring further. And it was worth exploring too. There's a cave at the end with the most superb stalactites. That's what I want to show you. You've never seen anything like it.

MARGOT. But I —

THELMA (*moving to boat*). Let me just get the tarpaulin off —

MARGOT (*not relishing the thought*). No, wait. I'd love to see it, Thelma. Really I would. But why not wait till Paul gets back? I know he'd want to be in on it too.

THELMA. Then we'll go again for his benefit. I never tire of visiting my cavern.

MARGOT. It's a bit cold down here too. I think perhaps it would be better if —

THELMA (*cuts in*). No problem there. Take my cardigan. I've got an old jacket in the boat. (*Handing it to her.*) Here.

MARGOT (*no option*). Thank you.

THELMA (*as she moves tarpaulin*). And it isn't really that cold. In winter it seems quite warm. (*Sound of her moving tarpaulin.*) It's a constant temperature you see. Watever goes on up there, down here nothing changes. I'll hold it steady while you get in.

MARGOT (*gingerly*). It is quite safe, the boat?

THELMA. Good heavens yes.

MARGOT (*trying to sound light*). Only I wouldn't fancy my chances if I had to swim.

THELMA. You're not a strong swimmer then?

MARGOT. I can't swim at all. Somehow I never learnt as a child. The boys tease me endlessly.

THELMA. Don't worry. You'll be safe in this. In you get now.

Creaking of boat as MARGOT gets in.

MARGOT. Oops.

THELMA. That's it. You sit in the front. I'll just undo the rope.

MARGOT (*already feeling slightly claustrophobic*). It's very narrow, the passage.

THELMA. Wide enough for four miners to work abreast. (*As she undoes the rope.*) All the same you're right. It's quite difficult to manoeuvre the boat in parts. I have to do it by pushing against the walls.

MARGOT. I really think it might be best to wait for Paul.

Sound of THELMA pushes off with the paddle.

THELMA. Too late now. We're underway.

Creak of boat as it moves off and lapping of water. Fade out.

Fade in Exterior. Hannah's Tor. Lambs bleating off.

EDGAR. Bearing up all right, Paul? Or do you want to stop for a breather before we tackle the last stretch?

PAUL. Just for a moment. (*Breathlessly.*) I'm going to have to take up squash again. Hadn't realised how out of training I was.

EDGAR. Old Rags keeps me in training. (*Subdued, remembering.*) Kept I should say.

PAUL. You must get another dog, Edgar.

EDGAR. Happen. It was nice of you to ask me along this afternoon.

PAUL. Was glad of your company.

EDGAR. *She* put you up to it didn't she?

PAUL. What?

EDGAR. Thelma. She asked you to take me out.

PAUL. Now what makes you think that?

EDGAR. I'm not so thick as I look.

PAUL. She didn't have to twist my arm.

EDGAR. Quite a woman that.

PAUL. I'm not doing you any favours. I'm really enjoying this.

EDGAR. How long have you known her?

PAUL. Thelma? We don't really know her that well. She's a friend of some neighbours of ours. We met her when she was staying with them. She was about to open this place as a guest house then and was singing its praises. Then she sent us a brochure when she got going in earnest.

EDGAR. Ah.

PAUL. So when we decided to take a break, we thought we'd give it a try.

EDGAR. It's a grand spot.

PAUL. Splendid.

EDGAR. I tumbled across it by chance. And Thelma couldn't have been kinder. See over there beyond. That's the reservoirs. Lady Bower, Derwent and Howden.

PAUL. Oh yes. Can see for miles can't you?

EDGAR. On a good day. It's a wonder she hasn't married again, Thelma.

PAUL (*with only a cursory interest*). Has she been a widow long?

EDGAR. Some years I think. But it still goes deep. You can tell. Does with me too. No one'll ever replace Evie. But I'm not cut out to be a single man. Once you've been married you lose the art of self-sufficiency.

PAUL. Mm.

EDGAR. And without Rags either. . . I'll be a dead loss.

PAUL (*lightly*). You ought to get together, you and Thelma.

EDGAR (*seriously*). Not a bad idea at that. Ready then?

PAUL. Okay.

EDGAR. Best foot forward. . .

PAUL. Is it my imagination or is the summit getting further away instead of nearer?

Edge out.

Fade in. Interior. Caves. Water lapping. Creaking of boat as THELMA *manoeuvres her way along.*

MARGOT. How much further?

THELMA. Not far now. If you look on the left by the next lamp you'll see a recess in the wall.

MARGOT. Oh yes.

THELMA. It was carved out by the miners. Somewhere to take refuge, when they were blasting or if the rock caved in.

MARGOT. But surely a tiny space like that wouldn't've held more than two or three people.

THELMA. Then some would've been unlucky.

A pause. Just the water lapping and the creaking of the boat.

MARGOT. I suppose lots of men must've lost their lives down here over the years. You can feel it can't you?

THELMA (*atmospherically*). You sense it too? Sometimes I picture them. Clawing their way through the debris. Their nails torn and bleeding.

MARGOT (*increasingly frightened*). Don't!

THELMA. Crying for help until their lungs are bursting. But no one hears them. And in the end they have to give up. Just lie there and wait to die. Slowly.

MARGOT. Stop it, please!

THELMA (*snapping out of it with convincing sympathy*). I'm sorry, my dear. I didn't mean to frighten you. I've always had a vivid imagination. One of the advantages of being an only child. You learn to draw on your own resources. Or is it a disadvantage, I wonder? You had brothers and sisters I suppose?

MARGOT. Yes there were three of us.

THELMA. One happy family. As *you* are now. (*Pointedly*.) You and Paul and Martin and Andrew.

MARGOT. Fancy you remembering their names. You couldn't've met them more than once.

THELMA. Oh I have a good memory.

Slight pause.

THELMA. It must be wonderful to be part of a proper family. It's what I always wanted. My father died you see when I was small. There was only my mother and me. (*With bitterness.*) And she wasted no time in casting me off when another man with no time for children came along.

MARGOT. How awful.

THELMA. Yes it was.

A flop as a rat moves in water.

MARGOT. What was that?

THELMA. What?

MARGOT. Something moved in the water there.

THELMA. I didn't see anything.

Another flop.

MARGOT. There. Again. (*With revulsion.*) Oh no, it's a rat.

THELMA. Possibly. There are some water rats down here.

MARGOT. Ugh. I can't stand rats.

THELMA. They're quite harmless.

MARGOT. Thelma — I know I'm being stupid — but d'you mind if we turn back?

THELMA. We're nearly at the cavern now.

MARGOT. I feel a bit claustrophobic and —

THELMA (*cuts in*). We can't turn back now. Not until you've seen the stalactites. . .

Dip of paddle in water. Creak of boat as it continues along. Fade.

Fade in. Exterior. Summit of Hannah's Tor. Wind blowing. Birds overhead.

PAUL. Phew. Quite windy up here isn't it? Sun's gone in too.

EDGAR. Aye. Strange the difference it makes. Sunlight. The Tor's quite eerie with the shadow across it.

PAUL. That's what Margot said.

EDGAR. Quite a view though isn't it? Worth the climb.

PAUL. I'll say.

EDGAR. Look out.

PAUL. What?

EDGAR. Don't go too near the edge there. It's a sheer drop down.

PAUL. I see what you mean.

EDGAR. Can't have you going the way of poor Hannah.

PAUL. Is that what happened to *her*?

EDGAR. Yes.

PAUL. Who was she anyway?

EDGAR. A lass from Bamford way. According to the guide books. She was promised to a local farmer. Handsome fellow who she doted on. Then he took up with someone else. Some flighty piece from Sheffield. She was that consumed with jealousy she murdered them both in their bed on the wedding night. Then she came up here, the blood still fresh on her hands, and threw herself over the edge. Hence Hannah's Tor.

PAUL. Poor old Hannah.

EDGAR. Mm. You know what they say, 'Hell hath no fury. . .

Edge out.

Fade in. Interior Caves, as before. Water lapping. Boat creaking.

THELMA. Look now, Margot. You can see the passage beginning to widen out at the end there.

MARGOT (*with relief*). Ah yes.

THELMA. That's where my cavern is. In a moment you'll be able to see the stalactites and then you'll consider the trip worthwhile after all.

MARGOT. You must think I'm very feeble.

THELMA. Of course not. I forget that everyone doesn't share my enthusiasm for the world under the ground. There. Look now.

Pause as the boat draws up along side the platform of the cavern.

MARGOT (*with a little gasp*). Oh! It's like a fairy-tale cave.

THELMA. Yes. Although the lamp light doesn't do them justice. See how delicate they are. Like beautiful candles. There's one in the corner — you can't quite see it from here — that's almost joined with a stalagmite on the ground. Another inch and they'll meet together and form a column. But that won't be in our lifetime. It'll take a thousand years or more.

MARGOT. As long as that?

THELMA. At least. All of them took thousands and thousands of years to grow like this.

MARGOT. Incredible.

THELMA. Drip, drip, drip. (*Peak the steady drip of the water which will continue in background throughout all cavern scenes.*) We'll get out and have a better look. Give you a chance to stretch your legs too. You go first. I'll hold the boat still.

MARGOT. All right.

THELMA. Can you manage?

MARGOT. Yes thank you. (*Getting out.*)

THELMA. You'll feel better on terra firma. I'll be with you in a minute. Just tie her up. That stalactite I told you about is over there.

MARGOT (*moves off*). Oh yes, I see.

THELMA. And have a look at some of the rock formations. Oh and that stone arch. I'm pretty sure it's Blue John. It's very like the one in Treak Cliff.

Over to MARGOT. *Dripping water continues in background.*

MARGOT. It's amazing isn't it? It all is. You *must* bring Paul. What a pity the boys aren't here. They'd be fascinated. Especially Andrew. He's always been interested in this sort of thing. I see what you mean about these rocks. What a strange shape that one there is. Like a bird's head. And that one over there too. It's rather like a witch on a broomstick. Have you ever though of opening this to the public? (*Turning.*) I said have you ever thought of —

She breaks off. We hear the creaking of the boat as THELMA *moves off.*

MARGOT (*beat*). Thelma?

No reply. Just the creaking.

MARGOT. Thelma? What're you doing?

THELMA (*in a strange tone*). It's time for me to go now.

MARGOT (*with complete incredulity*). Go?

THELMA. Yes. The other gusts'll be back soon. They'll be wanting their evening meal.

MARGOT (*beat, with disbelief*). Is this some sort of joke? Because if so I —

THELMA (*menacingly*). Oh no. I've never been more serious in my life.

MARGOT. What?

THELMA. I'm going to leave you here.

MARGOT (*as it begins to sink in, with utter horror*). No! You can't mean it.

THELMA. Oh yes I can.

MARGOT. But —

THELMA (*continues on*). I've been planning this moment for the last eighteen months. Eighteen *years* you might say.

MARGOT. I don't understand.

THELMA. No.

MARGOT. I didn't even know you till last year so how —

THELMA. Yes you did. But you chose to forget me didn't you? Just as Paul did.

MARGOT. Paul?

THELMA. Never mind the fact you ruined my life.

MARGOT. Thelma — please — you've made some awful mistake.

THELMA. Oh no, I've made no mistake. And my name's not Thelma either. It's Ann. Ann Milner. *Miss* Ann Milner. Spinster of this parish.

MARGOT. I don't know any Ann Milners.

THELMA. Don't you?

MARGOT. I promise you I don't. I've never —

THELMA (*cuts in*). What about the one who should've married Paul?

A long pause as it sinks in. Just the dripping water.

MARGOT (*slowly*). Oh my God. . .

THELMA. You remember now.

MARGOT. You were the girl who —

THELMA. Who he was going to marry before you came along.

MARGOT (*involuntarily*). But it can't be, you're too ol — (*She breaks off.*)

THELMA. Too old? Yes. . . There's nothing more ageing than grief.

MARGOT (*with incredulity*). But all that was —

THELMA (*obsessionally*). Eighteen years ago. Eighteen years, two months, three days to be exact. And how many times have you thought of me during those years?

MARGOT. We —

THELMA. Not once have you? You've been so wrapped up in your smug cocoon of happiness.

MARGOT. We felt dreadful about it to begin with.

THELMA. Oh yes. I still have the letter he wrote me. Full of abject apologies. Explaining how he'd met this little French tart and realised she was 'the real thing'. Well for me *he* was the real thing. He never even got in touch with me again.

MARGOT. He thought it was the best way.

THELMA. The best way for *him*. Close the book and forget the whole chapter. Well I didn't forget. Not for one day of the

eighteen barren years ahead. Each of these white hairs, each
of these lines, are my momentos. And there were always new
reminders weren't there? Cuttings from the *Telegraph* and
Times. 'To Paul and Margot Sutton, a son. Andrew Philip.'
That was the first time I took an overdose.

MARGOT (*horrified*). Because of Andrew?

THELMA (*intensely*). Because he should've been *mine*. It
should've been me happily married, with a baby. *Me* getting
letters from my devoted sons.

MARGOT (*with realisation*). You took that letter.

THELMA. Look what *you* took from *me*.

MARGOT. But surely — if you wanted — there must've been
other men you could've —

THELMA (*cuts in savagely*). I didn't *want* other men. (*The
echo takes it up.*) D'you think I could trust anyone else after
that? I'd already been through it once. I loved *her* and what
did she care?

MARGOT. Your mother?

THELMA. The man-crazy bitch. When I met Paul, everything
changed. I thought there was someone at last who. . . And then
you came along.

MARGOT. I —

THELMA (*obsessionally*). All I've wanted these last eighteen
years is my revenge. And now I'm going to have it. I shall
see you and he suffer as I've suffered.

MARGOT (*scarcely about to speak*). You're ill. . .

THELMA. And if I am, whose fault is that?

MARGOT. Please — listen — you need help.

THELMA. I've had 'Help'. D'you know how many times I've
been in and out of mental institutions? Almost as many times
as I was in and out of jobs. 'Talk' they say, and plug you with
pills, and wires and miracle drugs. In the end I told them all
the things they wanted to hear and they discharged me. 'You're
cured' they said. 'Make a new life for yourself.' And that's
what I've done. New life, new home, new name, new
appearance. *Old* score to settle. When Cousin Emily left me
this house it was the answer to my prayers. I remembered the
caves and knew what I was going to do. I knew because it

was what I'd planned for *her,* as a child, only then it could only be in my imagination.

Sound of frightened breathing from MARGOT.

THELMA. The only problem was getting you up here. I knew where you were living of course. I've always kept tabs on you. But I could hardly roll up and issue an invitation. That's when I decided to cultivate some neighbours of yours.

MARGOT. You mean — ?

THELMA. Oh yes, it wasn't by chance I got to know the Trents. Such tedious people. But they served their purpose didn't they. Very well indeed.

MARGOT (*with incredulity*). You did all that?

THELMA. I'm nothing if not thorough.

Creaking resumes as she starts to move off again.

MARGOT. No! Don't go!

Creaking continues.

MARGOT. Don't leave me here. Not on my own.

THELMA (*tauntingly*) You'll have the rats for company.

MARGOT. Please!

THELMA. And the ghosts of the miners.

MARGOT. I'll do anything. Anything. Just take me back.

Stop boat. Cut creaking.

THELMA. And spoil my plan? As a matter of fact you've got off lightly. I was going to tie you to the boat hook there, but since you can't swim, that won't be necessary will it?

MARGOT. I'll scream. They'll hear.

THELMA. From half a mile down?

MARGOT. Paul will come looking. He'll find the door in the cellar.

THELMA. I very much doubt it. No one has yet. I was afraid that dog of Edgar's might give the game away, but I dealt with him didn't I?

MARGOT. It was you — ?

THELMA. Yes. And then I dumped him in the stream so they wouldn't go searching. I suggested you went that way if you remember. You played right into my hands. Just as Paul did when he agreed to take Edgar out this afternoon.

MARGOT (*faintly*). No.

THELMA. And now I must say goodbye. The lamps should last for a few more hours.

MARGOT (*fearfully*). The lamps?

THELMA. I hope you're not afraid of the dark.

MARGOT. Oh no, no!

Sound as the boat creaks off.

MARGOT. Please! Don't go! Don't leave me!

She starts to scream hysterically. The echoes reverberate all around. Fade.

Fade in. Interior. Reception area. Hall. 'Larksmoor'. Sound as HESTER *and* ENID *come through outer door chatting together.*

EDGAR. Good evening, ladies.

HESTER. Hello, Mr Parsons.

ENID. Good evening.

HESTER. Had a good day?

EDGAR. Mr Sutton and I've been up on Hannah's Tor. Just got back.

HESTER. Lovely. We went over to Bakewell didn't we, Enid? Had lunch at the Rutland Arms.

ENID. Hester and I are great admirers of Jane Austen.

EDGAR (*politely*). Oh ay.

HESTER. She stayed there you know.

ENID. When she was writing *Pride and Prejudice*.

EDGAR. Is that so?

ENID. In fact they say two of the romantic scenes in the novel are actually set in the hotel.

EDGAR. Well I never. I always associate Bakewell with tarts. That is to say —

HESTER. Puddings.

EDGAR. That's right.

HESTER. *They* started life at the Rutland Arms too. Didn't they, Enid? (*As PAUL comes in.*) Oh good evening, Mr Sutton.

ENID. We hear you've had a stenuous afternoon.

PAUL (*joining them*). It was a bit. Have either of you seen my wife around?

ENID. No, but we've only just got back ourselves.

HESTER. From Bakewell. We were just telling Mr Parsons here about the famous puddings.

PAUL (*politely*). Really?

HESTER. How the original recipe was the result of a complete misunderstanding between the then mistress of the Rutland Arms —

ENID. A Mrs Greaves.

HESTER. — and her cook. You see instead of stirring the egg mixture into the pastry —

ENID. — and then filling the tart with jam —

HESTER (*not pleased to be interrupted*). — the cook put the *jam* into the tart —

ENID. — and then poured the egg mixture on to it.

HESTER. Who's telling the story, dear?

ENID (*deflated*). Sorry, Hester.

HESTER (*with a flourish*). Anyway the outcome was so successful the recipe was preserved. And believe it or not, they still use the same formula at the pudding shop today!

No response.

EDGAR (*lamely*). Well. . . you live and learn.

HESTER. Indeed you do. (*Going to stairs.*) Come on then, Enid. We'd better go and change.

EDGAR. Puddings!

PAUL. I wonder where Margot can've got to. Thought she'd be up in our room.

EDGAR. Have you tried the garden?

PAUL. Yes, and the TV room.

THELMA (*approaching*). Hello you two. Are you looking for Margot?

EDGAR. Hello, Thelma.

PAUL. Do you know where she is?

THELMA. Last I saw of her was at teatime. She was off to the village afterwards to post some letters.

PAUL. Ah. Perhaps I'll take a stroll down there. Probably meet her on the way. (*Moving off.*) Be seeing you later.

EDGAR. Ay.

Sound of outer door closing after him.

EDGAR. They're very devoted aren't they?

THELMA. Yes. . .

EDGAR. Refreshing in this age of self-service divorce.

THELMA. How was your walk?

EDGAR. Grand. Reckon I owe you a word of thanks.

THELMA. Me? Why?

EDGAR. Come off it. For getting him to dig me out of my room.

THELMA. I didn't like to see you stuck in doors.

EDGAR. Did me a power of good. You're a kind lass.

THELMA. Hardly a lass.

EDGAR. You can give me a few years. And you're still a handsome woman.

THELMA. Thank you.

EDGAR. I mean it.

THELMA (*turning to go*). I must go and see to the dinner.

EDGAR. No wait. It's not yet six o'clock. I want to talk to you. Happen it's not the best of times but —

Outer door opens as more guests return.

EDGAR 'Evening.

THELMA. Good evening.

EDGAR. Can we go into your sitting room? Fewer interruptions. Please.

THELMA. All right.

Over to sitting room.

THELMA. I can't stay long.

EDGAR. It won't take long.

THELMA. Sit down then.

EDGAR. I'd sooner stand. I suppose if I had any finesse I'd've picked my moment better. But I believe in speaking out while the spirit moves you. (*No reply.*) I'll get to the point then. I've an idea you're as lonely as I am, Thelma. We've both lost people we cared for. And I've been wondering — these last few days — if we couldn't make some sort of life together? I realise we haven't known each other long. . . but long enough for me to know I like what I've seen. I'd go further than that. (*Putting his hand on her arm.*) You're the first woman I've met since Evie died who —

THELMA (*pulling away at his touch, almost spitting out the words, betraying her revulsion*). No! Don't touch me.

Pause.

EDGAR (*shaken by her reaction*). I'm sorry. I didn't mean to — (*He breaks off.*) I hoped you might feel the same way.

THELMA (*with difficulty*). It isn't *you.* I couldn't with anyone. Never again.

Edge out.

Fade in. Interior. Hall. 'Larksmoor'. Sound of THELMA *ringing small gong to summon people to dinner.*

PAUL (*approaching, a note of concern*). Thelma —

THELMA. Hello, Paul. Did you find Margot all right?

PAUL. No. I went all the way down to the village.

THELMA. Perhaps she came back across the fields. It's a nice walk.

PAUL. She'd be here by now surely.

THELMA. Unless she's taken the wrong path. Up by the farm. It's not too well-signposted. That adds on half an hour at least.

PAUL. It's possible I suppose.

THELMA. She wouldn't be the first person to've done it.

(*Turns.*) Good evening. (*Back to* PAUL.) I'll hold your meal till she gets here shall I?

PAUL. Mm? Oh yes please.

THELMA (*moving off*). Would you mind taking the end table tonight, Mr Lumley?

Edge out.

Fade in. Interior. Cavern. Water dripping.

MARGOT (*her voice hoarse from shouting*). Help! Help! Someone help me. Please!

The echoes reverberate as before.

MARGOT (*as if trying to block out the sound*). Stop it! Stop it! Stop it!

Echo picks it up. 'Stop it. Stop it. Stop it.'

MARGOT *falls to her knees sobbing. The echoes die away. Only her deep low sobs. Then, as the last lamp starts to flicker.*

MARGOT. Uh? (*A gasp of horror.*) No! Not the lamp! No, no, please don't let it — (*Her voice peters out as it goes out.*) Oh God. Let someone hear me. Let them come. Don't let me die down here.

Hold on her sobs. Then fade.

Fade in. Dining room. Appropriate sounds in background.

THELMA. Won't you try to eat something, Paul?

PAUL. I couldn't.

THELMA. There's bound to be some simple explanation.

PAUL. That's what I keep telling myself.

THELMA. Perhaps she found a stray lamb. Went to the farm to report it.

PAUL. Then she'd've phoned. More likely she's been taken ill. She's always been delicate, and since this flu bug — (*Breaks off as* EDGAR *approaches.*) Hello, Edgar.

EDGAR. Still no sign of her?

PAUL. No.

EDGAR (*nods embarrassedly to* THELMA). Thelma.

PAUL. I'm afraid she may've been taken ill.

THELMA. She was feeling fine at tea time. She was saying how much better she felt.

PAUL. Had a fall then. If she'd wandered off the road no one would've found her.

EDGAR. I wouldn't look on the black side. She's not been gone that long.

PAUL. Over three hours. Doesn't take three hours to post a letter.

EDGAR. All the same —

PAUL. She could've been attacked. Anything.

EDGAR. Steady on.

PAUL. You read about these things.

EDGAR (*heartily*). I'm sure she'll turn up any minute. Safe and sound.

PAUL (*harshly*). Like your dog did?

Pause.

PAUL. Sorry. I shouldn't've said that.

EDGAR. Forget it.

THELMA. I tell you what. I'll go and ring the farm. See if they've seen anything of her.

EDGAR. Good idea. And if not we'll get up a bit of a search party. Go and look for her.

Edge out.

Fade in. Cavern. Just the monotonous drip of water and the sound of MARGOT's *tremulous breathing. Then we hear gradually the sound of the boat making its way through the water. Creaking its way nearer. The splash of the paddle.*

MARGOT. Who's that? Is someone there? (*With false optimism.*) Paul? Is that you? Paul? Paul?

The echoes fade away. Suddenly out of the dark comes the sound of the music box.

MARGOT (*catches her breath, then after a moment*). Thelma? Thelma, for Christ's sake, answer me. I know you're there.

THELMA *laughs a sinister little laugh quite near the platform of the cavern.*

MARGOT (*glad to have anyone there*). You've come back.

THELMA. Yes I've come back.

MARGOT. Thank God.

THELMA. All in the dark now are you? I thought I'd play you some music.

Peak music.

THELMA. Our music. His and mine. That's what he used to say.

Cut music as she shuts the box sharply.

MARGOT. I knew you couldn't mean it.

THELMA. What?

MARGOT. You wouldn't really leave me here. I knew it. I knew it.

THELMA. Then I'm afraid you were mistaken.

MARGOT. No.

THELMA. I merely came back to find out how you were.

MARGOT. Oh no. . . no.

THELMA. Let me get my torch so I can see.

Sound of her switching on torch.

MARGOT *lets out a little cry as the light blinds her momentarily.*

THELMA. Oh dear. I don't suppose Paul would find you so desirable now.

MARGOT. Please — take me back —

THELMA. But then *he's* not looking his best either. He didn't sleep at all last night you see. And he won't sleep tonight. Or tomorrow. Or the one after.

MARGOT *moans.*

THELMA. And *I* know how that feels. To lie awake endlessly. To close your eyes and see only the one face.

MARGOT *continues to moan softly.*

THELMA. Your disappearance has caused quite a stir up there you know. Edgar Parsons got up a search party last night. Quite the boy scout Edgar. (*Abstractedly to herself rather than* MARGOT.) He asked me to marry him. He thought he

was asking a woman, not an empty shell. Where was I? Oh
yes, the search party. It was really most amusing. Sending
them on false trails. Raising their hopes only to dash them.
Then we went back to 'Larksmoor', and I suggested ringing
round the hospitals. In case you'd been knocked down by a
car. I couldn't have been more helpful or concerned. I even
contacted the police for him this morning, and plied the
numbskull of a sergeant with coffee and red-herrings. I suppose
before long they'll be combing the peaks. What a silly waste
of the taxpayers' money.

MARGOT (*clutching at straws*). They'll find the other entrance
by the Tor.

THELMA. What if they do? It's all blocked over. No way in. They
won't connect it with your disappearance. Not at first
anyway. And later on, even if they were to look further, it'd
be too late wouldn't it? I give you a week in these conditions.

MARGOT. They'll search the house.

THELMA. Why should they do that?

MARGOT. They're bound to. They'll find the door in the cellar.

THELMA. But they think you were on your way to the village
when you disappeared. There's no reason to search the place.

MARGOT. Paul won't give up. He'll go on looking.

THELMA. Yes, and I shall be at his side to help him.

MARGOT. You'll give yourself away somehow. He may even
recognise you.

THELMA (*beat*). In that case I should have to kill him too.

MARGOT (*fearfully*). Oh no.

THELMA. It would be quite simple. A little climb up on the Tor.
I'd pretend I was taking him to you. In his state of mind it
wouldn't be surprising if he walked a little too near the edge.
They'd put it down to accidental death. Or suicide while the
balance of his mind was disturbed.

MARGOT (*pleading*). Listen Thelma — please — I understand
how you feel about Paul and me —

THELMA. Good.

MARGOT. But what'll you achieve by all this?

THELMA. Everything.

MARGOT. Will you? You let me die down here. You cause
Paul to crack up. Or worse. But it won't really alter anything
will it?

THELMA. It'll even the score a little.

MARGOT. They'll catch you in the end. You'll be imprisoned
for life.

THELMA. I already am. I must go now.

Creaking of boat starts again.

MARGOT (*a plan forming in her mind*). Wait — please wait —

THELMA. You won't make me change my mind.

MARGOT. At least — light the lamps again — it's worse in the
dark. If you could just light the one up here.

THELMA. You don't catch me that way.

MARGOT. The torch then. Leave me the torch. Anything.

THELMA (*taunting her*). Shall I, shan't I? Shall I, shan't I?

MARGOT. Please, Thelma —

THELMA. The name is Ann.

MARGOT. Ann!

THELMA. No. I don't think I will.

MARGOT. Please!

THELMA. Why should I make it easier for you?

MARGOT. I beg you.

THELMA. On the other hand it's customary to offer the
condemned person a last wish isn't it?

MARGOT. Just the torch. That's all I ask.

THELMA. Very well then. 'Ann the Magnanimous'. (*She laughs.*)
Here. (*Reaching out.*) Take it.

MARGOT (*as if reaching*). I can't reach.

THELMA. I'm not coming any closer.

Vocalised grunts from MARGOT *as she stretches further.*

THELMA. Got it?

MARGOT (*grabbing it and simultaneously making a jump for the
boat*). Yes I have!

THELMA. Oh no you don't — you little —

General commotion as they struggle together. Cries and groans. Creaking of boat as it rocks furiously.

THELMA (*at last*). Got you. (*As she gets her in grip.*) So you — thought you'd — trick me — did you?

MARGOT. Let go!

THELMA. Oh yes, I'll let you go. Over the side.

Splash and a scream from MARGOT *as* THELMA *pushes her over.*

MARGOT (*floundering in the water*). Help me — help me — I can't — I can't —

THELMA. You should've thought about that before.

A groan of effort from MARGOT *as she tries to grab the side of the boat.*

THELMA. Oh no you don't. (*She takes hold of the paddle and knocks her away with it.*) Get away. Take that. And that.

MARGOT *emits cries of pain as she is forced to let go.*

THELMA. That's better.

Gasps from MARGOT *as she flounders about in water.*

THELMA. You stupid bitch. Thought you'd get the better of me did you?

MARGOT *gulps as she takes a mouthful of water.*

THELMA. Well now you're worse off than before. You've two alternatives haven't you? Either stay there and drown among the rats.

A terrified gasp from MARGOT.

THELMA. Or climb back on the ledge and die of pneumonia. It's all one to me.

She starts to laugh uncannily as she moves the boat off. Fade on laughter.

Fade in. Interior. Near cellar door. 'Larksmoor'. Sound as the door creaks open.

EDGAR (*his attitude to* THELMA *is slightly restrained but he wants to make amends*). Been down below?

THELMA (*jumps*). Wha — Oh, Edgar. Hello. Yes. (*Quick improvisation*.) Had some trouble with the water tank.

EDGAR. You look a bit damp. Anything I can do?

THELMA. No. It's fixed now. Thank you all the same. (*Beat*.) You're wondering why I've got my music box. Took it down with me absent-mindedly. Must be senile decay.

Sound of her bolting door.

EDGAR. Thelma?

THELMA. Yes?

EDGAR. About yesterday — you know — what happened between us.

THELMA. I'd sooner forget it.

EDGAR. I've always been a bit ham-fisted.

THELMA. I over-reacted.

EDGAR. I shouldn't've sprung it on you like that. As I say you Southerners need longer to — Well anyway — (*Breaks off.*) So long as we're friends again.

THELMA. Of course. I must go and change out of these wet things. Or did you want something else?

EDGAR. I was looking for Paul. Thought he might be glad of some company.

THELMA. He went up to his room after lunch. I gave him a sleeping pill. I don't suppose it'll have done much good though.

EDGAR. No. Poor fellow. What d'you think's happened to her?

THELMA. One hears of cases of amnesia.

EDGAR. Out of the blue like that?

THELMA. We must try to be optimistic.

EDGAR. Ay.

THELMA. She may turn up in Chesterfield or somewhere.

EDGAR. I hope to God you're right. Because if anything's happened to that lass, I don't know what it'll do to Paul.

Edge out.

Fade in. Interior. PAUL's *bedroom.*

PAUL (*in a bad state now*). If only there was something I could do.

EDGAR. Ay.

PAUL. It's just sitting here waiting.

EDGAR. I'm sure the police'll have some news soon.

PAUL (*disparagingly*). The police! I don't even know if they're taking it seriously. Do you know what he asked me this morning, that Sergeant? He asked me if we were happily married. If we'd had any rows lately. I know what he was getting at.

EDGAR. They have to do their job, Paul.

PAUL. And while they're writing if off as some domestic tiff, what's happening to Margot?

EDGAR. Anyone could see how close you were. I'm sure they'll have questioned Thelma and she'll have told them that.

PAUL (*cuts in*). Why do you say 'Were'?

EDGAR. I didn't mean anything.

PAUL. You think something's happened to her too don't you?

EDGAR. Of course I don't. Nothing like what you're implying.

PAUL. Then where *is* she for Christ's sake?

Clean cut.

Fade in. Interior. Cavern. As before. The water drips. We hear MARGOT's *breath coming in sharp, painful gulps and her teeth chattering. She is now suffering from pneumonia and is in a state of near-delirium. The following 'Nightmare' sequence is a jumble of fact and fantasy to which the music box theme forms a background.*

MARGOT (*mutters, in her delirium*). Paul — Paul — don't leave me — please — Oh Paul.

In her mind she hears again the following sequence.

MARGOT. Oh Paul.

PAUL. I want you.

MARGOT. Again?

PAUL. Again and again and again. How can it be so good still?

MARGOT. I know.

PAUL. I've never stopped fancying you from the moment I first saw you. Or loving you.

Then THELMA's *voice cuts in harshly and tauntingly.*

THELMA. I don't suppose Paul would find you so desirable now.

MARGOT *lets out a little cry as if trying to block out* THELMA's *voice.*

THELMA (*persistently*). All I've wanted these last eighteen years is my revenge. And now I'm going to have it. I shall see you suffer as I've suffered.

MARGOT *lets out another little cry.*

MARGOT (*in her delirium*). No, no. . . Paul. . . (*We hear her teeth chattering as she shivers, then her thoughts drift to her children.*) Andrew — Andrew — Martin — Where are you? Come to Mummy. (*Then in her mind she hears again*).

THELMA. 'To Paul and Margot Sutton, a son. Andrew Philip.' That was the first time I took an overdose.

MARGOT. Because of Andrew?

THELMA. Because he should've been *mine!*

The words 'Mine, mine, mine' continue to reverberate all around and the echo picks them up in her imagination.

MARGOT (*in delirium*). No — no — don't let her take them away.

For a moment there is silence as the echo fades away. Only the dripping of water. Then in MARGOT's *imagination she hears a rumbling in the distance as if of falling rock and men's muffled voices calling for help.*

MARGOT (*in delirium*). Who's that? — who's calling? — Who is it?

THELMA (*as if answering*). Sometimes I picture them. Clawing their way through the debris. Their nails torn and bleeding. Crying for help until their lungs are bursting.

Peak the cries of the miners.

MARGOT (*in delirium, crying out with them*). Let me out — let me out.

THELMA. But no one hears them. And in the end they have to give up. Just lie there and wait to die, slowly.

Peak the mens' screams. Then gradually they become the squeaking of rats as in MARGOT's *imagination they clamber up out of the water and on to the ledge. Peak scratching sound as they claw their way up.*

MARGOT (*half conscious, makes terrified noises as she tries to brush the rats aside*). No — no — get away from me.

THELMA (*tauntingly*). You'll have the rats for company. The rats for company. The rats for company.

MARGOT (*moans petrified*). Get away! Get away!

THELMA *starts to laugh. At first a low sinister laugh which grows into an all-encompassing almost maniacal one that reverberates all around. Clean cut.*

Silence for a moment. Then fade in. Interior. Dining room. Sound of spoon on plate as EDGAR *finishes sweet.*

NANCY. Will you be wanting coffee, Mr Parsons?

EDGAR. Mm? What was that, Nancy?

NANCY. Cup of coffee after your sweet?

EDGAR. No thank you. Sorry. Are you waiting to clear?

NANCY. No hurry. I'll go and get Mr Sutton's tray first.

EDGAR. He had lunch up in his room did he?

NANCY. Mrs Weadon told me to take him some up. Not that he'll touch it. No more than he did his breakfast.

EDGAR. It's hardly surprising.

NANCY. No poor man. They say the police are up there today, scouring the hills.

EDGAR. Yes I heard.

NANCY. It don't bear thinking of. My mum won't let me walk up here on my own no more. Not until it's known what happened. She says if there is some maniac round these parts. . .

EDGAR. I don't suppose there is for a minute. It's probably all a storm in a teacup.

NANCY. That's what my brother says. He reckons she's gone off with another fellow. But she weren't like that were she?

EDGAR. I wouldn't have said so.

NANCY. They were real loving. That's why I was surprised when he went off without her that afternoon.

EDGAR. He was out walking with me. She wanted to take it easy.

NANCY. Oh was that it?

EDGAR. Did you see her after tea that day, Nancy?

NANCY. Me?

EDGAR. After you'd served tea, did you see her before she went out?

NANCY. Oh I weren't there that afternoon.

EDGAR. No? I thought *Wednesday* was your afternoon off.

NANCY. Mrs Weadon give me Monday too. Didn't even ask for it. My brother's home on leave see.

EDGAR. Ah.

NANCY. There wasn't no one else for tea but Mrs Sutton, and Mrs Weadon said she'd see to her.

EDGAR. I see.

NANCY. Nice of her wasn't it?

EDGAR. Mm.

Slight pause.

NANCY. She's ever so cut up about it herself.

EDGAR. What?

NANCY. Mrs Weadon. I can tell she is. Her mind's somewhere else all the time. Well she would be upset wouldn't she?

EDGAR. It's not a very pleasant thing to have happened at your guesthouse.

NANCY. And them being special friends of hers. I reckon she's wishing she hadn't put those other folks off now.

EDGAR. What was that?

NANCY. She cancelled this other booking so the Suttons could have the room.

EDGAR. Did she?

NANCY. The moment he rang up. Even though it were last minute.

EDGAR. I thought they only knew each other slightly. Through a mutual acquaintance.

NANCY. Then how come she put off someone else on their account? No, the Suttons are special so far as she's concerned. She said so.

Edge out.

Fade in. Interior. Sitting room. 'Larksmoor'.

ENID (*stifles a yawn*). Oh, I beg your pardon.

HESTER. I'm the same. I'll finish my chapter and then I'm off to bed.

ENID. Me too.

HESTER. Don't know when I felt so exhausted. Must be all that footwork.

EDGAR (*off slightly*). Where did you ladies go today?

HESTER. Into Sheffield. We were going to have a quiet day here. But we decided to go further afield.

ENID. To take out minds off poor Mrs Sutton.

EDGAR. Hm.

HESTER. No more news I gather?

EDGAR. I'm afraid not.

HESTER. I still say she'll turn up safe and sound. The way Agatha Christie did that time.

ENID. And Trixie Fancroft.

HESTER. Who, dear?

ENID. You remember. That part-time art teacher we had. She was always doodling coat-of-arms all over the staff room.

HESTER. Oh yes. (*To* EDGAR.) She disappeared one half term.

EDGAR. Really?

ENID. Turned up a week later in Windsor Great Park.

HESTER. Delusions of grandeur, poor girl.

ENID. And she couldn't remember a thing that happened in between. I can't help thinking that's what's happened to — (*She breaks off as she sees photo.*) — to Mrs Sutton.

HESTER. What's the matter, Enid?

ENID. Nothing. Just this photograph. Tumbled out of my book. The one I borrowed from Mrs Weadon.

HESTER. Of her is it?

ENID. No. Some young couple. It must've been taken a while back.

HESTER. Let's see.

ENID. Isn't that the New Look the girl's wearing?

HESTER. Mm. That was back in the fifties. What *did* we look like!

ENID. And see the young man's short back and sides.

HESTER. Probably been in the army. Pity they bon't bring back conscription.

ENID. Does he remind you of anyone, Hester?

HESTER. I don't think so.

ENID. He does me.

HESTER. Not young Mr Crow in the Science Department. It's his chin.

ENID. No. It's something about the eyes. I know. He's not unlike poor Mr Sutton. A younger version of course.

HESTER. I see what you mean.

EDGAR (*joining them*). May I look.

HESTER. There is a similarity.

EDGAR (*taking photo*). Thank you.

HESTER. What do you think, Mr Parsons?

EDGAR. Mm?

HESTER. Don't you think he's a bit like Mr Sutton?

EDGAR. I'm sorry. I was looking at the girl. . .

   Edge out.

Fade in. Interior. Hall. 'Larksmoor'. Sound of grandfather clock striking two. Then clock ticks away monotonously. After a while a door opens off upstairs. Footsteps on stairs as someone descends. Creak of a board, then a door opens off hall.

THELMA (*as if from sitting room door*). Who's that? Is someone there?

PAUL. Oh Thelma. You're up too.

THELMA. It's you, Paul.

PAUL (*He sounds absolutely worn out and is close to cracking point*) I came down to look for some cigarettes.

THELMA. Come into the sitting room, have one of mine.

Over to sitting room.

THELMA. Sit down.

PAUL. Thank you. (*Does so.*)

THELMA (*approaching with cigarettes*). Here we are. Help yourself. It's all right. I'll light it for you.

Sound of her doing so. He takes a long drag.

PAUL. And to think I'd given up smoking.

THELMA (*after a moment*). Couldn't you sleep either?

PAUL. I sometimes wonder if I'll ever sleep again.

THELMA (*with sympathy*). You must or you'll make yourself ill.

PAUL. If I shut my eyes I only see — her face — and imagine — (*His voice cracks as he breaks down.*) Oh God. (*He tries to control himself.*)

THELMA. No, let it out. Don't worry about me.

PAUL. If anything's happened to her. . . There's never been anyone else but Margot.

THELMA (*beat*). No one?

PAUL. No one that mattered. I was engaged to another girl before I met her, but that was nothing. I realised it as soon as I saw Margot. You don't know what it's like to love someone that much.

THELMA (*to herself rather than him*). No?

PAUL. I couldn't go on living without her.

THELMA. That's no way to talk.

PAUL. It's true. Without her I might just as well be dead. I'm sorry.

THELMA. I wish there was something I could do.

PAUL. There's nothing anyone can do.

THELMA. If only I'd never invited you up here.

PAUL. You weren't to know this'd happen. Whatever *has* happened. I wish to God the police'd — (*He breaks off.*) I think I'd rather hear something positive than go on like this.

THELMA. It must be dreadful for you.

PAUL (*drags on cigarette*). There's the boys too. And her parents. I haven't been in touch with them yet. I keep hoping.. . But I'll have to do something soon. They're due back next week. (*Gets up and starts pacing.*)

THELMA. I wouldn't worry about that yet.

PAUL *continuing over*). And how can I leave her until I know something definite? I couldn't go back to Wimbledon without her.

THELMA. You're welcome to stay here as long as you need.

PAUL. You'll be wanting the room.

THELMA. I can put someone off. You're my first concern. You need an ashtray.

PAUL. Oh — yes.

THELMA. There's one on the shelf there.

PAUL (*moves off*). It's all right. I'll get it.

THELMA (*continues*). If you'd like to bring the boys up here too when they get back. That is if things haven't resolved themselves — (*She breaks off as she sees him pick up the musical box.*) Let me take that.

PAUL. Is it a musical box?

THELMA. Yes. It shouldn't be on there. (*Moves to him.*)

PAUL. I once bought one like this. As a present for someone.

THELMA. Really? I expect there are heaps around. May I —

PAUL (*hanging on to it*). This is the first time I've seen one like it. The carving on top's the same too.

THELMA. May I have it please? I —

PAUL (*cutting in*). What tune does it play?

THELMA (*trying to take it from him*). It doesn't any more It's bro — (*She breaks off with a little cry as it slips from her hands.*)

PAUL. Careful!

A crash as it falls to the floor and opens, scattering contents. A second's pause. Then the sinister little tune starts to play. Silence except for the music.

PAUL (*eventually as music ends*). You're Ann Milner. . .

THELMA. I don't know what you're talking about.

PAUL (*kneeling to retrieve trinkets*). Then what are these? This ring and the letters.

THELMA. Nothing. Give them to me.

PAUL. It's my handwriting.

THELMA. Of course it isn't.

PAUL. Then let me see.

THELMA. No! They're private. They were from my husband.

But he wrenches them from her.

PAUL. And was *his* name Paul?

Pause.

THELMA. All right, I am Ann Milner. I've changed haven't I? You didn't even recognise me. That's what eighteen years of suffering does for you. People take me for fifty or more. Not the same age as your precious Margot.

PAUL (*with mounting horror, as things fall into place*). You know what's happened to her don't you?

THELMA (*continues on her own tack*). But then she's been spoilt and cossetted all these years.

PAUL. You planned all this.

THELMA. She's had all the love and care *I* should've had.

PAUL. You know where she is. (*Desperately*.) What've you done with her?

THELMA. Wouldn't you like to know?

PAUL. Just tell me she's safe, that's all I ask.

THELMA. What right have you to ask anything of *me*?

PAUL. I know I treated you badly, but I never thought for one moment —

THELMA. No you didn't, did you? You never thought about me. You just flung me aside like a cast-off glove.

PAUL (*pleading*). Where is she? Please, Ann, tell me.

THELMA. No!

PAUL. Tell me. I'll do anything if you'll tell me.

THELMA. There's nothing you can do for me now.

PAUL (*grovelling*). Please, Ann, please.

THELMA. Grovel as much as you like but it won't get you anywhere. You didn't take any notice of *my* pleas did you? You didn't answer my letters, you wouldn't speak to me on the phone.

PAUL (*aggressive now*). If you don't tell, so help me I'll —

THELMA. What?

PAUL. I'll —

THELMA. Nothing you can do can hurt me more than I've already been hurt.

PAUL (*shaking her*). Tell me, tell me or I'll kill you.

THELMA. Kill me then!

EDGAR (*who has come in unnoticed, topping them with authority*). No, Paul. Let her be.

PAUL (*spins round*). Edgar!

THELMA. You!

EDGAR (*to* PAUL, *with urgency*). I think I know where Margot is.

PAUL. Where for Christ's sake?

EDGAR. Though whether she's dead or alive remains to be seen.

PAUL. *Where?*

THELMA (*a last desperate plea before her mind cracks*). No! Don't tell him.

EDGAR (*gently*). I've got to Thelma. There's a door in the cellar leads to an old mineshaft.

THELMA *lets out a cry of anguish almost like an animal.*

EDGAR. It's filled with water but there's a boat there, been used recently.

PAUL. Oh my God.

EDGAR. One or two things made me suspicious. I came down tonight to investigate. Then I heard your voices.

PAUL. Quick — show me the way.

EDGAR. We'll need a lamp.

THELMA (*reverting to girlhood*). No, no, don't leave me, Paul.

PAUL (*throwing her aside*). Get away you —

EDGAR (*cuts in*). Easy with her. She can't help herself.

THELMA (*still pleading*). Don't go to *her.* Stay with me. Please Paul.

EDGAR. Come on.

They go out. The door closed behind them.

THELMA. You can't leave me. Not now. We're going to get married next month. I've got the dress and everything. It's such a beautiful dress too. When you see me in it, then you'll want me, not her. (*Beat.*) Paul? (*Pathetically.*) Don't leave me, Paul.

Edge out.

Fade in. Interior. Caves. Boat creaks along.

PAUL (*calls*). Margot! Margot! Margot!

Echo picks it up.

PAUL (*as echo dies away*). Can you hear anything?

EDGAR. Only that confounded echo.

PAUL. If she's alive she'd've heard me by now surely. Shouted back.

EDGAR. Depends on the state she's in.

PAUL. Or if she's drowned her. Oh my God, what sort of twisted mind would —

EDGAR. Looks like it's widening out now. Hold the lamp up higher. Sort of cave by the look of it.

PAUL (*calls*). Margot? Margot, are you there?

More echo.

EDGAR. Keep the lamp still. Ay, there's a ledge where you can tie up.

PAUL. Margot! It's me, Paul! Margot! — Ssh, what was that?

The echo fades. Silence. Only the water dripping.

EDGAR. Try again.

PAUL. Margot?

Echo.

EDGAR. Wait a minute. There's something over there.

PAUL. Where?

EDGAR. On the ground. By that kind of archway. Move the lamp round. That's it. There.

PAUL. It's her. It's Margot.

EDGAR. Easy. I'll get the boat alongside.

PAUL (*calls*) Margot?

EDGAR. Reach out for the edge.

PAUL. Margot, we're here!

EDGAR. Right. I'll hold the lamp while you get out.

PAUL (*as he goes out*). Oh God, let her be alive.

EDGAR. Here. Take it. I'll tie the boat up.

Over to ledge.

PAUL. Margot? Margot? It's me, Paul. Talk to me. Tell me you're alive. I love you, Margot.

MARGOT (*a faint whisper*). Paul —

PAUL. Oh thank God, thank God.

Edge out.

Fade in. Interior. ENID *and* HESTER's *room.*

ENID (*shaking* HESTER). Hester, Hester, wake up.

HESTER (*waking*). Oh — Enid, has the alarm gone?

ENID. No, it's only 3.00 a.m.

HESTER. Then what're you doing up? Aren't you well?

ENID. Yes but something strange just happened. I don't know what to make of it. I woke up and wanted to go to the bathroom. I was just crossing the landing when I saw Mrs Weadon. Only she wasn't like Mrs Weadon.

HESTER. What on earth do you mean?

ENID. She had this odd expression on her face. I said hello but she looked straight through me. Just went on down the stairs and then out the front door.

HESTER. Outside at this hour of the morning?

ENID. Yes.

HESTER. You've been dreaming, dear. It was that macaroni cheese last night.

ENID. No. And there was something else too. To begin with I thought she was wearing a nightgown, but when I got closer I saw it wasn't a nightie at all. It was a wedding dress.

Fade out.

Fade in. Interior. Room in hospital.

PAUL. Margot?

MARGOT (*weak*). Mm?

PAUL. It's me. Paul. Hello, sweetheart.

MARGOT. Where am I?

PAUL. In hospital. In Sheffield. You've had a pretty rough time, but you're going to be all right.

MARGOT. It was true then. It wasn't a nightmare.

PAUL. No. It was true.

MARGOT (*quietly*). Oh my God. . .

PAUL. My poor little love, what you must've gone through.

MARGOT (*not responding to him*). What has happened to — to her?

PAUL. We're not sure. She disappeared the night we found you. Hasn't been seen since. The police are looking for her.

MARGOT. What will they do when they find her?

PAUL. Put her away somewhere I hope. For her own sake as well as ours. She's quite mad.

MARGOT (*introspectively*). And *we* made her so.

The phone rings by the bed.

PAUL (*picking it up*). Hello. Yes, that's right. Oh thank you. Put him through. (*To* MARGOT.) It's Edgar.

MARGOT (*vaguely, still preoccupied*). Who?

PAUL. Edgar Parsons.

MARGOT. Oh yes.

PAUL. It was he who discovered where you were. (*On phone.*) Hello, Edgar. She's going to be fine now, aren't you, my love? (*Change of tone.*) What? I see. Yes I suppose so. Well thank you for letting me know. We'll be seeing you, Edgar.

He hangs up.

PAUL. They've found her.

MARGOT. Where?

PAUL. Dead. At the bottom of Hannah's Tor.

MARGOT (*slowly*). You mean she — she threw herself off.

PAUL. That's what they think. Like the girl in the legend.

MARGOT (*distantly*). Poor Ann. . .

PAUL. It's probably for the best.

MARGOT. Best for whom?

PAUL. For her. And for us. We can forget her now.

MARGOT (*appalled*). Forget her?

PAUL (*lovingly reassuring*). In time you will I promise. When you're back at home with the boys and everything —

MARGOT (*cuts in*). No.

PAUL. Darling.

MARGOT. Don't you understand, we killed her?

PAUL (*going to take her in his arms*). Come here let me hold y —

MARGOT (*pulling away with revulsion*). Stop it.

PAUL. What?

MARGOR (*same tone as* THELMA *used to* EDGAR *earlier*). Don't touch me.

PAUL. But —

MARGOT. I said don't. I don't want you near me.

PAUL. Margot.

MARGOT (*slowly*). You may be able to shrug her off as you did before. But I shan't forget her this time. Not as long as I live.

Bring in the music box theme under as though THELMA *is still manipulating them from beyond the grave.*

Credits.

Fade.

AFTERNOON THEATRE

POLARIS

by Fay Weldon

Polaris was first broadcast on BBC Radio 4 on 16th June 1978.
The cast was as follows:

CAPTAIN	Frederick Treves
MEG	Anna Calder-Marshall
TIMMY	Geoffrey Beevers
JIM	Mark Wing-Davey
ZELDA	June Barrie
TONY	Simon Callow
NURSE (MOTHER/POLLY/ background murmurs)	Jennifer Piercey
MILKMAN/DOCTOR	Robert Trotter
POSTMAN/ENGINE ROOM	Andrew McCulloch
FARMER	Ken Drury

Producer: Shaun MacLoughlin

Fay Weldon was born in Worcestershire, brought up in New
Zealand, educated at St Andrew's University, is married with
four children and lives in Somerset. She has written half a
dozen novels — among them *Down Among the Women, Female
Friends* and *Remember Me*, all of which went into paperback —
several stage and radio plays — of which *Spider* won the Writers'
Guild Award for the Best Radio Play of 1973 — and upwards of
twenty plays for television. Among these are *The Visiting Hour,
Office Party* and *The Tale of Timothy Bagshot*, as well as a
six-part adaptation of *Pride and Prejudice* for BBC-TV and
contributions to series such as *Six Women* and *Upstairs
Downstairs*.

We are in the control room of a Polaris submarine, in dock, on the surface. The CAPTAIN *and* JIM, *the First Lieutenant, are completing a daily-user check, and exchanging a murmured conversation over assorted whirrs, clicks and the sound of Radio 1: 'Rudolph the red-nosed reindeer'. The Captain is a suave and easy fellow: rather too much so for his First Lieutenant.*

CAPTAIN. Hydroplane system. One-man-control?

JIM. A OK sir —

CAPTAIN. Plotting tables?

JIM. All complete, sir —

CAPTAIN. Sounder?

JIM. Hold on, sir —

Silence. Then ping-ping-ping from the echo sounder.

JIM. A OK sir.

That seems to be that. The play proper, as it were, begins.

CAPTAIN. Anything else on the radio, Number One?

JIM. It will all be Christmas, sir, up and down the dial. (*But he changes the programme.*)

CAPTAIN. We are not immune to Christmas, Mr First Lieutenant. 'He shall have dominion also from sea to sea, and from the rivers unto the ends of the earth.'

JIM. I just meant, sir, Christmas starts so early these days.

Radio 4: 'Deck the halls with fern and holly, 'Tis the season to be jolly.'

CAPTAIN. You should remember that, Mr First Lieutenant. 'Tis the season to be jolly.'

JIM. Yes, sir. But it's only December 10th.

CAPTAIN. Daily-user check complete, then, Number One?

JIM. That's right, sir.

CAPTAIN. Everyone on board? We could do the fast cruise early.

JIM. All but one, sir.

CAPTAIN. And who's that?

JIM. The navigator, sir. He rang. He's on his way.

CAPTAIN. He'd better be, hadn't he? I detected a squeak on the periscope.

JIM. You did, sir.

CAPTAIN. Turn through eight-five degrees. Wait, I'll do it. What's the matter with Mr Navigator? Young Timmy's usually first in, not last.

JIM. He's just got married, sir.

CAPTAIN. Ah. What's she like?

JIM. Small, sir. Friend of my wife. Young, sir.

CAPTAIN. But sensible?

JIM. Have to be, won't she, sir?

The CAPTAIN *cries out.*

JIM. What's the matter, sir?

CAPTAIN. The sun's rising over the loch. It dazzled me, that's all. 'Ah, the Lord reigneth: let the people tremble: let the earth be moved.'

JIM. No squeak, sir?

CAPTAIN. No squeak.

JIM. Cold as cold out there, sir. Snug as a bug in here.

CAPTAIN. Snug as a bug. User check complete. Down periscope. Goodbye, God's eye. See you in three months. Take care. Small you said, and learning to be sensible. Ah!

Radio 4: 'Deck the halls with fern and holly'.

CAPTAIN. She won't be lonely?

JIM. They have a dog.

Cut to: THOMPSON, *the dog, half springer, half Alsation, which makes him amiable and enormous, slurps and grunts over the sleeping* MEG's *face. The bedroom is a bare place, sparsely furnished, as yet without carpets. The bedside radio is tuned to Radio 4 and continues from previous scene in the new acoustic. Radio 4: 'Tis the season to be jolly'.*

THOMPSON. Phloph.

MEG. Go away, Thompson: get off this bed. You're not allowed on the bed. Get off! Timmy, get him off. Timmy, get him off. Timmy? Oh Timmy, you're gone. I forgot. Three months. Oh Thompson, you stupid dog, what will I do? Sleep. ' 'Tis the season to be jolly.' Thompson get your great paws off of me. And stop licking my face.

The bedside telephone rings. MEG *answers it.*

TIMMY (*slight distort*). Meg.

MEG. Timmy, where are you?

TIMMY (*slight distort*). What are you doing?

MEG. Fighting with Thompson.

TIMMY (*slight distort*). Aren't you up, yet? I've been up for ever. Look after yourself. I wish we'd got the carpets down before I left.

MEG. We spent too much time in bed.

TIMMY (*slight distort*). Think of me on Christmas Day, at eleven thirty. I must go.

MEG. Where are you?

TIMMY (*slight distort*). Shouldn't say. But I'm not on board yet. I've been hanging around waiting for this telephone. Meg, perhaps I should get a shore job.

MEG. It's only three months. I can just think of you for that long, and survive. The sun's rising over the hill. There's a line of dazzle beneath the blind — wait a moment — (*She pulls the blind. It rattles open.*)

TIMMY (*slight distort*). You're not wearing your nightie, are you. I can see you in my mind. I can feel you in my mind.

MEG. It's a wonderful morning. Frost on the hills so you can't tell a sheep from the grass, and brilliant sun, and shiny loch. Why does it have to be today you go? All the other days it's been raining. What's it like where you are?

TIMMY (*slight distort*). Grey wharf, shiny wet, bright sea. Enough said.

MEG. I suppose it's dark at the bottom of the sea.

TIMMY (*slight distort*). I don't get to look out, Meg. Submarines don't have windows.

MEG. No? I thought of it somehow as Nautilus, and you as Captain Nemo, and the fishes swimming past the windows. You mean there's nothing to see but plastic and steel?

TIMMY (*slight distort*). And the faces of men. I've got to go. Don't forget to order the wood. Don't miss any more driving lessons. And keep the deep freeze full in case you get snowed up.

MEG. Snowed up?

TIMMY (*slight distort*). Well, you might.

MEG. Don't be silly. It wouldn't do that to me. Don't eat too much and get fat.

TIMMY (*slight distort*). There's nothing else to do, but eat.

MEG. And think of me.

TIMMY (*slight distort*). True. I'd better go. (*More slurping from* THOMPSON.) I don't want to be last on board.

MEG. Thompson, get out! Why are there no peep-peeps?

TIMMY (*slight distort*). I put in five ten pees, that's why.

MEG. You are extravagant. Thompson wants to talk, I think.

TIMMY (*slight distort*). I don't want to talk to him, tell him. I love you. Go back to sleep. Oh hell. Goodbye.

MEG. I'm not supposed to ask when you're actually leaving.

TIMMY (*slight distort*). No. But we'll lie about on the bottom of the loch for a while, in any case.

MEG. What a funny way to live. It doesn't seem natural.

TIMMY (*slight distort*). It would be to a fish.

MEG. Yes. But you're a man.

TIMMY (*slight distort*). Goodbye.

MEG. Goodbye.

TIMMY (*slight distort*). See you in three months.

MEG. See you in three months.

> TIMMY *puts down his receiver.* MEG *puts down hers. She turns up the radio and sings along, snivelling. The front door bell goes,* THOMPSON *barks.*

MEG. Oh hell. Where's my dressing-gown. Do shut up dog. I haven't got any slippers. Where are they? The floor's cold. Oh, the Aga's gone out.

> MEG *goes downstairs and opens the door.* THOMPSON *goes first. Distant bleating of sheep and other Scottish hill noises where they can be heard between dog barking.*

MEG. Quiet, you idiot dog. Don't worry, he won't bite.

POSTMAN. He'd better not, or you won't be getting your letters any more. Recorded delivery: sign here. You ought to keep that door properly latched. There's prowlers about. A young woman like yourself, your husband off —

MEG. How do you know he's off?

POSTMAN. First crew are back, that's why. He's second crew, isn't he? So he's off.

MEG. It's supposed to be secret.

POSTMAN. We're all friends up here. Don't fuss yourself. It's a bill, is it?

MEG. I don't know. It's for Timmy.

POSTMAN. You'll have to open it, lassie.

MEG. But it's for my husband.

POSTMAN. You're married to a sailor, now, You'll catch your death without your shoes.

MEG. I couldn't find them. Do you want some coffee?

POSTMAN. I won't wait. I've got to collect from the Base. The minute the husbands go, the wives start writing. I'll come up every day, though, to see how you are, letters or no. You're too isolated up here. You'd have done better to have chosen nearer the Base, with the others. But that's your affair. (*He goes.*)

MEG. I didn't want to be near the others. I wanted us all alone, just the two of us. Oh Timmy.
'God rest you, merry gentleman,
Let nothing you dismay.'

(THOMPSON *joins in, howling.*) Be quiet, Thompson, you stupid dumb dog. If you could talk there'd be some point to you.

Slight edge out. Down in the Polaris: ping-ping-ping.

CAPTAIN. 'God rest us, merry gentlemen,
            Let nothing you dismay' —
Glad to see you, Timmy, Now perhaps we can get on with the fast cruise.

TIMMY. Morning, sir. I was last aboard. That's never happened before.

CAPTAIN. You've never been married before.
            'Remember Christ our Saviour
            Was born on Christmas day' —
Mr First Lieutenant, Jim, have you checked the turkeys are on board?

JIM. Yes, sir. A OK sir. And a goose too.

CAPTAIN. Only one? One goose doesn't go very far, Mr First Leiutenant.

JIM. Special Christmas Eve dinner for you, me and Timmy, Sir. Captain, First Lieutenant.and Navigator, sir. Instruction through from Base on last routine, sir —

CAPTAIN. They like to keep us happy, don't they? We'll have a prune stuffing with the goose, I think. You've remembered your glasses, Mr Navigator? — Mr Navigator, I said, have you remembered your glasses?

TIMMY. Yes, sir. Or at any rate the wife did.

CAPTAIN. The wife. How's it feel, Timmy? I've forgotten.

TIMMY. Pretty good, sir.

JIM. Prune stuffing, sir? I'm not sure there are any prunes aboard.

CAPTAIN. Check it, please, Number One. Not so good being away this time, I suppose, Timmy?

TIMMY. What, sir? No, sir.

CAPTAIN. Naval family?

TIMMY. No, sir. She's from London.

CAPTAIN. I'm a Plymouth man, myself. The wife's a county councillor. Pretty chilly up here in the north. I'm always glad when we get below. Isn't it lunch time yet? Find out what it is, will you, Timmy.

TIMMY. Eggs à la grecque, pork chops and apple, chocolate mousse, sir. I asked cook on the way in.

JIM. Prunes on board, sir.

CAPTAIN. Close the hatches.
     'To save us all from sin and shame
     When we are gone astray,
     Oh, tidings of comfort and joy, comfort and joy.'

Ping-ping-ping goes the sounder.

CAPTAIN. Begin the fast cruise.

Slight edge out. MEG's *riddling the Aga.*

MEG. It's all clinkered up. No wonder it's gone out. Thompson, that's my kindling. Oh, come back.

Door bell goes again. The dog barks.

MEG. Where's my other shoe? You horrible dog, you've had them again, haven't you? Stop making that terrible noise. It's only the milkman. If I was a dog, I suppose I'd bark at the milkman. (*She opens the door, together with* THOMPSON.) What is it?

MILKMAN. You'll be wanting less milk, Mrs Lee-Fox.

MEG. Will I?

MILKMAN. With your husband off. Before we had the Base at least we knew where we were. Now it's chop and change all the time. Six pints on one day, three the next. And vice versa. It's the night time cocoa. Navy men get a taste for cocoa, I suppose, and the wives drink it to keep them company, and the very day they're off, they revert.

MEG. How do you know he's gone? No-one's supposed to know.

MILKMAN. I'm sure we're all to be trusted, Mrs Lee-Fox, with secrets of state. We don't want no commies taking over, any more than the government does.

MEG. But it's not — oh, well. One pint a day will do, I suppose.

MILKMAN. If you had kiddies, they'd keep you company.

MEG. I'm only just married.

MILKMAN. I'd get on with it, all the same. All the navy wives do round here. You haven't put in your Christmas order. It would save me inconvenience if you did. I left a form.

MEG. Sorry, I hadn't thought about it.

MILKMAN. Hadn't thought about Christmas?

MEG. It's come so quickly. Did you leave a form? I expect the dog got it.

MILKMAN. You'll be wanting cream, I suppose, for Sundays.

MEG. Well —

MILKMAN. It's a long way to come trailing up here, just for one pint of silver-top a day.

MEG. Make it gold-top. Cream on Sundays.

MILKMAN. Double or single?

MEG. Double.

MILKMAN. Snow's forecast. Got chains for the car?

MEG. I don't drive. Well, I'm learning.

MILKMAN. Don't drive?

MEG. In London, there seems no point. You could always get a taxi anyway.

MILKMAN. Oh, London. I can't stand here chatting all morning.

MEG. I'm sorry.

MILKMAN. The way I look at it, this is a welfare job. Someone for lonely wives to talk to. I don't suppose that dog bites.

MEG. No. Only barks.

MILKMAN. He'll need to do more than that. Prowlers about. You need to get that road fixed before the snow makes it worse.

MEG. How do you mean, fixed?

MILKMAN. Potholes. Getting worse. Nearly broke my bottles on the way up. The council can make you keep it in good repair, you know.

MEG. We can't possibly be expected to mend a road.

MILKMAN. If you will live this far out, instead of near the Base with the other wives, what can you expect? Well, of course, they rent. You went and bought. I don't get paid to stand here chatting. You ought to do something about that dog.

He goes. MEG *closes the door.*

MEG. Get your great claws off me, Thompson. I swore I'd never have a dog, and I was right. I don't want to be down there with the other wives. What have I got in common with the other wives? You silly dog, stop grinning at me. What do you know that I don't? What does a fish know that Timmy doesn't? Lying on the bottom of the loch, like some sleeping whale. The new leviathan.

Slight edge out. It's dinner time in the mess at the bottom of the loch. Ping-ping goes the sonar sounder as cutlery clashes and hungry men murmur.

CAPTAIN. What's the cook thinking of? Oeufs à la grecque for lunch, and now eggs mayonnaise for dinner? Too many eggs spoil the cook. Can your wife cook, Mr Navigator. What is it, Number One?

JIM. Routine from Base, sir.

CAPTAIN. Hand it over. Timmy. Mr Navigator. Mr Lee-Fox. Wake up.

TIMMY. What, sir? Sorry, sir. Dreaming, sir.

CAPTAIN. We're off. Come along.

They leave the mess and make for the bridge.

TIMMY. I forgot to remind her about Thompson's conditioning tablets.

CAPTAIN. You have to get used to forgetting. Otherwise a sailor's life is all remorse.

TIMMY. Yes, sir. Sorry, sir.

CAPTAIN. Got your glasses, Mr Navigator? We don't want to end up in the Black Sea.

JIM. Or up the Yangtze River, sir. Worse.

CAPTAIN. That's a matter of opinion. That's for the politicians to decide. But I'm glad to hear you making a joke, Mr First Lieutenant, so early in the patrol. We're usually half way round the world before you so much as smile. Is it the land that depresses you, or the sea?

JIM. The land, sir, I think, sir.

CAPTAIN. And you, Mr Navigator?

TIMMY. The sea, I think, sir. Being married makes a difference.

CAPTAIN. Being newly married does. I've been married a long, long time. Living down on the Base, is she?

TIMMY. No, sir. We bought a croft out on the hills. We're in the middle of converting it.

CAPTAIN. In the middle?

TIMMY. Ran out of money, sir.

CAPTAIN. Engine Room.

ENGINE ROOM. Sir?

CAPTAIN. Stand by. Ready, Mr Navigator?

TIMMY. Not yet, sir. Sorry, sir. They've changed the code.

CAPTAIN. Engine Room —

ENGINE ROOM. Sir —

CAPTAIN. Stand down. Get a move on, Mr Navigator. The cheese soufflé will be sinking. Trust the cook to make a cheese soufflé first night out, when we're bound to be interrupted. Base has got eyes in the back of its head: it knows when we sit down to eat. All right, Mr Navigator?

TIMMY. No. Not really. I must have brought my wife's glasses, I think, not my own. Yes, I have. It's all right, sir. I can see. I'll just get headaches.

CAPTAIN. Seeing with her eyes, while she sees with yours. Ah, young love. Don't let it happen again. Engine Room?

ENGINE ROOM. Sir.

CAPTAIN. Stand by. (*Sings.*)
>   'We won't go until we get some,
>   We won't go until we get some.
(*Massed choirs join in.*)
>   We won't go until we get some
>   So bring some out here' —

The ping-ping changes its note as Polaris sets off.

CAPTAIN. 'The floods have lifted up, oh Lord, the floods have lifted up their voice: the floods lift up their waves. The Lord on high is mightier than the noise of many waters — yea, than the mighty waves of the sea' — we're off.

Cut to: MEG's kitchen. MEG sings as she re-lights the Aga.

MEG (*sings*). 'We won't go until we get some,
        We won't go until we get some' —
Beastly dog, Thompson. How can I light the fire if you've eaten the newspaper? How can I cook your meat if I haven't lit the fire? Stupid. Timmy, you're going, aren't you? I can feel you. A great dark fish moving out of the loch, away from the land into the open sea. Leviathan. Goodbye Timmy. You idiot dog Thompson, you've jumped in the ash. It's all over everywhere. You're worse than a child. If you were a child there'd be some point to you. But you'll never amount to anything. Never.

Cut to: Ping-ping goes the echo sounder. The attack crew are in the mess, naturally.

CAPTAIN. Number One, tell the cook kindly not to put garlic in all the vegetables.

JIM. I don't think he does, sir. I think the galley's watertank has somehow got polluted. My bet is he wiped it out with a garlicky cloth. Hygiene isn't his strong point.

CAPTAIN. It's not meant to be. Cooking is. Tell him to go over to Number Two and be more careful in future. Timmy!

TIMMY. Yes, sir. Sorry, sir. Dreaming, sir.

CAPTAIN. Timmy, we've got the world's destiny in our hands. You, me and Number One here form an attack team. You mustn't dream.

TIMMY. Sorry sir, I forgot, sir.

CAPTAIN. I just thought I'd mention it.

JIM. Routine, sir.

CAPTAIN. What?

JIM. Russian sub operating in our vicinity.

CAPTAIN. When were they ever not? Someone go and pinch the radar lad.

JIM (*hurt*). Sir, he is fully alert.

CAPTAIN. Of course he is, Mr First Lieutenant. I was joking.
(*Ping-ping-ping.*)
'Holy night, silent night,
All is calm, all is still' – Then – Crash! One British and one
Russian sub, lying crippled on the North Sea bed. Leviathans
with broken heads.

TIMMY. We're out of the North, sir –

JIM. Sir, I wish you wouldn't joke.

CAPTAIN. I do my best to entertain you all. 'Lord God of
host, who breakest the heads of the dragons in the waters.
Thou breakest the heads of leviathans in pieces' – Do you
plan to have any children, Mr Navigator?

TIMMY. Not yet awhile, sir.

CAPTAIN. Why not?

TIMMY. All kinds of things, sir – money, mortgage. And besides,
sir, Meg says, well, she wants time to think. I mean, sir, is the
point of life just to hand it on?

CAPTAIN. Woman's libber, is she?

TIMMY. Oh no, sir, nothing like that, sir. We just want to live
by principle: think things out for ourselves, not just do things
because others do them.

CAPTAIN. 'The fool hath said in his heart, there is no God.
Corrupt are they, and have one abominable iniquity.' What's
for lunch, Mr First Lieutenant?

JIM. Mulligatawny soup, quiche lorraine, coleslaw and pomme
anna, apple pie and cream.

Cut to: THOMPSON *barks. The telephone rings.* MEG
answers it.

MEG. Hello. Hello, is that you, Zelda. Oh Zelda, I'm so miserable.
Timmy's been gone too long.

ZELDA (*slight distort – a fluty officer's wife voice*). What two
weeks? Jim's been gone just as long – well, that stands to
reason, but I'm not complaining. I can get on.

MEG. What do you mean, get on?

ZELDA (*slight distort*). You haven't been married long enough,
or you'd know.

MEG. Zelda, listen Zelda, Thompson do go away — Thompson stop it, sorry Zelda, he got the cord. Zelda, something terrible, when I went to take my pill this morning —

ZELDA (*slight distort*). None of us take the pill, Meg. I mean, three months off and three months on. If you're on the pill it means, well — so most of us have the coil —

MEG. Zelda listen.

ZELDA (*slight distort*). I don't know why you always have to be so special, Meg.

MEG. Zelda listen, all my dates are out, I've missed at least four pills somehow.

ZELDA (*slight distort*). Of course you've missed at least four. You want a baby. It's your unconscious.

MEG. I don't want a baby, I want Timmy.

ZELDA (*slight distort*). You can't have Timmy, so his baby will do.

MEG. But Zelda, supposing I'm pregnant.

ZELDA (*slight distort*). I am. That's why I rang. I had a test back today. But Jim won't know for another two months and two weeks.

MEG. Can't you tell him, through the family telegrams?

ZELDA (*slight distort*). They only pass on good news. Bad news waits until they're back on shore.

MEG. I suppose your good news and Jim's good news aren't necessarily the same.

ZELDA (*slight distort*). That's right.

MEG. Will you come up for lunch?

ZELDA (*slight distort*). I've got my mother. Why don't you come down here?

MEG. I'd have to cycle.

ZELDA (*slight distort*). How are your driving lessons?

MEG. I forgot again. Well, the cancellation fee's cheaper than the lesson.

ZELDA (*slight distort*). What's for lunch?

MEG. Sausages and mash and beans.

ZELDA (*slight distort*). On the other hand if you came to me, you'd meet Tony.

MEG. Who's Tony?

ZELDA (*slight distort*). He's a spare man, dear, from second crew. His wife's visiting relatives in New Zealand and she doesn't understand him, even when she's here. He mends fuses and walks dogs and lends a sympathetic ear, and all the husbands trust him. He might cheer you up.

MEG. No thank you.

ZELDA (*slight distort*). Why not?

MEG. I don't think Timmy would like it.

ZELDA (*slight distort*). I don't think submariners are very possessive men, actually. Or they wouldn't be away so much, would they?

MEG. No, you come up here, Zelda.

ZELDA (*slight distort*). If you promise Thompson won't knock me over.

MEG. I wish it felt more Christmassy.

Cut to: ping-ping-ping. The action crew are in the mess.

CAPTAIN. 'Where a mother laid a baby,
           In a manger for a bed' —
Timmy, why does cook always serve mulligatawny soup at lunch and curry for dinner on the same day?

TIMMY. Because he's got the curry can out, sir, I suppose.

CAPTAIN. Brilliant. Have some more lemon meringue pie, Timmy.

TIMMY. No thank you, sir.

CAPTAIN. Why not, man? What's the matter with you?

TIMMY. I don't want to get fat, sir. I don't think Meg would like it.

CAPTAIN. Got your instructions, have you, Timmy?

TIMMY. Yes, sir. I suppose so, sir. But even so, sir, no thank you, sir. No second helping of lemon meringue pie.

Edge out. MEG's *door bell rings.* THOMPSON *barks.*
ZELDA *enters.*

ZELDA. Meg? Down, Thompson! Meg, you promised me!
Meg, where are you? You ought to get that dog put down.
I've got mud all over my suit. Meg?

MEG. Upstairs, papering. Careful of your heels, one of the stairs
is broken. Are you wearing your heels?

ZELDA. Of course I'm wearing my heels. I don't slop around
like some.

MEG. And little hat and matching gloves. It's like the thirties
back again. You never used to be like this. When you were at
college you were a mess like me.

ZELDA. You'll learn.

MEG. Learn what?

ZELDA. Officers' wives set an example.

MEG. I'm not an officer's wife. I'm Timmy's wife.

ZELDA. Timmy is an officer.

MEG. But he's Timmy first.

ZELDA. No. Not on board. He's a man who could blow up the
world.

MEG. How do you mean?

ZELDA. Well, if the routine comes through from Base, blow
up Moscow, or Hanoi, or Peking, or whatever, then the Captain,
and my Jim and your Timmy, all sit down and push their
button at the same time and whee — off goes the missile as
programmed. That's an attack team. Can we eat? Little and
often, the doctor said.

MEG. But that routine never does come through.

ZELDA. It hasn't so far, but I suppose it must one day. I mean,
in your experience, if a thing's there, it gets used, doesn't it?
If you own a pair of nut crackers, you tend to crack nuts.
Why are you looking like that? You know all this. You knew
from the beginning. When I introduced you, I said this is
Jim's friend Timmy — he's on Polaris too.

MEG. Everything happened so fast. I mean, I hardly heard. I
just looked, and I knew — and we couldn't even be apart.

We could hardly talk: and then we were married and got this home, and it's all taken three months and two weeks from start to finish and I haven't had time to think, Zelda.

ZELDA. You'll get plenty of time to think. At intervals. Why is the floor covered with splinters of wood?

MEG. I shut Thompson in while I went for a walk. He tried to chew down the door.

ZELDA. Why didn't you take Thompson with you. Dogs are meant to go for walks.

MEG. He chases sheep. Supposing the farmer shoots him. He shot the dog of the last people who were here. Timmy would never forgive me.

ZELDA. Take him on a lead.

MEG. He's stronger than me. I'm only small.

ZELDA. You'll have to learn to be large.

MEG. I've run out of baked beans.

ZELDA. Are you coming to me for Christmas day? Tony will be there, carving the turkey. Well, someone's got to carve the turkey. You can't have Christmas alone, Meg.

MEG. I don't mind being alone. I've always wanted to be alone. I've always been so crowded. You don't know how I always wanted peace and quiet, and space and time.

ZELDA. Now you've got it. Oh shut up Thompson. He's worse than a child. I should let him chase the sheep, Meg.

MEG. I know you would.

Edge out. Ping-ping-ping, goes the sounder.

TIMMY. She's got her best friend on the Base. That's Jim's wife Zelda. She won't be lonely.

CAPTAIN. In Singapore the naval wives ran a white brothel. Highly successful. Could be rather embarrassing, though. Meeting up with old friends. Well, wives of old friends.

TIMMY. I imagine it would, sir.

CAPTAIN. Submariners' wives are a different kettle of fish, of course.

Edge out. pling-plong go ZELDA's *doorbell chimes.*

MEG. Zelda! It's me, Meg. I'm only here for a minute.

ZELDA. You won't catch anything, Meg.

MEG. I'm not so sure. It's ever so warm in here.

ZELDA. It won't be for long if you go on standing in the door. And it's not that this house is warm, it's just that yours is so cold.

MEG. And so tidy.

ZELDA. Again, it's only by comparison.

MEG. Where are the children?

ZELDA. Gone to stay with my mother.

MEG. She must like children.

ZELDA. Of course she likes children.

MEG. There's no of course. My mother didn't like me. Timmy's mother didn't like him much. I think that gives us something in common.

ZELDA. Coffee will warm you.

MEG. All right.

ZELDA. You're lonely, I suppose.

MEG. Just days without talking. Except the postman and the milkman, and they talk too much.

ZELDA. Yes they do.

MEG. Did you hear about it? The credit-card business?

ZELDA. Of course. Everyone did.

MEG. What do I do?

ZELDA. Go to the Families Officer and tell him you tried to buy wallpaper on your husband's credit card but when they rang through to check they wouldn't allow you credit. Facilities had been withdrawn. Your husband forgot to pay the last instalment.

MEG. It's such a public disgrace.

ZELDA. Aren't you furious?

MEG. No. Just humiliated. I'd no idea life was so practical. No stars, just washing up. Anyway, I can't be angry. I have a kind of responsibility. Timmy knows what I'm thinking and feeling.

I have such a sense of his presence, Zelda. I don't want him to blow up the world, or anything silly, because of me. I can't be angry. I won't be angry. I love him. I must love him, do you hear?

ZELDA. You're going loony, up there by yourself. Come to Christmas dinner tomorrow. Come on.

MEG. All right. Is Tony coming?

ZELDA. Yes. Of course. Why?

MEG. I don't know.

ZELDA. You mightn't even like him.

MEG. I think I will, somehow. I'm frightened. Everything rocks and reels beneath me. I don't know what's happening.

Fade. Ping-ping-ping, goes the echo sounder. The attack crew are in the Control Room

CAPTAIN. What's the time?

JIM. Eleven-thirty, sir.

CAPTAIN. One and a half hours to Christmas dinner. Turkey is a very dry bird. Of course, chestnut stuffing helps. Is cook doing chestnut stuffing, Number One?

JIM. Yes sir. I think so, sir. And prune and walnut the other end.

CAPTAIN. It sounds all right. But last night's goose was on the fatty side. And why a gooseberry purée instead of prunes? Do you think it was a practical joke on the part of Base to give me indigestion? Or worse, a kind of plot? Timmy? I said Timmy?

TIMMY. What sir? Sorry, sir.

CAPTAIN. What are you doing?

TIMMY. Thought transmitting, sir. It's eleven-thirty on Christmas morning. I'm thinking of Meg, and she's thinking of me.

Edge out. Fade up. The sound of splashing and barking.

MEG. Shut up, you horrible dog. How can I think of Timmy if you're trying to get in the bath with me? And you've walked all over my Christmas clothes and you've been outside and they're covered with mud. Timmy, help me! Timmy, I can't remember your face.

Edge out. Fade back: to Polaris and last scene.

CAPTAIN. I don't want you going loony on me, Timmy. We can't afford loonies on board. Not this boat. Can we, Number One?

JIM. No, sir. But sir, thought transference in young lovers is not an unknown phenomenon. I mean, you lie awake and think of them, and you know they're thinking of you. Mr Navigator is not necessarily loony, sir. I'm even thinking of Zelda, sir, and I'm pretty sure she's thinking of me. I wonder who's carving the turkey today?

CAPTAIN. Ask Steward if he'll bring up a few savoury crackers. It might settle my indigestion.

JIM. I don't know how you manage to keep so thin, sir.

CAPTAIN. I hope that's not a criticism, Mr First Lieutenant. I keep thin because of the responsibility I bear, and don't any of you forget it. (*Roaring.*) Timmy! Did you hear what I said?

TIMMY. Yes, sir. At once, sir.

CAPTAIN. What's she doing now?

TIMMY. Meg? She's walking, with the dog. He's half Alsatian, half Springer. Bigger than her, almost.

Edge out. Fade up: outdoors. MEG *walks the dog.*

MEG. Thompson, now come on. We've got to get to Zelda's. It's this way, not that way, idiot. Please let me keep to the path. Now I've dropped the sprouts. You made me. It's your fault. Look, I'll let you off the lead if you promise to be good. But don't chase the sheep. Heel, boy. Now heel. Why don't you walk along quietly like other dogs? Come back, Thompson. It's Christmas Day. On this day a child was born. Oh go on, I don't care, chase the sheep, have it as a Christmas treat. What farmer's going to be out today, with his gun? Run the profit off them, Thompson. How dare he keep animals for profit. We're going to be late.

Edge out. Pling-plong go ZELDA's *door chimes. She opens the door.*

ZELDA. Oh it's you, Tony. I thought it was Meg with the sprouts. She's always late these days. She never used to be.

TONY. Got the carving knives ready, Zelda?

ZELDA. There she is, coming down the road. Oh dear me, she's brought the dog. Can you cope with a dog, Tony?

TONY. I can cope with anything, Zelda, but I would rather cope with you.

ZELDA. Well, you can't. You're getting altogether too moony for your own good. Moony and loony. You look at me with soppy eyes. I can't stand it. Jim never looks at me like that. My mother will notice.

TONY. If you weren't serious you should never have started. I do have feelings, Zelda, even though I am a man. You can't just palm me off with a friend.

ZELDA. She's a lovely girl and ever so lonely — you know what navy wives are. And precariously balanced in her mind.

MEG. I'm sorry I'm late. I suppose you're Tony.

ZELDA. I'm not giving Thompson any turkey.

MEG. I bought him some liver as a treat, but when I fell it got all mixed up with the brussels sprouts.

Cut to: choir singing 'God rest you merry gentlemen, Let nothing you dismay.'

Cut to Polaris acoustic.

CAPTAIN. 'Lord God of hosts deliver us.
        Lord God of hosts show thy mercy on us.
        The floods have lifted up, oh Lord,
        The floods have lifted up their voice.'

TIMMY. Oh Meg.

MEG. Oh Timmy.

Cut to ZELDA's Christmas table.

ZELDA. More stuffing, Tony? Mother? Meg? Polly? No? What about you Thompson, sprouts? No?

MEG. He's so strong, you see. He pulls and I fall. He's a cross between a Springer and an Alsatian.

TONY. That's why it's so big. Alsatian crosses usually are. It sounds to me as if he needs a man's hand.

MEG. He's used to one, that's the trouble. He's Timmy's dog, you see. He's very fond of me, but he acts as if I was his sister, not his mistress. He has no real respect.

TONY. Perhaps I'd better come round and see what I can do with him? Tomorrow?

MEG. Well. All right. That's Boxing Day.

Fade. Ping-ping-ping. The attack crew's in the Control Room.

TIMMY. I wonder what time it is up above? Are they having breakfast on the surface, or dinner or tea?

JIM. Doesn't make much difference, does it?

TIMMY. I'd like to know.

JIM. Haven't you got one of those watches?

TIMMY. Yes. But it only gives Tokyo and New York and Sydney. It wasn't meant for 200 miles South of Tierra del Fuego.

JIM. Is that where we are?

TIMMY. I certainly hope so. Well, to me it's four-thirty on Boxing Day. It's dark at home. I hope she's remembered Thompson's conditioning powders. And he ought to have as much fresh meat as possible. Meg has a terrible tendency to be lazy and open tins. Or else not cook the liver.

Cut to: MEG's *bedroom. Champagne cork opens.* THOMPSON *snuffles.*

TONY. Do you think Thompson would like some champagne?

MEG. Ask him.

TONY. No. Tell me why you married Timmy.

MEG. I loved him.

TONY. Did you love him before you went to bed with him?

MEG. No. I went to bed with him and fell in love with him at the same time.

TONY. Is he good looking?

MEG. Not as good looking as you are.

TONY. And he's left you?

MEG. Yes. All alone.

TONY. I suppose you spent most of the three months in bed.

MEG. That's right.

TONY. And then it stopped, just like that?

MEG. That's right.

TONY. Isn't that hard?

MEG. Of course it's bleeding hard.

TONY. Well then.

MEG. Well then what? — I was thinking about radioactivity and
nuclear power stations and critical piles. Which is a collection
of nothings which when brought together, make something,
and such a something that everything explodes. And people
fade away and die, in the face of that collection of nothings.

TONY. Have some more champagne.

MEG. It's difficult and it's lonely and it's cold and he didn't
pay his credit card and I don't understand anything and
all right, yes.

Cut to: ping-ping-ping, down in Polaris.

JIM. Routine, sir.

CAPTAIN. What is it?

JIM. NATO reports US nuclears manoeuvring in our area.

CAPTAIN. When were they ever not? We're outnumbering the
blue whale. American, Russian, Chinese by the hundred. We're
the rarity. Only five with GB plates. Every city in the world,
and a missile pointed straight at it. From Christchurch,
New Zealand, to Moose Jaw, Ontario. We just provide extra
cover for the major capitals, of course. A face saver. Are we
under the ice-cap? Timmy?

TIMMY. No, sir. Not yet, sir.

CAPTAIN. You were paying attention, Timmy? What's the matter?

TIMMY. I don't know, sir. I feel back in the here and now, sir.
My mind's emptied out; it is now fit to receive new impressions.

CAPTAIN. Number One, what's for Boxing Day tea? Mr First
Lieutenant, what's the matter with you? You're miles away.
You've caught it from Mr Navigator.

JIM. Sorry sir. I was thinking of Zelda. What was it? Tea, sir?
Waffles, I think, sir with Canadian maple sauce.

CAPTAIN. 'A man hath no better thing under the sun, than
to eat and to drink and to be merry, for that shall abide with
him of his labour all the days of his life.'

Cut to: MEG's bedroom. THOMPSON wuffles and barks.

TONY. Meg, get that animal away.

MEG. No. You get away.

TONY. Wait on now —

MEG. No. You wait on. I'm sorry. I'm not. I can't. I've changed my mind.

TONY. You can't change your mind.

MEG. I can. I have. Sorry. Unless you want to make it rape.

TONY. What's the matter with you?

MEG. I don't know. What's the matter with you? Worming your way in here, taking advantage of me —

TONY. It was you as much as me.

MEG. That's what's so terrible. Nothing's going to be the same again. How could you — in my husband's bedroom and he's in the navy too. Have you no loyalty at all? One day it will happen to you and then what will you feel like? Off on a six-month mission and your wife at the mercy of men like you —

TONY. It's already happened. You're right, of course you're right, women are always right, but couldn't you have said it all downstairs not waited until now — get that dog away from me. Tell him I'm going, tell him I'm sorry, I'm lost, I'm defeated. Tell him I'm a nice feller really.

MEG. Thompson, he's a nice man. He really is.

TONY. Just at the moment rather provoked, and liable to bark back.

MEG. Shall I help you with your shirt buttons? You are clumsy.

TONY. Surprise, surprise. I'll come up every morning and walk the dog. He needs more exercise.

MEG. All right.

TONY. What are you going to do all by yourself up here, being faithful to an absent husband?

MEG. There's lots to do. Didn't you have a tie? No? There's the wallpapering once I've got the credit card sorted out, and one and a half acres to dig over, and a compost heap to get started, and already the days are longer and soon Timmy will be back — first the snowdrops — soon the crocuses — then the daffodils — then Timmy.

'Nymphs and Shepherds' sing the choir. 'Come away', fading in and out and around voices, signalled by pings, barks and door chimes. More barks.

MEG. Oh Thompson, Thompson, that was a crocus, not an enemy. See what you've done. Thompson, come back, come back, you'll get shot. Thompson, I didn't hit you. I didn't beat you, I only reproached you. Why are you so sensitive?

Choir sings: 'Come, come, come away'. Ping-ping-ping.

CAPTAIN. There's a way of cooking ham with apricots we must get cook to try. 'There is nothing better for a man than that he should eat and drink.' Ecclesiastes 2. 'This also I saw, that it was from the hand of God.'

Choir sings: 'In this bower, in this bower.' THOMPSON *slurps.*

MEG. Yes but doctor I only missed four pills. I can't really be pregnant. Can I?

Choir sings: 'Let's sport and play'. Ping-ping-ping.

JIM. Routine sir. Time to go home, sir.

Choir sings: 'Let's sport and play'. Ping-ping-ping.

TIMMY. Of course the service is my mother and my father. Always has been.

Choir sings: 'Let's sport and play'. Ping-ping-ping.

CAPTAIN. 'They shall be afraid of that which is high, and fears shall be in the way, and the almond tree shall flourish, and desire shall fail, because man goeth to his long home.' Plymouth and the County Council: the little death, not yet the greater.

Door chimes.

MEG. I wonder if the daffodils will be yellow or white, Zelda.

ZELDA. Daffodils on the Base are all yellow. Yours are bound to be white, Meg. Is it Timmy's baby, or Tony's?

Silence.

MEG. It's Timmy's. How could it be Tony's? What made you think there was any doubt?

ZELDA. 'Take back your mink
Take back your pearls
What made you think
That I was one of your girls.'

MEG. I'm going to be sick.

Choir sings: 'For this is Flora's holiday'. Ping-ping-ping.

CAPTAIN. What's cook thinking of? Setting off to sea without green peppercorns. What's a steak au poivre when the pepper-corns are black? Well, it's the last meal of the patrol. He hasn't done too badly.

Choir sings: 'This is Flora's holiday'. THOMPSON barks excitedly.

MEG. Look, the daffodils are showing. They're white! I love white daffodils. Timmy, see, the first daffodils! Timmy, you're back. I thought I would die with you away. Three months took so long.

TIMMY. Two different lives. One here. One there. No time seems to have passed at all.

Choir sings: 'This is Flora's Hol-i-day'. Fade. MEG's bedroom. THOMPSON snuffling.

MEG. Champagne in bed in the afternoon!

TIMMY. Champagne stops you feeling hungry. I have to lose some weight.

MEG. You're ever so pale.

TIMMY. No. The rest of the world is just over-coloured.

MEG. What do they give you to eat at sea? Under the sea. Baked beans and spam?

TIMMY. More or less.

MEG. I made us a nice cottage pie. If I'd known when you were coming back — but there was nothing in the house.

TIMMY. It's all a plot, to catch you unawares.

MEG. I think it might be. Put your hand on my tummy.

TIMMY. It doesn't feel any different.

MEG. But it is. It's all going on, down there — growing and feeling and changing and thinking.

TIMMY. I'm glad you forgot your pills.

MEG. How much did the champagne cost?

TIMMY. Don't be so practical.

MEG. I have to be practical.

   Choir sings: 'In spring time, in spring time,
                The only pretty ring-time.'

TIMMY. Do you always let Thompson in the bedroom?

MEG. Well, yes.

TIMMY. I wish you wouldn't. He's not a house dog. A poodle or anything. He's a gun dog.

MEG. All right. I'm sorry. It's just he likes it and I sleep better for the sound of his snores and his scratching.

TIMMY. He hasn't got fleas.

MEG. No. He hasn't got fleas. No more than most dogs. Relax. You come back all nervy and twitchy and worried. Zelda says Jim does too.

   Choir sings: 'When Lambs do spring
                Hey ding-a-ding-a-ding,
                Sweet lovers love the spring.'

TIMMY. I must really get to work on the garden.

   Fade: TIMMY *and* MEG *are in the garden.*

TIMMY. Perhaps we should get a rotivator?

MEG. Can't afford it. No. You dig. I weed. All those holes are Thompson.

TIMMY. I hope you take him for walks.

MEG. He's so strong now. And I'm afraid of falling. And if he's not on the lead he might worry the sheep. Tony comes up sometimes and walks him.

TIMMY. Who?

MEG. Tony. I told you. Jim and Zelda's friend.

TIMMY. Oh yes. Surely it's not beyond your capacity to take a dog for a walk?

MEG. Sorry, I'm sure.

TIMMY. Give us a kiss.

Choir sings: 'In spring time, in spring time' —

Fade. TIMMY and MEG are in the kitchen. The noise of the Aga being riddled.

TIMMY. You've let it get clinkered up, Meg. No wonder it keeps going out. It needs cleaning out properly every couple of weeks.

MEG. You pull out the damper too early, that's all. Do please stop telling me how to do things.

TIMMY. Sorry.

MEG. No. I'm sorry. I'm not to upset you. You're not to be worried.

TIMMY. Who says?

MEG. The Families Officer.

TIMMY. Why did you go to him anyway? Why didn't you see the Bank?

MEG. Don't upset your husband, the Families Officer said. Save him from financial worry. One third of an attack team. For the sake of the navy, the sake of the country, for the sake of the world. See my smile? That's my smile, set fair for you.

TIMMY. Is Zelda like this when she's pregnant?

Choir sings: 'When flowers do spring.
Hey ding-a-ding-a-ding.

Fade. MEG and TIMMY are in bed.

MEG. What's Thompson doing under the bed?

TIMMY. Eating the rug. It's ever so dusty under there.

MEG. I know. I'm sorry.

TIMMY. When I lay my hand on your tummy, it's on a hill-slope. I wish I didn't have to go. It'll be any day now. Back in June, with any luck. In time for the peas and the strawberries.

MEG. But you will be here when the baby's born?

TIMMY. I don't know, my love. How can I know?

MEG. But you must be. Babies are real life. The other's just games. Men's games.

TIMMY. What do you mean?

MEG. What I say. Schoolboy games. Pranks and japes and the honour of the school.

TIMMY. There's nothing funny about a Polaris missile, or schoolboy in being responsible for one. Is that what you think of me?

MEG. No. No. Oh yes. Three fingers on the trigger. Bang. Up goes the world. You're ridiculous.

TIMMY. Only a part of it. Who'd ever want to blow up the whole world?

MEG. Not me. Not me. (*The phone goes.* MEG *answers it.*) For you.

We hear a voice at the other end of the phone, but cannot make out any words.

MEG. Come here, Thompson, ridiculous dog. You'll look after me, won't you? (TIMMY *replaces the receiver.*) Is it them?

TIMMY. That's right.

MEG. When?

TIMMY. Can't say exactly.

MEG. That's silly.

TIMMY. That's security. Come on, we'll finish up the champagne. (*Pop goes the champagne cork.*)

MEG. Last bottle.

TIMMY. I timed it well. What's Thompson got?

MEG. I don't know.

TIMMY. It's a tie. Who wears a red tie with yellow stars upon it?

MEG. I don't know. Who wears a red tie with yellow stars upon it? (*Silence.*) I told you. Tony. He came up on Boxing Day and made a pass. That's all.

TIMMY. I don't call his tie under my bed a pass. I don't think many men would.

MEG. Nothing happened.

TIMMY. I don't believe you.

MEG. Then believe what you like.

TIMMY. It's not my baby, is it?

MEG. Of course it is.

TIMMY. No. It doesn't feel like my baby. Nothing's been right since I've been home. Nothing.

MEG. Where are you going?

TIMMY. Back to work, to earn money to keep you in the whoredom you're accustomed to. I don't know who you are or what you are. I never have. Now I'm beginning to.

MEG. Timmy, you can't go like this. Saying things like that to me, then just going — Timmy, I'm pregnant.

TIMMY. Then complain to the father.

MEG. Timmy!

TIMMY. At least try and look after the dog properly.

TIMMY *goes,* MEG *cries,* THOMPSON *whines.*

Choir sings: 'Fa-la-la-la-la-la-la-la-la-la,
    Fa-la-la-la-la-la-la-la-la-la.

Fade. Ping-ping-ping.

CAPTAIN. 'Truly the light is sweet, and a pleasant thing it is for the eyes to behold the sun.' Being the fast cruise. You see these lumps on my eyelids, Mr Navigator? Cholesterol spots, they say. According to the MD I have to cut down on animal fats. You were first on board, Mr Navigator. Have a good leave?

TIMMY. No, sir.

CAPTAIN. 'As thou knowest not what is the way of the spirit, nor how the bones do grow in the womb of her that is with child, even so thou knowest not the works of God, who maketh all. ' You'll settle down to it, so will she, Mr Navigator. Have some lemon tea, with saccharine?

TIMMY. No thank you, sir.

CAPTAIN. Quite right.

TIMMY. It's not that I don't like lemon tea, sir, I just want to get on with my work.

Cut to: pling-plong. It's ZELDA's *new doorbell. Four chimes instead of three. She runs to open it.*

ZELDA. Meg! Don't you love my new doorbell? Four chimes and not just three. Woodland bells, they're called. All the houses have them, of course. If only you lived down here you too could have woodland bells.

MEG. I don't want woodland bells.

ZELDA. Where's Thompson? (THOMPSON *rushes past. Crash.*) Ah, there's Thompson. I'm afraid that's the hall stand. Why are your eyes red, Meg? No, don't tell me. You had a row with Timmy, and he walked off with a harsh word on his lips.

MEG. Yes.

ZELDA. And you won't see him for another three months. Never mind., it always happens. You get used to it. What did Jim say this time? Oh, I can't remember, it doesn't matter. Something perfectly horrid. I've been offered a part-time job and Jim said if I took it I'd grow even more of a moustache than I have already. He doesn't find working wives feminine.

MEG. But supposing, supposing —

ZELDA. Supposing something happens to Timmy and the last words he heard from you were those — whatever they were.

MEG. No. Supposing something happens to me, and the last words I have from him is him denying he's the father of my child.

ZELDA. Is he?

MEG. Yes.

ZELDA. That's not what I told Jim.

MEG. Zelda!

ZELDA. I was only teasing. Just think how much worse things might be. You really are very egocentric, Meg. Always thinking of yourself, when you should be thinking of Timmy. Of course he didn't mean it. He'll have forgotten it all completely already.

MEG. I don't think so.

ZELDA. But men always do. They have no memory for insults given, only for those received. Did you say anything terrible to him?

MEG. No.

ZELDA. That will be next leave. Jim and I take it in turns. We all do.

MEG. I'm not all. I'm different.

ZELDA. Did he sort out the credit card business?

MEG. No. And he bought a case of champagne out of the joint account, and I don't know how I'm going to manage on what's left.

ZELDA. If you cry about money, you'll never stop crying all your life.

MEG. No. It's not money. I thought I'd left home, I thought I'd left my mother's house, I thought I'd got away. But wherever I go it's going to be the same. You ask for bread, and are given stones. Worse, you offer all you have, and are looked at coldly and despised.

Cut to: ping-ping-ping.

CAPTAIN. 'There is an evil which I have seen under the sun, and it is common among men. A man to whom God hath given riches, wealth and honour, so that he wanteth nothing for his soul, yet God giveth him not the power to eat thereof.'

JIM. Sir, your blood pressure will rise. If you ask me, your blood pressure has been up through the whole patrol.

CAPTAIN. I do not like my eggs fried in corn oil because I am forbidden butter; and since Base will not supply first-grade olive oil but only third I do not even have that consolation. I should never have joined the navy. If you lads have any sense you'll get back to civvy street and sleep next to your wives the year round.

TIMMY. I prefer the navy. You can trust the navy. You know what to expect. Order and system and loyalty. Real friendship. A man's world.

JIM. Routine, sir.

CAPTAIN. What?

JIM. Three new oil rigs, sir. Submersibles at work.

CAPTAIN. Manned or unmanned?

JIM. Unmanned, sir.

CAPTAIN. Then they'll have to take their chances.

JIM. Sir?

CAPTAIN. The bottom of the North Sea is getting to be like Oxford Circus in the rush hour. Take a look at the radar screen, Number One. The more you dodge, the more you hit. Engine Room!

ENGINE ROOM. Sir —

CAPTAIN. Gently starboard —

ENGINE ROOM. Sir —

Crash.

CAPTAIN. Told you so. Emergency lighting. Thank you, Number One. Mr Navigator — well done. Base makes such false economies. They ought to be aware by now that it pays to keep us happy; otherwise reactions slow down. If I had my eggs properly cooked, this wouldn't have happened. Damage?

JIM. Minimal, sir.

TIMMY. Slight dent, I imagine, sir.

JIM. Lighting's back on, sir.

CAPTAIN. Thank you, Number One. What are you laughing at, Mr Navigator?

TIMMY. I must say, sir, I like it down here.

Edge out. Springtime countryside noises.

*Choir sings 'Where the bee sucks, There suck I,
In a cowslip's bell I lie' —*

MEG. Thompson! Oh Thompson. Hell! Come back.

FARMER. That your dog, then Mrs Lee-Fox?

MEG. Yes. I'm afraid it is.

FARMER. Something's got to be done about him —

*Choir sings: 'There I couch while owls do fly,
While owls do fly —*

POSTMAN. Hello, Thompson. Down dog. Morning Misses. How's the little one?

MEG. Growing thank you.

POSTMAN. I can see that. Now what have we got this morning?

That's from your mother, I think, down South. And this one's the telephone bill.

MEG. Oh no.

POSTMAN. Living out here, it's bound to be high. If you were down on the Base you could pop round. Legs are cheaper than wires.

MEG. Thank you.

Choir sings: 'When owls do cry,
After summer, merrily'.

MILKMAN. Down, Thompson. There's a good dog. You ought to be taking an extra pint, Mrs Lee-Fox, calcium, you know. You don't have to lose a tooth with every child — that's an old wives' tale. Oh dear, dear. You crying? Got you up suddenly, did I? It's too bad, you shut up here by yourself, no-one to look after you. You should be down on the Base with the others. Save my legs, too, I can tell you, trailing all the way up here, and the garden's going to rack and ruin.

MEG. I do my best but I can't bend.

Choir sings: 'Merrily, merrily,
After summer, merrily' —

Edge out. THOMPSON *barks. Choir sings 'Come unto these yellow sands, and then take hands'.* NURSE SANDERS *knocks and calls out.*

NURSE. Mrs Lee-Fox! Mrs Lee-Fox! Are you there? It's the midwife. Are you all right?

MEG. Fine.

NURSE. You don't look it. Down, dog!

MEG. I'm a bit tired, that's all.

NURSE. I can see that. Two o'clock on a fine summer's day and you in your dressing-gown. Well, why not? Twenty-six weeks, isn't it?

MEG. Six months, yes.

NURSE. Sit down, dear. You didn't come to the clinic, and I rang and the phone was out of order so I thought I'd just pop round. Quite a road, that, isn't it? Someone ought to do something. I must say, you do have a good watch-dog there.

MEG. He's all bark, no bite. He loves one's enemies, even more than one's friends.

NURSE. I'm sure you don't have enemies, dear. On the sofa. That's right. Feet up. Now let's just take your blood pressure. Hubby away, I suppose?

MEG. Yes.

NURSE. And we mustn't ask when he's due back, I suppose?

MEG. No. And he couldn't be fetched back, even if I was dying. He might miss the end of the world.

NURSE. It's not like that, now.

MEG. Isn't it?

NURSE. Dear, dear. It is up. How about your mother? Can she come?

MEG. No. She's a make-your-bed-and-lie-on-it person. My father was in the airforce. I went to sixteen different schools. Then he left us. Anyway she doesn't like dogs. Neither do I. Horrible smelly disgusting Thompson. Do you know what it costs me to feed him? And he's fussy. Only the expensive brands. I lug them all the way up the hill and cut my hands on the lids because the tin opener's so blunt and then he just tosses it all over the carpet and walks off. I hate dogs. I always have. I wish he was dead.

NURSE. Please now. Calm down. What about the telephone?

MEG. It's been cut off. We can drink champagne but not pay the telephone.

NURSE. Have you seen the Families Officer?

MEG. No.

NURSE. Why not?

MEG. Because my husband says I shouldn't.

NURSE. You're cutting off your nose to spite your face. Start thinking of baby, not yourself.

MEG. Don't tell me what I'm doing; don't tell me who to think of.

NURSE. Can't you go to your mother?

MEG. No. How can I leave the dog?

NURSE. You can put him in kennels.

MEG. Timmy wouldn't have that. He thinks more of the dog than of me. I could go to kennels, of course.

NURSE. Why are your legs so scratched?

MEG. Thompson pulled me through a hedge. I was taking him for a walk.

NURSE. But you're six months pregnant. If he pulls let him go.

MEG. Then he'll get shot for worrying sheep.

NURSE. Then don't take him for walks.

MEG. Timmy says I have to.

NURSE. Get someone else to take him.

MEG. Oh no. We've tried that. And how did that end?

NURSE. I think I'd better get doctor up, Mrs Lee-Fox. We can't have you in this state.

MEG. Bang. Pow. Three schoolboys with their fingers on the trigger. Men, Nurse Sanders, men! Nurse Sanders, where are you going?

NURSE. For some water, so you can take a couple of tranquillizers.

MEG. Don't go. Stop Thompson licking my face. You can get terrible things from dogs and I don't want the baby harmed. Nurse, please.

NURSE. You're only a baby yourself.

Choir sings: 'Foot it featly here and there;
And, sweet sprites, the burden bear'.

Cut to: ping-ping-ping.

TIMMY. It's different for me. You and Zelda, well. . . The thing is, I wasn't my father's child. I was his best friend's. Then my mother died, and my father remarried and I ended up on the edges of a family with whom, when I come to think of it, I had no blood ties. And then I met Meg, and I thought it's going to be different, it doesn't have to be like that at all. People can be happy. Quiet and orderly. But one can never quite dispel the notion that chaos lies on the edges of one's world, ready to break through. The axe, about to fall. Destroy everything. Well, it fell, all right.

JIM. Because of Tony's tie? Under the bed? Your dog took it up there, I should say. Tony's not like that. I wouldn't have him near Zelda, would I, if I didn't trust him? He does odd jobs for lots of the wives. What's the matter with you?

TIMMY. I don't know. It doesn't feel like my baby. And all I feel for Meg is hate.

Edge out. MEG *walks the dog.* THOMPSON *barks.*

Choir sings: 'Hark, hark, the watch-dogs bark' —

MEG. Thompson, stop it. Thompson, heel. Thompson, please. No, I'm not getting through there, I can't. Stop pulling, you'll choke yourself to death. Oh all right. Go. There you are! Run yourself silly. Get yourself killed. I wish you would. Thompson, come here. Not in with the sheep — oh, you can't. Thompson, Thompson, come back.

A shot. Silence.
Voice sings: 'I leant my back upon a thorn
I thought it was a trusty tree' —

Edge out. Pling-ping-pling. It's ZELDA's *front door.*
Voice sings: 'But first it bent and then it broke' —

ZELDA. What's the matter? Dear God, Meg, come in. Quick, Tony, down here, it's Meg, Meg Lee-Fox. Put her on her side — Meg, what's the matter — Tony, get the doctor, oh what does it matter, you're only cleaning the windows, what does any of it matter, oh dear God supposing she loses the baby?

MEG. Thompson's dead. His head's all in bits.

ZELDA. Hush, hush.

MEG. I have a terrible pain, Zelda.

ZELDA. What's Timmy going to say?

MEG. Oh shut up, Zelda!

Voice sings: 'But first it bent and then it broke
As my true love did unto me.'

DOCTOR. Because it's acute abdominal pain it doesn't mean she's losing the baby. What are all these women doing here? Get them out. Someone get an ambulance. Apart from the pain, she's perfectly all right.

Voice sings: 'Hark, hark! I hear,
The strain of strutting Chanticleer' —

MEG. I want to end it, do you hear. I want everything to end. I want the world to end. It's none of it any use. I hate you, God, for your creation. If I could end it now, I would. Finish it, now.

Voice sings: 'Hark, hark! I hear
The strain of strutting Chanticleer' —

NURSE. I imagine it's only muscular. Now if you'll relax, dear. That's better.

MEG. What happened? What was all that?

NURSE. A pain, dear. Just one of those things. It happens sometimes. Acute abdominal, with no apparent cause.

MEG. I thought I'd blown up the world.

NURSE. Takes more than you, dear.

MEG. The dog, Thompson. Was that true?

NURSE. I'm afraid so.

MEG. I killed him.

NURSE. No dear. The farmer did.

MEG. What's Timmy going to say?

NURSE. Stop being such a baby. Or how ever are you going to look after your own?

MEG. I don't want to go home. It's going to be so quiet.

Choir sings: 'I leant my back upon a thorn,
I thought it was a trusty tree,
But first it bent, and then it broke,
As my true love did unto me' —

NURSE. I'll leave you now, dear, all tucked in. In your own safe home.

MEG. Thompson, Thompson. I seem to see you out of the corner of my eye. On the stairs or in your basket. You're not there and yet you are. Well, you'll be off soon. Did you die on purpose? Did I kill you for a cause? Is there a lesson to be learned? Mother saw a lesson in everything. Perhaps she was right, and not so mean and cold and boring as I thought. Thompson, shadow of Thompson, I was not grateful for what I had. Your noisy, voiceless company. I expect too much. I expected a talking, grateful dog, I expected a knight in shining armour for a husband, and not a man of flesh and blood. I expected my father again; my perfect father before I came to know his imperfections. It is conceit, nothing but conceit, which makes me feel I deserve to be happier than anyone else. We should have lived down on the Base, like anyone else. We were not so special, after all. And the truth of the matter is, I was in this bed with Tony, and threw him out not because of any lack of desire, but because of fear of the consequences. I betrayed Timmy in thought, if not in deed; the baby is Timmy's, but might be anyone's, and if I didn't feel so guilty, I wouldn't have taken such offence. Thompson, shadow of Thompson, take your spirit to the bottom of the sea, where the big dark ships glide in and out, and tell your master I'm sorry.

Choir sings: 'Hark, hark, the watch-dogs bark' —

Edge out. Ping-ping-ping.

CAPTAIN. Custom is, my boy, to leave bad news to the last day of the tour. What's the point of knowing before? Since there's nothing anyone can do about it.

TIMMY. All the same, sir. I'm edgy, sir.

CAPTAIN. Your wife's all right. Dog got killed, though. Sorry. Shot by a farmer. Worrying sheep. Timmy, you all right? Only a dog. Timmy? Shouldn't have told you.

TIMMY. That's all right, sir. Poor Meg, she'll miss him. All by herself up there.

CAPTAIN. She's young and healthy, why should anything go wrong?

TIMMY. Did you hear barking then, sir?

CAPTAIN. Of course I didn't hear barking, Mr Navigator.

TIMMY. I was just thinking of Thompson, I suppose.

Choir sings (distant): 'Hark, hark, the watch-dogs bark' —

MEG. Sorry, Timmy.

TIMMY. Sorry, Meg.

Choir sings (distant): 'Hark, hark, the watchdogs bark' —

CAPTAIN. I said, take a message to the galley, Mr Navigator. Are you dreaming again?

Choir sings: 'Hark, hark! I hear,
The strain of strutting Chanticleer.'

CAPTAIN. Mr Navigator!

TIMMY. Sorry, sir.

CAPTAIN. Tell them to forget about the cholesterol. Let's have a short life and a merry one. Butter, cream and cheese. Mr Navigator, I said Mr Navigator — roast potatoes and sweet and sour pork. 'Go thy way, saith the preacher, eat thy bread with joy, and drink they wine with a merry heart, for God now accepteth thy works.'

Choir sings: 'Merrily, merrily, shall I live now
                Under the blossom that hangs on the bough' —

MEG. Hello, Timmy.

TIMMY. Hello, Meg. Thank you, Thompson.

Choir sings: 'Under the blossom that hangs on the bough'.

End.

THIRTY MINUTE THEATRE

IS IT SOMETHING
I SAID?

by Richard Harris

Is It Something I Said? was first broadcast on BBC Radio 4 on
9th May 1978. The cast was as follows:

WALLACE	Peter Jeffrey
ARTHUR	John Hollis
STELLA	Hilda Kriseman

Director: Cherry Cookson

Richard Harris is 44 and was born and bred in West London.
Grammar school-educated, he worked as an insurance clerk before
doing National Service in the RAF — an experience that must have
shaken a few marbles because on resuming civilian life he was
given the sack from job after job. Dividends would seem to have
been payed in 1959 however when he wrote his first play and sold
it to H.M. Tennent Globe Productions. Since then he has written
innumerable television plays and series episodes, many films, and
eight plays for the theatre, two of which have been staged in
London. A television play — *Reasonable Suspicion* — was
published in the 'People In Conflict' anthology series. *Is It
Something I Said?* is his first radio play.

The reception counter of a clean but third rate hotel near Paddington station.

ARTHUR. If you would care to sign the register, Mr . . . er . . . ?

WALLACE. Wallace. Mr Wallace. By all means. Certainly.

ARTHUR. Just a formality, of course.

> WALLACE *hums tunelessly, cheerfully, somewhat inanely, as he writes. This tuneless humming should punctuate all of the earlier exchanges.*

Were you recommended?

WALLACE. Sorry?

ARTHUR. Are you here as the result of a recommendation?

WALLACE. No, no — purely on the off-chance. Shall we say — in passing, as it were. (*Resumes his humming.*) There. All done.

ARTHUR (*reading*). Leslie William Wallace, Number 33 Park View Crescent, Croydon. What's this? Oh, I see . . . you've included your telephone number.

WALLACE. Have I? Oh yes, so I have. Might I have the key to my room?

ARTHUR. I'll show you up . . . it's number thirty-three.

WALLACE (*brightly*). Aha!

> *Footsteps ascending lino-covered stairs.* WALLACE *humming, but somewhat breathlessly.*

ARTHUR (*puffing*). We do have a lift of course but unfortunately it was vandalised in celebration of the Scottish victory at Wembley last week.

WALLACE. I don't understand these people, truly I don't.

ARTHUR. I'm often at a loss myself. Good as gold they were before kick-off. I remember saying to my wife . . . what a nice class of supporter they've brought down this year . . . twenty-four hours later, there's our lift poised between the second and third floors like a gaping wound. Anyway, you'll enjoy number thirty-three . . . I've just had it re-decorated . . .

Door opens — light switched on. Fade up sound of tap dripping and, from outside, the slow clank-clanking of a goods train. All the scenes in this room will be punctuated by railway noises, including perhaps the sound of an approaching and slowing inter-city express.

WALLACE. Oh yes, very pleasant . . . very pleasant indeed. (*He begins humming again.*)

ARTHUR. Where would you like your case?

WALLACE. Ummm . . . on the bed for the moment, I think.

ARTHUR. Brand-new mattress. Interior sprung. Sleep like the dead.

WALLACE (*stops humming instantly*). I notice there's a gas-fire.

ARTHUR. We try to make the rooms as cosy as pos — some of these places you go to . . .

WALLACE (*interrupts*). What's that thing over the bed?

ARTHUR. That is part of the intercommunication system.

WALLACE. It looks very useful, I must say.

ARTHUR. Should you require anything — that is, until eleven o'clock p.m. — up with the switch like so . . . direct contact with reception.

WALLACE. Aha!

ARTHUR. *Will* you be requiring anything, do you think?

Pause.

WALLACE. The thing is, I don't want to be disturbed. I've had a very long day. I've been travelling, you see. From Cornwall. *South* Cornwall. This is by way of being an overnight stop before I continue my journey up North. Newcastle-upon-Tyne. As soon as you're out of this room I shall be into that bed and fast asleep.

ARTHUR. And there's me keeping you chatting.

WALLACE. Normally I enjoy a good conversation.

ARTHUR. I can see that.

WALLACE. I'll bid you goodnight then.

ARTHUR. I shall personally see to it that you're not disturbed. (*He moves to the door.*)

WALLACE. On the other hand . . .

ARTHUR. . . . yes?

WALLACE. A glass of hot milk would be most acceptable.

ARTHUR. Milk.

WALLACE. And — er — here's a pound note. I would like some change for the gas.

ARTHUR. For the gas.

WALLACE. What coins does it take?

ARTHUR. Fivepenny pieces.

WALLACE. So that's fives into . . . that's twenty . . . no, forty . . . no twenty . . . yes . . . I'll have twenty fivepenny pieces if you would be so kind.

ARTHUR. Twenty.

WALLACE. Yes.

ARTHUR. That's a glass of hot milk and twenty fivepenny pieces.

WALLACE. Yes.

ARTHUR. Right. (*Sighs.*) I'll bring it up.

WALLACE. There's no . . . (*Door closes.*) . . . hurry. (*Pause.*) WALLACE *sighs then, as he begins the humming again. . . Fade down.*)

Fade up sound of milk being poured into saucepan, gas being lit under it.

STELLA (*entering*). You're not stuffing yourself again, I trust?

ARTHUR. No, my dear, I'm preparing a glass of hot milk for our new guest.

STELLA. Oh yes? When did *he* arrive?

ARTHUR. Just . . .

STELLA. Why didn't you say? You know I like to give our guests a personal welcome.

ARTHUR. You were lying down with your migraine.

STELLA. I would have *risen*.

ARTHUR. Anyway . . . it seems to have passed over.

STELLA. Don't make light of my suffering, Arthur, it doesn't become you.

ARTHUR. No my dear. Will you be going out this evening?

STELLA. I shall take a bath and see how I feel . . . (*Going.*) and don't use a mug, Arthur — not for the guests. Put it in the blue . . . the nice new blue.

ARTHUR. Certainly, my dear. The blue . . . the nice new blue . . .

Fade down.

Fade up.

WALLACE (*hums a moment*). Now then. What shall I say? Err. . . (*Sound of pen on paper.*) Dear . . . Irene . . . I cannot go on and have therefore decided to end it. All. End it all. Err . . . *dammit.* (*Sound of paper being screwed into a ball.*)

Intercom buzzer.

ARTHUR. Reception?

WALLACE. Umm . . . this is . . . er . . . Mr Wallace in room . . . err . . .

ARTHUR. . . thirty-three.

WALLACE. Yes . . . room thirty-three. I wonder if I might — er — bother you for — er — a little something to eat.

ARTHUR. What had you in mind?

WALLACE. Err . . . something like a biscuit.

Slight pause.

ARTHUR. I'll bring one up with the milk and the fivepenny pieces.

WALLACE. Thank you so much.

Sound of intercom switch clicking up and ARTHUR moving away.

Fade up.

WALLACE (*reading*). My Dearest Irene . . . this is the only way out. Please understand . . . and forgive me . . . If I cause you pain . . . no . . . for the pain I am causing you. No. You and the children. Err . . . no . . . causing *you*. Your ever-loving Leslie. (*Sound of paper being folded, put into envelope, licked and sealed. Knock at the door.*) One moment, please! (*Footsteps across — door opening.*) Ah!

ARTHUR (*breathless*). I managed a couple of digestives.

WALLACE. You're very kind.

ARTHUR. Milk . . . and twenty . . . fivepenny pieces . . . (*Coins clinking.*)

WALLACE. I wonder if you'd be so kind as to put the tray on the table?

ARTHUR (*still breathless*). Eh? Oh — yes — certainly, certainly . . . (*Crosses room.*)

WALLACE. I'll just move this letter — make it easier for you.

ARTHUR. Oh. You've been — er — you've been writing a letter, have you?

WALLACE. Oh you noticed? Yes. I *have* just written a letter, you're quite right — to my wife. More of a *note*, really. Er . . . what I was going to say is . . . should I happen to forget it tomorrow — that is, in my haste — I was wondering if you could make sure she gets it. Personally. She'll be wondering where I *am*, you see.

Slight pause.

ARTHUR. Yes.

Sound of door closing. WALLACE sighs. Sips the milk. Sound of coins jingling. Footsteps across. Coin going into gas money slot . . . the knob turning, the money falling . . . another coin going in . . . same procedure . . . .
Fade down.

Fade up sound of tea being poured from large pot into large mug.

STELLA (*entering*). You're not drinking more tea, are you? And the colour of it . . . how many spoonfuls do you put in? I dread to think of the state of your stomach, I do, I really do.

And don't leave that awful pot on the reception counter,
Arthur . . . it's 'ardly a work of art, 'ardly conducive to good
public relations now, is it? Anyway . . . I *shall* be popping
out . . . just for half an hour or so.

ARTHUR. Oh yes, my dear?

STELLA. Don't say it like that, Arthur . . . if I don't get my
little break from the wear and tear of this place I shall have
a breakdown, I know I will — and I shall be needing the car —
where've you put the keys?

ARTHUR. They'll be in your bag — you took the car last night
if you remember.

STELLA. I don't think I like your tone of voice, Arthur.

ARTHUR. I was simply trying to point out . . .

STELLA. It is quite clear, Arthur, that as far as you are concerned,
life is nothing but a bowl of innuendoes. I sometimes wonder
what goes on in that head of yours. I do, I really do . . .

Fade.

*Fade up sound of tape being pulled out from the roll and,
at the same time, the sound of* WALLACE's *humming.*

WALLACE. Right. That's the window done . . . now the door . . .
(*Moves across, a chair is set down.*) The thing is . . . have I got
enough tape? Mmm. Oh yes. . . I should think so . . . anyway
. . . *they'll* have some. Bound to. Now then . . . where shall I
start? Along the top I think . . . (*The sound of him humming,
tape being pulled out, torn off, stuck down.*) Mustn't forget
the keyhole. Must not . . . forget . . . the key . . . hole . . .
(*Further sounds of tape. Fade.*)

Fade up.

STELLA. You'll be all right then, will you?

ARTHUR. You won't be long, will you?

STELLA. I've *said.* If number seventeen gets up to his tricks
again, tell him he'll have *me* to answer to.

ARTHUR. What time might I expect you then?

STELLA. Don't fuss, Arthur; if it looks like I shall be detained
I'll give you a tinkle. What's that you're reading?

ARTHUR. One of my brochures.

STELLA (*moving away*). I wish you wouldn't read brochures, Arthur — you know how it unsettles your system . . .

Main door closes. A moment's silence. Then the sound of the huge teapot being poured out. Fade down.

Fade up WALLACE *humming.*

WALLACE. Now then . . . money in the meter . . . letter to Irene . . . windows and door . . . that's it. Nothing more. Just . . . turn on the tap . . . like . . . so . . . like *so* . . . (*Even more effort.*) Like . . . Oh! (*Hand slips.*) Damn thing . . . damn rotten thing . . .

Sound of intercome buzzing.

ARTHUR. Reception.

WALLACE (*distort*). Err . . . this is Mr Wallace in room thirty-three.

ARTHUR. Oh yes?

WALLACE. I wonder if you would be so kind as to spare me a minute.

ARTHUR. You mean come up?

WALLACE. Err . . . yes.

ARTHUR. Is something wrong?

WALLACE. Err . . . I'd rather not discuss it on the — er — the thing.

A pause.

ARTHUR. I'll come up then.

Sound of intercome switch off — ARTHUR *breathlessly mounting the stairs — knocking on the door.*

WALLACE (*other side of door*). Who's that?

ARTHUR (*breathless*). Me.

WALLACE. Oh. One moment please.

The tape ripped from around the door frame . . . WALLACE'S *exertions as he does so . . .* ARTHUR *puffing . . . the key turning in the lock . . . the door opening.*

ARTHUR. Oh.

WALLACE. Excuse me . . . I'll — er — (*Moving away.*) I'll just put this sellotape in the wastepaper basket.

ARTHUR. Er . . . I take it that the — er — the room was a bit — er — draughty for you, was it?

WALLACE (*cheerfully*). The — er — the thing is . . . the gas doesn't work.

ARTHUR. Gas?

WALLACE. Yes. I was lying down — that is, I was about to lie down — when I suddenly felt a bit chilly.

ARTHUR. The tap's stuck.

WALLACE. So I discover. (*He gives a little laugh.*)

ARTHUR (*more to himself*). I should have put you in number twenty-seven.

WALLACE. Should have what?

ARTHUR. I say I can move you into number twenty-seven.

WALLACE. It works in number twenty-seven, does it?

ARTHUR. A guaranteed one hundred percent flow.

WALLACE. Ah. I don't think a move will be necessary, thank you. I just wanted you to know that I tried to turn on the gas and it didn't work. I just wanted you to know that. Should your — future clientele — wish to make use of it. I just wanted you to know — to make clear — that I did try and it didn't work. I did *try*. Excuse me . . . I'll just put the — er — the sellotape and my scissors back in my suitcase. Excuse me. (*He does so.*)

ARTHUR. It would work in number twenty-seven.

WALLACE. Yes. that reminds me. I heard this joke yesterday. Did you hear about the Scotsman who was so mean that he broke into the house next door to gas himself?

ARTHUR. No.

WALLACE. Yes. The point being, of course, to show just how far a human being will sink when he's at the end of his tether. Even a Scotsman.

ARTHUR. I wouldn't have said gas was a very good idea, myself. No. People can smell gas, don't they? Raise the alarm. Gas can creep. Through gaps. Round the door, for example.

WALLACE. I'm not saying he succeeded, this Scotsman — all I'm saying is that at least he *tried*.

ARTHUR. He would have done a lot better in number twenty-seven. No-one ever goes down that end of the corridor.

WALLACE (*increasingly irritable*). He could still have been talked *out* of it.

ARTHUR. On the other hand, there would seem very little point in going *into* it.

WALLACE. Why not?

ARTHUR. Because we have been converted. And natural gas is not what they call toxical. All he would have got, this Scotch friend of yours, would be a nasty headache.

WALLACE (*disappointed*). Oh.

ARTHUR. Yes. I'll leave you to it then.

WALLACE. Before you go . . .

ARTHUR. Yes?

WALLACE. This *is* the third floor.

ARTHUR. Third floor, yes.

WALLACE. Might I ask what is outside that window?

ARTHUR. A sheer drop.

WALLACE. Leading where?

ARTHUR. In what way?

WALLACE. As the crow flies — always assuming of course that this particular crow has given up the effort.

ARTHUR. In that case it would find itself plummeting towards a solid concrete area surrounded by metal railings.

WALLACE. With very little chance of survival.

ARTHUR. None — at — all.

WALLACE. Just a heap of mincemeat and feathers.

ARTHUR. See for yourself. (*Sounds of his exertions as he tries without success, to raise the window.*)

WALLACE (*smug*). It would appear to be stuck.

ARTHUR. It's those painters. . . if there's one thing I can't stand it's shoddy workmanship.

WALLACE. I might say that I was hoping to look out of that window . . . get a breath of fresh air before turning in.

ARTHUR. I'll fetch a hammer — loosen it up a bit.

WALLACE. I would of course have to be very careful and not lean out too far — suffering as I do from heavy vertigo.

ARTHUR. Let me fetch my hammer. (*Sound of him moving to the door.*)

WALLACE. I've changed my mind.

ARTHUR. Two minutes.

WALLACE. What I would really like is a piece of rope.

ARTHUR. What had you in mind?

WALLACE. I want to tie up my suitcase.

ARTHUR. I might manage a piece of flex.

WALLACE. Something about . . . this long . . . say about six feet . . . yes . . . big enough to tie a knot in.

ARTHUR. I'll have a look in my tool-bag.

WALLACE. Yes — flex might do the trick . . . heavy-duty flex, of course. They say it's very strong, flex. They *say* that if you were to tie it up somewhere . . . say that curtain rail . . . and hang a heavy weight on the other end . . . say something about my size . . . heavy-duty electrical flex would stand the strain with no trouble *at all*.

ARTHUR. Just the job.

WALLACE. In that case . . . forget the hammer, I'll settle for the flex.

ARTHUR. Right.

WALLACE. On the other hand . . . what about the rail? We know all about the flex, but would that curtain rail stand the strain?

ARTHUR. That rail is fixed by six four-inch number twelves. I installed it myself. That rail would support a horse.

WALLACE. So what you are saying is . . . that if a horse were suspended from that rail by a length of heavy-duty electrical flex, it could do so with a certain amount of grace and with little fear of that rail collapsing and thus breaking its *neck*.

ARTHUR. No chance.

WALLACE. That horse could dangle there all night, without fear of breaking its neck and without fear of being disturbed.

ARTHUR. I would personally guarantee it.

WALLACE. Would your guarantee hold good if *I* decided to suspend myself from that rail and forget about the horse?

ARTHUR. I didn't hear that.

WALLACE. I'll re-phrase it then. I am going to kill myself.

ARTHUR. Yes.

WALLACE. Is that *it? Yes?*

ARTHUR. I mean . . . oh yes?

WALLACE (*menacing*). Oh *yes?* Oh *yes?* Where's your sense of duty?

ARTHUR (*affronted*). I made you a cup of hot *milk.*

WALLACE. You have a *duty* to save my life.

ARTHUR. Why?

WALLACE. Pardon?

ARTHUR. *Why?*

WALLACE. Because people *do.*

ARTHUR. I've never met you before.

WALLACE. What's that got to do with it?

ARTHUR. A perfect stranger interfering with your personal decisions — no, mate, it's not *on.*

WALLACE. People get *medals.*

ARTHUR. *Interfering* people.

WALLACE. *Heroes.*

ARTHUR. I did my bit during the war.

WALLACE. You've known all along, haven't you? You knew as soon as I walked *in* this place.

ARTHUR. Well whose fault was that?

WALLACE. Whose *fault?*

ARTHUR. You book in — you put your full name and address *and* your phone number — I'm surprised you didn't put your next-of-kin and be done with it . . . then you pay in advance and when I offer early morning tea you refuse it. No-one refuses early morning tea. It's one of the joys.

WALLACE (*deflating fast*). I haven't *done* this sort of thing before.

ARTHUR. You should have done a bit of *research* — found out. They *always* pay in advance — leave the house in order you might say — minimise the problems of the bereaved. I mean, can you imagine me going up to your wife and saying 'Excuse me, Mrs Wallace, your husband's just done himself in and can I have one pound seventy-five for the room'. Carry on like that and I'd be bankrupt. That you *did* pay in advance. is a question of human nature and nothing to do with research. It's like throwing yourself under a train — you don't buy a return ticket because you won't be needing it. That's human *nature*. You should have researched that and, in order to throw me off the scent, left the bill till the *morning, ordered* your tea. The Daily Express. Left your *shoes* out. (*Sighs.*) I try to close my eyes — let you get on with it — and what do I get? Abuse.

Pause.

WALLACE. I still say that having found out, you should have prevented it.

ARTHUR. Who am *I* to tell you what to do with your life?

WALLACE. It's my death I'm talking about.

ARTHUR. It's bound to happen sooner or later. The only thing you can bank on in life is death.

WALLACE. There's no need to be morbid.

ARTHUR. Life is like being on a train. Sooner of later we all have to get off. You happen to have chosen to get off three stops early.

WALLACE. Yes, but I could have changed my mind. I might have done it and found out I didn't fancy it after all.

ARTHUR. How do you know that you won't walk out of here, go down to the station and fall under the very train you're supposed to be travelling on?

WALLACE. You're talking about an accident.

ARTHUR. Exactly: what *you* have done is come to a decision. Eliminated the unforeseen. It's not *my* fault you chose to do it in a room where the gas doesn't work. *I* had you chalked down as a pills man.

WALLACE. I *never* take pills.

ARTHUR. I made a *mistake:* I'm *sorry.*

WALLACE. Yes. Well. But I could have prevented all this if she'd packed my razor.

ARTHUR. The wife?

WALLACE. Can't rely on her to do anything.

ARTHUR (*full scorn*). Typical.

Pause.

WALLACE. I didn't mean to be offensive.

ARTHUR. I can see you're very depressed.

WALLACE. There doesn't seem much point in going on.

ARTHUR. Let me see if I can get that window open.

WALLACE. I didn't really fancy it, to tell the truth.

ARTHUR. Don't give up hope: try and look on the dark side.

WALLACE. I'm a bit confused.

ARTHUR. You'd made up your mind on the gas.

WALLACE (*gloomily*). I put twenty fivepenny pieces in that meter.

ARTHUR. I know; I had to go round to the off-licence to get 'em.

WALLACE. Oh — sorry.

ARTHUR. No, no, no.

WALLACE. Skinned my knuckles something terrible trying to get that tap open. Look . . .

ARTHUR (*sucks in air*). You want to look after that.

WALLACE. And it was the wrong sort of gas anyway.

ARTHUR. Still — you can't think of *everything,* can you?

WALLACE *sighs heavily.*

That's the — er — that's the note, is it?

WALLACE. To the wife.

ARTHUR. Might I?

WALLACE. *Please.*

Sounds of letter being opened, unfolded. A moment.

ARTHUR. Mmmm.

WALLACE. No good?

ARTHUR. Typical really. I mean, you take this bit: 'This is the only way out'. Typical.

WALLACE. Well . . . it's how I felt at the time.

ARTHUR. What I mean is . . . way out of what?

WALLACE. My problems.

ARTHUR. Money?

WALLACE. Income tax. It's murder for the small trader nowadays.

ARTHUR. That's your reason, is it?

WALLACE. I can't go on.

ARTHUR. *I* see.

Pause.

WALLACE. What d'you mean . . . *I* see?

ARTHUR. No, no . . .

WALLACE. What are you implying?

ARTHUR. Nothing.

WALLACE. I don't like your tone.

ARTHUR. Ha! Neither does *she.*

WALLACE. What?

ARTHUR. If you think that's why you're killing yourself, that's fair enough . . .

WALLACE. I *know* that's why I'm killing myself. It's *me* who's doing it, you know.

ARTHUR. All I'm saying is . . . that if everyone who had trouble
  with the taxman did away with himself, the government could
  go into the funeral business. More than likely it'd be the only
  department to make a profit. I think you might be on to
  something: consider the possibilities . . . The Ministry of
  Labour gets you a job . . . when you're over the hill the
  taxman puts on the pressure, you do yourself in and the
  government fixes you up with a state funeral. Well, a funeral
  on the state. In that way they could control the labour force
  of the country and minimise the outlay on pensions something
  rotten.

WALLACE. I'm not doing myself in for my country, you know —
  I've got problems of my *own*.

ARTHUR. Financial problems.

WALLACE. It's a fact.

ARTHUR. It's a cover-up.

WALLACE. For what?

ARTHUR. For what is known as the awful reality of your
  situation. Still . . . you know best.

WALLACE. No, come on, come on . . .

ARTHUR. I've said — it's not for me to interfere in your
  personal decisions.

WALLACE. I'm *asking* you.

ARTHUR. You've obviously been blotting it out for years.

WALLACE. Blotting what out?

ARTHUR. Well . . . your wife for a start.

WALLACE. I love my wife.

ARTHUR. That I don't doubt; but does she love you?

WALLACE. She thinks the world of me.

ARTHUR. She didn't pack your razor.

WALLACE. She had other things on her mind.

ARTHUR. Such as what?

WALLACE. Such as . . . her needlework classes.

ARTHUR. Goes to evening classes, does she?

WALLACE. Three times a week. Got a very lively mind, my wife.

ARTHUR. So three times a week you go without your dinner.

WALLACE. I don't mind.

ARTHUR. Ah! You *say* you don't mind . . . but inside . . .
  inside . . .

WALLACE. I *like* her going to evening classes.

ARTHUR. As long as you're sure that's where she goes.

WALLACE. Of course she goes.

ARTHUR. Have you seen her then?

WALLACE. I don't *have* to see her.

ARTHUR. So you've only got her word for it.

WALLACE (*unsure*). I trust her.

ARTHUR. Of course you trust her. We all trust her. But we
  don't know, do we? We don't *know*. Got her own car, has
  she?

WALLACE. *She* cleans it.

ARTHUR. She could be out there now . . . driving around . . .
  laughing and joking . . . and where do you enter into her
  philosophy? Nowhere. No — *where*. She should be here . . .
  at home . . . giving you a decent hot dinner . . . helping you
  run the rotten business . . . instead of which, you're stuck
  here, working yourself to the bone, running up and down
  those lousy stairs while she's sipping sherry with that Flash
  Harry of a furniture representative.

WALLACE (*off on his own track*). Where's her samples?

ARTHUR. What happened to all those dreams.

WALLACE. She used to bring home samples of her handiwork.

ARTHUR. A man's entitled to his dreams.

WALLACE. In the past few weeks — nothing. What's going on?

ARTHUR. Deliberately flaunting it in your face.

WALLACE. I *knew* it . . . I *knew* it.

  A moment, both back on the same track now.

ARTHUR. When was the last time she slept in the marital bed?

WALLACE. She always sleeps there.

ARTHUR. Hair in curlers — pair of your winter pyjamas.

WALLACE. I wouldn't know; I sleep in the spare room.

ARTHUR. Ever since her migraine started.

WALLACE. Her back. She gets trouble with her back.

ARTHUR. And what do *you* get?

WALLACE. *Nothing.*

ARTHUR. *Women.*

WALLACE. I hate her . . . I hate her.

ARTHUR. We *all* do.

WALLACE. It's not just her — I could put up with her, it's the kids.

ARTHUR. Never talk to you.

WALLACE. Treat me like dirt.

ARTHUR. Their own father.

WALLACE. I walk into a room and they walk out of it.

ARTHUR. You work and slave to give 'em a decent education and when they've got it you're not good enough for 'em.

WALLACE. They'll be gone soon — lives of their own.

ARTHUR. Dropping in, once a month, Sunday tea, like they're doing you some big favour.

WALLACE. At least there'll be *some* sort of conversation. The rest of the time, just me and *her*.

ARTHUR. It doesn't bear thinking about.

WALLACE. Kill myself? I wouldn't give her the satisfaction.

ARTHUR. When did she ever give *you* any?

WALLACE. And there's me blaming it all on the Inland Revenue.

A pause as they consider.

ARTHUR. Mind you . . . you *are* a failure. I mean, I wouldn't like you to get the wrong idea. I wasn't trying to stop you killing yourself . . . all *I* wanted to do was make quite sure you're doing it for the right reasons.

WALLACE. Oh?

ARTHUR. It's all very well blaming the family but what is loud and clear is that they've got no respect for you. What you must ask yourself is why haven't they? Respect is something you *earn*. What have you achieved? I would say — just from hearing you talk — that if a man is measured by his achievements, you go about a pound and a quarter. I mean, you can't even do a decent job of putting yourself out of your misery. You don't mind me talking like this, do you? You do understand that I'm just trying to be helpful.

ARTHUR (*somewhat bewildered*). Thank you.

ARTHUR. What it all comes down to is personality defects. Take, for example, your reasons for choosing this hotel. Why choose this hotel?

WALLACE. Well . . . it seemed as good as any . . .

ARTHUR. What I'm getting at is — why not do it at home?

WALLACE. I was thinking of the wife.

ARTHUR. Coming home and finding you.

WALLACE. I've always tried to be considerate.

ARTHUR. Didn't matter about *me* though — you were quite prepared for *me* to find you.

WALLACE. Well I had to do it *somewhere*.

ARTHUR. So why not in the comfort of your own home? You say it was consideration for your good wife . . . *I* say it was self-pity. 'Poor old Leslie . . . why did he have to do it *there*? A second-rate hotel in Paddington. He didn't want to upset the wife. Trust old Les: thoughtful to the end'.

WALLACE. Whose side are you *on*?

ARTHUR. There could of course be another reason. A hotel means people and people means a chance of being discovered. Saved in the nick of time. Where's your determination? Where's your pride? No wonder they've got no respect for you . . .

WALLACE. I had every intention. . .

ARTHUR. You take that Colonel What's-his-name in number eighteen. One of residents. Seventy-four years of age and unable to move a step without the use of about fifteen tons of aluminium scaffolding. That man used to play scrum-half for the Saracens . . . leader of men he was — he's still got the moustache for it. All those years fighting for his country, all those years bringing up a family — and who cares tuppence for him now? Cries himself to sleep every night on a mixture of Irish whiskey and lager. I said to him, last New Year's Eve. . . 'What's the point of going on?' I said. 'What is the *point*?' And all he does is shake my hand and tell me what a lovely fellah I am. You just can't *help* these people.

WALLACE *has sunk into gloom.*

WALLACE. What would you suggest?

ARTHUR. Do away with yourself by all means, but make it a bit harder on her.

WALLACE. The wife?

ARTHUR. Make the cow suffer. Now, is there anyone you detest — outside your immediate family of course.

WALLACE. Only Kenwright.

ARTHUR. Who's he?

WALLACE. The tax inspector.

ARTHUR. Perfect. It's just a matter of re-writing that note. Something like this . . . 'My Dear Irene . . . I have found out about you and Mr Kenwright. I am doing the noble thing. Yours sincerely, Leslie'. How does that sound?

WALLACE. To be honest, a bit spiteful. I mean, he's only doing his job.

ARTHUR. All right — try this. You write another note, using a heavily disguised handwriting and signing off with an unusual signature. L.W. Wallace. William. Willy. Something like that. Then you do away with yourself in a way that *could* suggest foul play. Think of it . . . all those coppers . . . post-mortem, ruthless interrogation of the nearest and dearest . . . skeletons protruding from every conceivable cupboard. . . you could be the centre of her misery for *months*.

WALLACE. She'd never forgive me.

ARTHUR. That's the beauty of it. Les the suicide . . . ten a penny . . . but Les the *murder* victim . . . mystery, hidden depth . . . all there for the taking.

Pause.

WALLACE. I'll do it.

ARTHUR. I *knew* it.

WALLACE. Only not *here*. (*Sound of him packing his suitcase. Starts to hum again.*)

ARTHUR. Waddya mean — not here?

WALLACE. I'll do it — but not here. It wouldn't be fair. You're quite right. I'm too considerate. I couldn't involve *you* — you've been too helpful — no, it wouldn't be right.

ARTHUR. You can't walk out of here just like that . . .

WALLACE. I owe it to you — as a friend.

ARTHUR. But no-one *ever* commits suicide here. They come through that door, full of good intentions, but they never *do* it. What's *wrong* with these people?

WALLACE. Yes — well — that's it then — I expect you'll be reading about me in the local paper.

ARTHUR. I'm *always* reading about it in the local paper. They go down like ninepins. Foreigners even. They come to this country for the specific purpose . . . but not once do they do it *here*. It's not as if I'm not amenable. Am I or am I not amenable?

WALLACE. Anyway . . . thanks very much. I've got to admit, when I came here, I wasn't sure. If it hadn't been for you, I would never have made up my mind. Well . . . cheerio then . . . I'll — er — cheerio . . .

Sound of door closing . . . ARTHUR moving quickly across to open it again.

ARTHUR (*calls*). Wait!

WALLACE (*descending stairs*). I *will* . . . yes . . . I *will*. . .

The sound of him hurrying down the stairs. Then of the door closing. ARTHUR heaves a sigh. The sound of the intercom buzzing. Sound of ARTHUR moving quickly to answer it.

ARTHUR. Hello?

STELLA (*distort*). Are you *there*, Arthur? (*A slight moment.*) I said . . .

ARTHUR. You've come back then, have you, my dear?

STELLA. I've been ringing all over for you. (*Voice changes tone.*) Goodbye, sir, have a pleasant journey.

WALLACE. Thank you. I *will* do it, I promise you.

STELLA. As long as you enjoy yourself. (*The voice changes back to its shrewish tone.*) What are you *doing* up there?

ARTHUR. I'm thinking about killing myself.

STELLA. That'll be the day. Come down here and get these books sorted out. My head is bursting, truly bursting it is. Are you *listening* to me Arthur?

ARTHUR. Yes, dear. I'm listening.

Sound of intercom switching off.

ARTHUR. Just *one,* that's all. And then I'll do it. (*A moment. Then the sound of the intercom being switched on. Shouts.*) I will!

Sound of intercom switching off.
He sighs. A moment. Then the sound of him crossing the room, opening and closing the door. A moment.
The sound of a train clanking slowly by.
Fade.